Friedrich Wi  his
soundlisten) or 15 ; a
German philosopl nd
philologist whose ￼ on
modern intellectual history. He began his career as a classical
philologist before turning to philosophy. He became the
youngest person ever to hold the Chair of Classical Philology
at the University of Basel in 1869 at the age of 24.Nietzsche
resigned in 1879 due to health problems that plagued him
most of his life; he completed much of his core writing in
the following decade.In 1889, at age 44, he suffered a collapse
and afterward a complete loss of his mental faculties. He lived
his remaining years in the care of his mother until her death
in 1897 and then with his sister Elisabeth Förster-Nietzsche.
Nietzsche died in 1900.

FRIEDRICH NIETZSCHE

ON THE GENEALOGY OF MORALS

MORALS

&

THE BIRTH OF

TRAGEDY

DELHI OPEN BOOKS

ON THE GENEALOGY OF MORALS
&
THE BIRTH OF TRAGEDY
by FRIEDRICH NIETZSCHE

Edition copyright © Delhi Open Books, 2020

Published by

Delhi Open Books

G/F, 4771/23, Bharat Ram Road, Daryaganj, New Delhi-110002
Ph.: 91-11-42408081
E-mail: delhiopenbooks2016@gmail.com

ISBN: 978-81-947472-5-3

Cover, Typesetting, and Book Design by **ROHIT**

Contents

ON THE GENEALOGY OF MORALS

FIRST ESSAY.
"GOOD AND EVIL," "GOOD AND BAD."

    1

SECOND ESSAY.
"GUILT," "BAD CONSCIENCE,
" AND THE LIKE.   **34**

THIRD ESSAY.
WHAT IS THE MEANING
OF ASCETIC IDEALS?   **79**

PEOPLES AND COUNTRIES.   **150**

THE BIRTH OF TRAGEDY

AN ATTEMPT AT SELF-CRITICISM   **163**

FOREWORD TO RICHARD WAGNER   **175**

APPENDIX   **306**

ON THE GENEALOGY OF MORALS

FIRST ESSAY. "GOOD AND EVIL," "GOOD AND BAD."

1.

Those English psychologists, who up to the present are the only philosophers who are to be thanked for any endeavour to get as far as a history of the origin of morality—these men, I say, offer us in their own personalities no paltry problem;—they even have, if I am to be quite frank about it, in their capacity of living riddles, an advantage over their books—they themselves are interesting! These English psychologists— what do they really mean? We always find them voluntarily or involuntarily at the same task of pushing to the front the partiehonteuse of our inner world, and looking for the efficient, governing, and decisive principle in that precise quarter where the intellectual self- respect of the race would be the most reluctant to find it (for example, in the vis inertiæ of habit, or in forgetfulness, or in a blind and fortuitous mechanism and association of ideas, or in some factor that is purely passive, reflex, molecular, or fundamentally stupid)—what is the real motive power which always impels these psychologists inprecisely this direction? Is it an instinct for human disparagement somewhat sinister, vulgar, and malignant, or perhaps incomprehensible even to itself? or perhaps a touch of pessimistic jealousy, the mistrust of disillusioned idealists who have become gloomy, poisoned, and bitter? or a petty subconscious enmity and rancour against Christianity (and Plato), that has conceivably never crossed the threshold of consciousness? or just a vicious taste for those elements of life which are bizarre, painfully paradoxical, mystical, and illogical? or, as a final alternative, a dash of each of these motives—a little vulgarity, a little gloominess, a little anti-Christianity, a little craving for the necessary piquancy?

But I am told that it is simply a case of old frigid and tedious frogs crawling and hopping around men and inside men, as if they were as thoroughly at home there, as they would be in a swamp.

I am opposed to this statement, nay, I do not believe it; and if, in the impossibility of knowledge, one is permitted to wish, so do I wish from my heart that just the converse metaphor should apply, and that these analysts with their psychological microscopes should be, at bottom, brave, proud, and magnanimous animals who know how to bridle both their hearts and their smarts, and have specifically trained themselves to sacrifice what is desirable to what is true, any truth in fact, even the simple, bitter, ugly, repulsive, unchristian, and immoral truths—for there are truths of that description.

2.

All honour, then, to the noble spirits who would fain dominate these historians of morality. But it is certainly a pity that they lackthe historical sense itself, that they themselves are quite deserted by all the beneficent spirits of history. The whole train of their thought runs, as was always the way of old-fashioned philosophers,on thoroughly unhistorical lines: there is no doubt on this point. The crass ineptitude of their genealogy of morals is immediately apparent when the question arises of ascertaining the origin of the idea and judgment of "good." "Man had originally," so speaks their decree, "praised and called 'good' altruistic acts from the standpoint of those on whom they were conferred, that is, those to whom they were useful; subsequently the origin of this praise was forgotten, and altruistic acts, simply because, as a sheer matter of habit, they were praised as good, came also to be felt as good—as though they contained in themselves some intrinsic goodness." The thing is obvious:—this initial derivation contains already all the typical and idiosyncratic traits of the English psychologists—we have "utility," "forgetting," "habit," and finally "error," the whole assemblage forming the basis of a system of values, on which the higher man has up to the present prided himself as though it were a kind of privilege of man in general. This pride must be brought low, this system of values must lose its values: is that attained?

Now the first argument that comes ready to my hand is that the real homestead of the concept "good" is sought and located in the wrong place: the judgment "good" did not originate among those to whom goodness was shown. Much rather has it been the good themselves, that is, the aristocratic, the powerful, the high-stationed, the high-minded, who have felt that they themselves were good, and that their actions were good, that is to say of the first order, in contradistinction to all the low, the low-minded, the vulgar, and the plebeian. It was out of this pathos of distance that they first arrogated the right to create values for their own profit, and to coin the names of such values: what had they to do with utility? The standpoint of utility is as alien and as inapplicable as it could possibly be, when we have to deal with so volcanic an effervescence of supreme values, creating and demarcating as they do a hierarchy within themselves: it is at this juncture that one arrives at an appreciation of the contrast to that tepid temperature, which is the presupposition on which every combination of worldly wisdom and every calculation of practical expediency is always based—and not for one occasional, not for one exceptional instance, but chronically. The pathos of nobility and distance, as I have said, the chronic and despotic esprit de corps and fundamental instinct of a higher dominant race coming into association with a meaner race, an "under race," this is the origin of the antithesis of good and bad.

(The masters' right of giving names goes so far that it is permissible to look upon language itself as the expression of the power of the masters: they say "this is that, and that," they seal finally every object and every event with a sound, and thereby at the same time take possession of it.) It is because of this origin that the word "good" is far from having any necessary connection with altruistic acts, in accordance with the superstitious belief of these moral philosophers. On the contrary, it is on the occasion of the decay of aristocratic values, that the antitheses between "egoistic" and "altruistic" presses more and more heavily on the human conscience—it is, to use my own language, the herd instinct which finds in this antithesis an expression in many ways. And even then it takes a considerable time for this instinct to become sufficiently dominant, for the valuation to be inextricably dependent on this antithesis (as is the case in contemporary Europe); for to-day that prejudice is predominant, which, acting even now with all the intensity of an obsession and brain disease, holds that "moral," "altruistic," and "désintéressé" are concepts of equal value.

3.

In the second place, quite apart from the fact that this hypothesis as to the genesis of the value "good" cannot be historically upheld, it suffers from an inherent psychological contradiction. The utility of altruistic conduct has presumably been the origin of its being praised, and this origin has become forgotten:—But in what conceivable way is this forgetting possible! Has perchance the utility of such conduct ceased at some given moment? The contrary is the case. This utility has rather been experienced every day at all times, and is consequently a feature that obtains a new and regular emphasis with every fresh day; it follows that, so far from vanishing from the consciousness, so far indeed from being forgotten, it must necessarily become impressed on the consciousness with ever-increasing distinctness. How much more logical is that contrary theory (it is not the truer for that) which is represented, for instance, by Herbert Spencer, who places the concept "good" as essentially similar to the concept "useful," "purposive," so that in the judgments "good" and "bad" mankind is simply summarising and investing with a sanction its unforgotten and unforgettable experiences concerning the "useful-purposive" and the "mischievous-non- purposive." According to this theory, "good" is the attribute of that which has previously shown itself useful; and so is able to claim to be considered "valuable in the highest degree," "valuable in itself." This method of explanation is also, as I have said, wrong, but at any rate the explanation itself is coherent, and psychologically tenable.

4.

The guide-post which first put me on the right track was this question— what is the true etymological significance of the various symbols for the idea "good" which have been coined in the various languages? I then found that they all led back to the same evolution of the same idea—that everywhere "aristocrat," "noble" (in the social sense), is the root idea, out of which have necessarily developed "good" in the sense of "with aristocratic soul," "noble," in the sense of "with a soul of high calibre," "with a privileged soul"—a development which invariably runs parallel with that other evolution by which "vulgar," "plebeian," "low," are made to change finally into "bad." The most eloquent proof of this last contention is the German word "schlecht" itself: this word is identical with "schlicht"—(compare "schlechtweg" and "schlechterdings")—which, originally and as yet without any sinister innuendo, simply denoted the plebeian man in contrast to the aristocratic man. It is at the sufficiently late period of the

Thirty Years' War that this sense becomes changed to the sense now current. From the standpoint of the Genealogy of Morals this discovery seems to be substantial: the lateness of it is to be attributed to the retarding influence exercised in the modern world by democratic prejudice in the sphere of all questions of origin. This extends, as will shortly be shown, even to the province of natural science and physiology, which, prima facie is the most objective. The extent of the mischief which is caused by this prejudice (once it is free of all trammels except those of its own malice), particularly to Ethics and History, is shown by the notorious case of Buckle: it was in Buckle that that plebeianism of the modern spirit, which is of English origin, broke out once again from its malignant soil with all the violence of a slimy volcano, and with that salted, rampant, and vulgar eloquence with which up to the present time all volcanoes have spoken.

5.

With regard to our problem, which can justly be called an intimate problem, and which elects to appeal to only a limited number of ears: it is of no small interest to ascertain that in those words and roots which denote "good" we catch glimpses of that arch-trait, on the strength of which the aristocrats feel themselves to be beings of a higher order than their fellows. Indeed, they call themselves in perhaps the most frequent instances simply after their superiority in power (e.g. "the powerful," "the lords," "the commanders"), or after the most obvious sign of their superiority, as for example "the rich," "the possessors" (that is the meaning of arya; and the Iranian and Slav languages correspond). But they also call themselves aftersome characteristic idiosyncrasy; and this is the case which now concerns us. They name themselves, for instance, "the truthful": this is first done by the Greek nobility whose mouthpiece is found in Theognis, the Megarian poet. The word which is coined for the purpose, signifies etymologically "one who is," who has reality, who is real, who is true; and then with a subjective twist, the "true," as the "truthful": at this stage in the evolution of the idea, it becomes the motto and party cry of the nobility, and quite completes the transition to the meaning "noble," so as to place outside the pale the lying, vulgar man, as Theognis conceives and portrays him— till finally the word after the decay of the nobility is left to delineate psychological noblesse, and becomes as it were ripe and mellow. In the word κακός as in δειλός (the plebeian in contrast to the the cowardice is emphasised. This affords perhaps an inkling on what lines the etymological origin of the very ambiguous is to be investigated. In the Latin malus (which I place side by side with μέλας) the vulgar man can be distinguished as the dark-coloured, and above all as the black-haired ("hic niger est"), as the pre-Aryan inhabitants of the Italian soil, whose complexion formed the clearest feature of distinction from the dominant blondes, namely, the Aryan conquering race:—at any rate Gaelic has afforded me the exact analogue—Fin (for instance, in the name Fin-Gal), the distinctive word of the nobility, finally—good, noble, clean, but originally the blonde- haired man in contrast to the dark black-haired aboriginals. The Celts, if I may make a parenthetic statement, were throughout a blonde race; and it is wrong to connect, as Virchow still connects, those traces of an essentially dark-haired population which are to be seen on the more elaborate ethnographical maps of Germany with any Celtic ancestry or with any admixture of Celtic blood: in this context it is rather the pre- Aryan population of Germany which surges up to these districts. (The same is true substantially of the whole of Europe: in point of fact, the subject race has finally again obtained the upper hand, in complexion and the shortness of the skull, and perhaps in the intellectual and social qualities. Who can guarantee that modern democracy, still more modern anarchy, and indeed that tendency to the "Commune," the most primitive form of society, which is now common to all the Socialists in Europe, does not in its real essence signify a monstrous reversion—and that the conquering and master race—the Aryan race, is not also becoming inferior physiologically?) I believe that I can explain the Latin *bonus* as the "warrior": my hypothesis is that I am right in deriving *bonus* from an older *duonus* (compare *bellum* = *duellum*= *duen-lum*, in which the word *duonus* appears to me to be contained). *Bonus* accordingly as the man of discord, of variance, "entzweiung" (duo), as the warrior: one sees what in ancient Rome "the good" meant for a man. Must not our actual German word *gut* mean "the godlike, the man of godlike race"? and be identical with the national name (originally the nobles' name) of the Goths?

The grounds for this supposition do not appertain to this work. 6.

Above all, there is no exception (though there are opportunities for exceptions) to this rule, that the idea of political superiority always resolves itself into the idea of psychological superiority, in those cases where the highest caste is at the same time the priestly caste, and in accordance with its general characteristics confers on itself the privilege of a title which alludes specifically to its priestly function. It is in these cases, for instance, that "clean" and "unclean" confront each other for the first time as badges of class distinction; here again there develops a "good" and a "bad," in a sense which has ceased to be merely social.

Moreover, care should be taken not to take these ideas of "clean" and "unclean" too seriously, too broadly, or too symbolically: all the ideas of ancient man have, on the contrary, got to be understood in their initial stages, in a sense which is, to an almost inconceivable extent, crude, coarse, physical, and narrow, and above all essentially unsymbolical. The "clean man" is originally only a man who washes himself, who abstains from certain foods which are conducive to skin diseases, who does not sleep with the unclean women of the lower classes, who has a horror of blood—not more, not much more! On the other hand, the very nature of a priestly aristocracy shows the reasons why just at such an early juncture there should ensue a really dangerous sharpening and intensification of opposed values: it is, in fact, through these opposed values that gulfs are cleft in the social plane, which a veritable Achilles of free thought would shudder to cross. There is from the outset a certain diseased taint in such sacerdotal aristocracies, and in the habits which prevail in such societies—habits which, averse as they are to action, constitute a compound of introspection and explosive emotionalism, as a result of which there appears that introspective morbidity and neurasthenia, which adheres almost inevitably to all priests at all times: with regard, however, to the remedy which they themselves have invented for this disease—the philosopher has no option but to state, that it has proved itself in its effects a hundred times more dangerous than the disease, from which it should have been the deliverer. Humanity itself is still diseased from the effects of the naïvetés of this priestly cure. Take, for instance, certain kinds of diet (abstention from flesh), fasts, sexual continence, flight into the wilderness (a kind of Weir-Mitchell isolation, though of course without that system of excessive feeding and fattening which is the most efficient antidote to all the hysteria of the ascetic ideal); consider too the whole metaphysic of the priests, with its war on the senses, its enervation, its hair-splitting; consider its self-hypnotism on the fakir and Brahman principles (it uses Brahman as a glass disc and obsession), and that climax which we can understand only too well of an unusual satiety with its panacea of nothingness (or God:—the demand for a unio mystica with God is the demand of the Buddhist for nothingness, Nirvana—and nothing else!). In sacerdotal societies every element is on a more dangerous scale, not merely cures and remedies, but also pride, revenge, cunning, exaltation, love, ambition, virtue, morbidity:—further, it can fairly be stated that it is on the soil of this essentially dangerous form of human society, the sacerdotal form, that man really becomes for the first time an interesting animal, that it is in this form that the soul of man has in a higher sense attained depths and become evil—and those are the two fundamental forms of the superiority which up to the present man has exhibited over every other animal.

7.

The reader will have already surmised with what ease the priestly mode of valuation can branch off from the knightly aristocratic mode, and then develop into the very antithesis of the latter: special impetus is given to this opposition, by every occasion when the castes of the priests and warriors confront each other with mutual jealousy and cannot agree over the prize. The knightly-aristocratic "values" are based on a careful cult of the physical, on a flowering, rich, and even effervescing healthiness, that goes considerably beyond what is necessary for maintaining life, on war, adventure, the chase, the dance, the tourney—on everything, in fact, which is contained in strong, free, and joyous action. The priestly- aristocratic mode of valuation is—we have seen—based on other hypotheses: it is bad enough for this class when it is a question of war!

Yet the priests are, as is notorious, the worst enemies—why? Because they are the weakest. Their weakness causes their hate to expand into a monstrous and sinister shape, a shape which is most crafty and most poisonous. The really great haters in the history of the world have always been priests, who are also the cleverest haters—in comparison with the cleverness of priestly revenge, every other piece of cleverness is practically negligible. Human history would be too fatuous for anything were it not for the cleverness imported into it by the weak—take at once the most important instance. All the world's efforts against the "aristocrats," the "mighty," the "masters," the "holders of power," are negligible by comparison with what has been accomplished against those classes by the Jews—the Jews, that priestly nation which eventually realised that the one method of effecting satisfaction on its enemies and tyrants was by means of a radical transvaluation of values, which was at the same time an act of the cleverest revenge. Yet the method was only appropriate to a nation of priests, to a nation of the most jealously nursed priestly revengefulness. It was the Jews who, in opposition to the aristocratic equation (good = aristocratic = beautiful = happy = loved by the gods), dared with a terrifying logic to suggest the contrary equation, and indeed to maintain with the teeth of the most profound hatred (the hatred of weakness) this contrary equation, namely, "the wretched are alone the good; the poor, the weak, the lowly, are alone the good; the suffering, the needy, the sick, the loathsome, are the only ones who are pious, the only ones who are blessed, for them alone is salvation—but you, on the other hand, you aristocrats, you men of power, you are to all eternity the evil, the horrible, the covetous, the insatiate, the godless; eternally also shall you be the unblessed, the cursed, the damned!" We know who it was who reaped the heritage of this Jewish transvaluation.

In the context of the monstrous and inordinately fateful initiative which the Jews have exhibited in connection with this most fundamental of all declarations of war, I remember the passage which came to my pen on another occasion (Beyond Good and Evil, Aph. 195)—that it was, in fact, with the Jews that the revolt of the slaves begins in the sphere of morals; that revolt which has behind it a history of two millennia, and which at the present day has only moved out of our sight, because it—has achieved victory.

8.

But you understand this not? You have no eyes for a force which has taken two thousand years to achieve victory?— There is nothing wonderful in this: all lengthy processes are hard to see and to realise. But this is what took place: from the trunk of that tree of revenge and hate, Jewish hate,—that most profound and sublime hate, which creates ideals and changes old values to new creations, the like of which has never been on earth,—there grew a phenomenon which was equally incomparable, a new love, the most profound and sublime of all kinds of love;—and from what other trunk could it have grown? But beware of supposing that this love has soared on its upward growth, as in any way a real negation of that thirst for revenge, as an antithesis to the Jewish hate! No, the contrary is the truth! This love grew out of that hate, as its crown, as its triumphant crown, circling wider and wider amid the clarity and fulness of the sun, and pursuing in the very kingdom of light and height its goal of hatred, its victory, its spoil, its strategy, with the same intensity with which the roots of that tree of hate sank into everything which was deep and evil with increasing stability and increasing desire.

This Jesus of Nazareth, the incarnate gospel of love, this "Redeemer" bringing salvation and victory to the poor, the sick, the sinful—was he not really temptation in its most sinister and irresistible form, temptation to take the tortuous path to those very Jewish values and those very Jewish ideals? Has not Israel really obtained the final goal of its sublime revenge, by the tortuous paths of this "Redeemer," for all that he might pose as Israel's adversary and Israel's destroyer? Is it not due to the black magic of a really great policy of revenge, of a far-seeing, burrowing revenge, both acting and calculating with slowness, that Israel himself must repudiate before all the world the actual instrument of his own revenge and nail it to the cross, so that all the world—that is, all the enemies of Israel—could nibble without suspicion at this very bait?

Could, moreover, any human mind with all its elaborate ingenuity invent a bait that was more truly dangerous? Anything that was even equivalent in the power of its seductive, intoxicating, defiling, and corrupting influence to that symbol of the holy cross, to that awful paradox of a "god on the cross," to that mystery of the unthinkable, supreme, and utter horror of the self-crucifixion of a god for the salvation of man? It is at least certain that sub hoc signo Israel, with its revenge and transvaluation of all values, has up to the present always triumphed again over all other ideals, over all more aristocratic ideals.

9.

"But why do you talk of nobler ideals? Let us submit to the facts; that the people have triumphed—or the slaves, or the populace, or the herd, or whatever name you care to give them—if this has happened through the Jews, so be it! In that case no nation ever had a greater mission in the world's history. The 'masters' have been done away with; the morality of the vulgar man has triumphed. This triumph may also be called a blood- poisoning (it has mutually fused the races)—I do not dispute it; but there is no doubt but that this intoxication has succeeded. The 'redemption' of the human race (that is, from the masters) is progressing swimmingly; everything is obviously becoming Judaised, or Christianised, or vulgarised (what is there in the words?). It seems impossible to stop the course of this poisoning through the whole body politic of mankind—but its tempo and pace may from the present time be slower, more delicate, quieter, more discreet—there is time enough. In view of this context has the Church nowadays any necessary purpose? has it, in fact, a right to live? Or could man get on without it? Quæritur. It seems that it fetters and retards this tendency, instead of accelerating it. Well, even that might be its utility. The Church certainly is a crude and boorish institution, that is repugnant to an intelligence with any pretence at delicacy, to a really modern taste. Should it not at any rate learn to be somewhat more subtle? It alienates nowadays, more than it allures.

Which of us would, forsooth, be a freethinker if there were no Church? It is the Church which repels us, not its poison— apart from the Church we like the poison." This is the epilogue of a freethinker to my discourse, of an honourable animal (as he has given abundant proof), and a democrat to boot; he had up to that time listened to me, and could not endure my silence, but for me, indeed, with regard to this topic there is much on which to be silent.

10.

The revolt of the slaves in morals begins in the very principle of resentment becoming creative and giving birth to values—a resentment experienced by creatures who, deprived as they are of the proper outlet of action, are forced to find their compensation in an imaginary revenge. While every aristocratic morality springs from a triumphant affirmation of its own demands, the slave morality says "no" from the very outset to what is "outside itself," "different from itself," and "not itself": and this "no" is its creative deed. This volte-face of the valuing standpoint—this inevitable gravitation to the objective instead of back to the subjective—is typical of "resentment": the slave-morality requires as the condition of its existence an external and objective world, to employ physiological terminology, it requires objective stimuli to be capable of action at all—its action is fundamentally a reaction. The contrary is the case when we come to the aristocrat's system of values: it acts and grows spontaneously, it merely seeks its antithesis in order to pronounce a more grateful and exultant "yes" to its own self;—its negative conception, "low," "vulgar," "bad," is merely a pale late-born foil in comparison with its positive and fundamental conception (saturated as it is with life and passion), of "we aristocrats, we good ones, we beautiful ones, we happy ones."

When the aristocratic morality goes astray and commits sacrilege on reality, this is limited to that particular sphere with which it is not sufficiently acquainted—a sphere, in fact, from the real knowledge of which it disdainfully defends itself. It misjudges, in some cases, the sphere which it despises, the sphere of the common vulgar man and the low people: on the other hand, due weight should be given to the consideration that in any case the mood of contempt, of disdain, of superciliousness, even on the supposition that it falsely portrays the object of its contempt, will always be far removed from that degree of falsity which will always characterise the attacks—in effigy, of course—of the vindictive hatred and revengefulness of the weak in onslaughts on their enemies. In point of fact, there is in contempt too strong an admixture of nonchalance, of casualness, of boredom, of impatience, even of personal exultation, for it to be capable of distorting its victim into a real caricature or a real monstrosity. Attention again should be paid to the almost benevolent nuances which, for instance, the Greek nobility imports into all the words by which it distinguishes the common people from itself; note how continuously a kind of pity, care, and consideration imparts its honeyed flavour, until at last almost all the words which are applied to the vulgar man survive finally as expressions for "unhappy," "worthy of pity" (compare δειλο, δείλαιος, πονηρός, μοχθηρός]; the latter two names really denoting the vulgar man as labour-slave and beast of burden)—and how, conversely, "bad," "low," "unhappy" have never ceased to ring in the Greek ear with a tone in which "unhappy" is the predominant note: this is a heritage of the old noble aristocratic morality, which remains true to itself even in contempt (let philologists remember the sense in which used to be employed). The "well-born" simply felt themselves the "happy"; they did not have to manufacture their happiness artificially through looking at their enemies, or in cases to talk and lie themselves into happiness (as is the custom with all resentful men); and similarly, complete men as they were, exuberant with strength, and consequently necessarily energetic, they were too wise to dissociate happiness from action—activity becomes in their minds necessarily counted as happiness (that is the etymology of—all in sharp contrast to the "happiness" of the weak and the oppressed, with their festering venom and malignity, among whom happiness appears essentially as a narcotic, a deadening, a quietude, a peace, a "Sabbath," an enervation of the mind and relaxation of the limbs,—in short, a purely passive phenomenon. While the aristocratic man lived in confidence and openness with himself "noblee- born," emphasises the nuance "sincere," and perhaps also "naïf"), the resentful man, on the other hand, is neither sincere nor naïf, nor honest and candid with himself. His soul squints; his mind loves hidden crannies, tortuous paths and back-doors, everything secret appeals to him as his world, his safety, his balm; he is past master in silence, in not forgetting, in waiting, in provisional self-depreciation and self- abasement. A race of such resentful men will of necessity eventually prove more prudent than any aristocratic race, it will honour prudence on quite a distinct scale, as, in fact, a paramount condition of existence, while prudence among aristocratic men is apt to be tinged with a delicate flavour of luxury and refinement; so among them it plays nothing like so integral a part as that complete certainty of function of the governing unconscious instincts, or as indeed a certain lack of prudence, such as a vehement and valiant charge, whether against danger or the enemy, or as those ecstatic bursts of rage, love, reverence, gratitude, by which at all times noble souls have recognised each other. When the resentment of the aristocratic man manifests itself, it fulfils and exhausts itself in an immediate reaction, and consequently instills no venom: on the other hand, it never manifests itself at all in countless instances, when in the case of the feeble and weak it would be inevitable.

An inability to take seriously for any length of time their enemies, their disasters, their misdeeds—that is the sign of the full strong natures who possess a superfluity of moulding plastic force, that heals completely and produces forgetfulness: a good example of this in the modern world is Mirabeau, who had no memory for any insults and meannesses which were practised on him, and who was only incapable of forgiving because he forgot. Such a man indeed shakes off with a shrug many a worm which would have buried itself in another; it is only in characters like these that we see the possibility (supposing, of course, that there is such a possibility in the world) of the real "love of one's enemies." What respect for his enemies is found, forsooth, in an aristocratic man—and such a reverence is already a bridge to love! He insists on having his enemy to himself as his distinction. He tolerates no other enemy but a man in whose character there is nothing to despise and much to honour! On the other hand, imagine the "enemy" as the resentful man conceives him—and it is here exactly that we see his work, his creativeness; he has conceived "the evil enemy," the "evil one," and indeed that is the root idea from which he now evolves as a contrasting and corresponding figure a "good one," himself—his very self!

11

The method of this man is quite contrary to that of the aristocratic man, who conceives the root idea "good" spontaneously and straight away, that is to say, out of himself, and from that material then creates for himself a concept of "bad"! This "bad" of aristocratic origin and that "evil" out of the cauldron of unsatisfied hatred—the former an imitation, an "extra," an additional nuance; the latter, on the other hand, the original, the beginning, the essential act in the conception of a slave- morality—these two words "bad" and "evil," how great a difference do they mark, in spite of the fact that they have an identical contrary in the idea "good." But the idea "good" is not the same: much rather let the question be asked, "Who is really evil according to the meaning of the morality of resentment?" In all sternness let it be answered thus:— just the good man of the other morality, just the aristocrat, the powerful one, the one who rules, but who is distorted by the venomous eye of resentfulness, into a new colour, a new signification, a new appearance. This particular point we would be the last to deny: the man who learnt to know those "good" ones only as enemies, learnt at the same time not to know them only as "evil enemies" and the same men who inter pares were kept so rigorously in bounds through convention, respect, custom, and gratitude, though much more through mutual vigilance and jealousy inter pares, these men who in their relations with each other find so many new ways of manifesting consideration, self-control, delicacy, loyalty, pride, and friendship, these men are in reference to what is outside their circle (where the foreign element, a foreign country, begins), not much better than beasts of prey, which have been let loose.

They enjoy there freedom from all social control, they feel that in the wilderness they can give vent with impunity to that tension which is produced by enclosure and imprisonment in the peace of society, they revert to the innocence of the beast-of-prey conscience, like jubilant monsters, who perhaps come from a ghastly bout of murder, arson, rape, and torture, with bravado and a moral equanimity, as though merely some wild student's prank had been played, perfectly convinced that the poets have now an ample theme to sing and celebrate. It is impossible not to recognise at the core of all these aristocratic races the beast of prey; the magnificent blonde brute, avidly rampant for spoil and victory; this hidden core needed an outlet from time to time, the beast must get loose again, must return into the wilderness—the Roman, Arabic, German, and Japanese nobility, the Homeric heroes, the Scandinavian Vikings, are all alike in this need. It is the aristocratic races who have left the idea "Barbarian" on all the tracks in which they have marched; nay, a consciousness of this very barbarianism, and even a pride in it, manifests itself even in their highest civilisation (for example, when Pericles says to his Athenians in that celebrated funeral oration, "Our audacity has forced a way over every land and sea, rearing everywhere imperishable memorials of itself for good and for evil"). This audacity of aristocratic races, mad, absurd, and spasmodic as may be its expression; the incalculable and fantastic nature of their enterprises, Pericles sets in special relief and glory the of the Athenians, their nonchalance and contempt for safety, body, life, and comfort, their awful joy and intense delight in all destruction, in all the ecstasies of victory and cruelty,—all these features become crystallised, for those who suffered thereby in the picture of the "barbarian," of the "evil enemy," perhaps of the "Goth" and of the "Vandal." The profound, icy mistrust which the German provokes, as soon as he arrives at power,—even at the present time,—is always still an aftermath of that inextinguishable horror with which for whole centuries Europe has regarded the wrath of the blonde Teuton beast (although between the old Germans and ourselves there exists scarcely a psychological, let alone a physical, relationship). I have once called attention to the embarrassment of Hesiod, when he conceived the series of social ages, and endeavoured to express them in gold, silver, and bronze. He could only dispose of the contradiction, with which he was confronted, by the Homeric world, an age magnificent indeed, but at the same time so awful and so violent, by making two ages out of one, which he henceforth placed one behind each other—first, the age of the heroes and demigods, as that world had remained in the memories of the aristocratic families, who found therein their own ancestors; secondly, the bronze age, as that corresponding age appeared to the descendants of the oppressed, spoiled, ill-treated, exiled, enslaved; namely, as an age of bronze, as I have said, hard, cold, terrible, without feelings and without conscience, crushing everything, and bespattering everything with blood. Granted the truth of the theory now believed to be true, that the very essence of all civilisation is to train out of man, the beast of prey, a tame and civilised animal, a domesticated animal, it follows indubitably that we must regard as the real tools of civilisation all those instincts of reaction and resentment, by the help of which the aristocratic races, together with their ideals, were finally degraded and overpowered; though that has not yet come to be synonymous with saying that the bearers of those tools also represented the civilisation. It is rather the contrary that is not only probable—nay, it is palpable to-day; these bearers of vindictive instincts that have to be bottled up, these descendants of all European and non- European slavery, especially of the pre-Aryan population—these people, I say, represent the decline of humanity! These "tools of civilisation" are a disgrace to humanity, and constitute in reality more of an argument against civilisation, more of a reason why civilisation should be suspected. One may be perfectly justified in being always afraid of the blonde beast that lies at the core of all aristocratic races, and in being on one's guard: but who would not a hundred times prefer to be afraid, when one at the same time admires, than to be immune from fear, at the cost of being perpetually obsessed with the loathsome spectacle of the distorted, the dwarfed, the stunted, the envenomed? And is that not our fate? What produces to-day our repulsion towards "man"?—for we suffer from "man," there is no doubt about it. It is not fear; it is rather that we have nothing more to fear from men; it is that the worm "man" is in the foreground and pullulates; it is that the "tame man," the wretched mediocre and unedifying creature, has learnt to consider himself a goal and a pinnacle, an inner meaning, an historic principle, a "higher man"; yes, it is that he has a certain right so to consider himself, in so far as he feels that in contrast to that excess of deformity, disease, exhaustion, and effeteness whose odour is beginning to pollute present-day Europe, he at any rate has achieved a relative success, he at any rate still says "yes" to life.

12.

I cannot refrain at this juncture from uttering a sigh and one last hope. What is it precisely which I find intolerable? That which I alone cannot get rid of, which makes me choke and faint? Bad air! bad air! That something misbegotten comes near me; that I must inhale the odour of the entrails of a misbegotten soul!—That excepted, what can one not endure in the way of need, privation, bad weather, sickness, toil, solitude? In point of fact, one manages to get over everything, born as one is to a burrowing and battling existence; one always returns once again to the light, one always lives again one's golden hour of victory— and then one stands as one was born, unbreakable, tense, ready for something more difficult, for something more distant, like a bow stretched but the tauter by every strain. But from time to time do ye grant me— assuming that "beyond good and evil" there are goddesses who can grant—one glimpse, grant me but one glimpse only, of something perfect, fully realised, happy, mighty, triumphant, of something that still gives cause for fear! A glimpse of a man that justifies the existence of man, a glimpse of an incarnate human happiness that realises and redeems, for the sake of which one may hold fast to the belief in man! For the position is this: in the dwarfing and levelling of the European man lurks our greatest peril, for it is this outlook which fatigues—we see to-day nothing which wishes to be greater, we surmise that the process is always still backwards, still backwards towards something more attenuated, more inoffensive, more cunning, more comfortable, more mediocre, more indifferent, more Chinese, more Christian—man, there is no doubt about it, grows always "better" —the destiny of Europe lies even in this—that in losing the fear of man, we have also lost the hope in man, yea, the will to be man. The sight of man now fatigues.—What is present-day Nihilism if it is not that?—We are tired of man.

13.

But let us come back to it; the problem of another origin of the good—of the good, as the resentful man has thought it out—demands its solution.

It is not surprising that the lambs should bear a grudge against the great birds of prey, but that is no reason for blaming the great birds of prey for taking the little lambs. And when the lambs say among themselves, "These birds of prey are evil, and he who is as far removed from being a bird of prey, who is rather its opposite, a lamb,—is he not good?" then there is nothing to cavil at in the setting up of this ideal, though it may also be that the birds of prey will regard it a little sneeringly, and perchance say to themselves, "We bear no grudge against them, these good lambs, we even like them: nothing is tastier than a tender lamb." To require of strength that it should not express itself as strength, that it should not be a wish to overpower, a wish to overthrow, a wish to become master, a thirst for enemies and antagonisms and triumphs, is just as absurd as to require of weakness that it should express itself as strength. A quantum of force is just such a quantum of movement, will, action—rather it is nothing else than just those very phenomena of moving, willing, acting, and can only appear otherwise in the misleading errors of language (and the fundamental fallacies of reason which have become petrified therein), which understands, and understands wrongly, all working as conditioned by a worker, by a "subject." And just exactly as the people separate the lightning from its flash, and interpret the latter as a thing done, as the working of a subject which is called lightning, so also does the popular morality separate strength from the expression of strength, as though behind the strong man there existed some indifferent neutral substratum, which enjoyed a caprice and option as to whether or not it should express strength. But there is no such substratum, there is no "being" behind doing, working, becoming; "the doer" is a mere appanage to the action. The action is everything. In point of fact, the people duplicate the doing, when they make the lightning lighten, that is a "doing-doing": they make the same phenomenon first a cause, and then, secondly, the effect of that cause.

The scientists fail to improve matters when they say, "Force moves, force causes," and so on. Our whole science is still, in spite of all its coldness, of all its freedom from passion, a dupe of the tricks of language, and has never succeeded in getting rid of that superstitious changeling "the subject" (the atom, to give another instance, is such a changeling, just as the Kantian "Thing-in-itself"). What wonder, if the suppressed and stealthily simmering passions of revenge and hatred exploit for their own advantage this belief, and indeed hold no belief with a more steadfast enthusiasm than this—"that the strong has the option of being weak, and the bird of prey of being a lamb." Thereby do they win for themselves the right of attributing to the birds of prey the responsibility for being birds of prey: when the oppressed, down-trodden, and overpowered say to themselves with the vindictive guile of weakness, "Let us be otherwise than the evil, namely, good! and good is every one who does not oppress, who hurts no one, who does not attack, who does not pay back, who hands over revenge to God, who holds himself, as we do, in hiding; who goes out of the way of evil, and demands, in short, little from life; like ourselves the patient, the meek, the just,"—yet all this, in its cold and unprejudiced interpretation, means nothing more than "once for all, the weak are weak; it is good to do nothing for which we are not strong enough"; but this dismal state of affairs, this prudence of the lowest order, which even insects possess (which in a great danger are fain to sham death so as to avoid doing "too much"), has, thanks to the counterfeiting and self-deception of weakness, come to masquerade in the pomp of an ascetic, mute, and expectant virtue, just as though the veryweakness of the weak—that is, forsooth, its being, its working, its whole unique inevitable inseparable reality—were a voluntary result, something wished, chosen, a deed, an act of merit. This kind of man finds the belief in a neutral, free-choosing "subject" necessary from an instinct of self-preservation, of self-assertion, in which every lie is fain to sanctify itself. The subject (or, to use popular language, the soul) has perhaps proved itself the best dogma in the world simply because it rendered possible to the horde of mortal, weak, and oppressed individuals of every kind, that most sublime specimen of self-deception, the interpretation of weakness as freedom, of being this, or being that, as merit.

Will any one look a little into—right into—the mystery of how ideals are manufactured in this world? Who has the courage to do it? Come!

Here we have a vista opened into these grimy workshops. Wait just a moment, dear Mr. Inquisitive and Foolhardy; your eye must first grow accustomed to this false changing light—Yes! Enough! Now speak! What is happening below down yonder? Speak out that what you see, man of the most dangerous curiosity—for now I am the listener.

"I see nothing, I hear the more. It is a cautious, spiteful, gentle whispering and muttering together in all the corners and crannies. It seems to me that they are lying; a sugary softness adheres to every sound. Weakness is turned to merit, there is no doubt about it—it is just as you say."

Further!

"And the impotence which requites not, is turned to 'goodness,' craven baseness to meekness, submission to those whom one hates, to obedience (namely, obedience to one of whom they say that he ordered this submission—they call him God). The inoffensive character of the weak, the very cowardice in which he is rich, his standing at the door, his forced necessity of waiting, gain here fine names, such as 'patience,' which is also called 'virtue'; not being able to avenge one's self, is called not wishing to avenge one's self, perhaps even forgiveness (for they know not what they do—we alone know what they do). They also talk of the 'love of their enemies' and sweat thereby."

Further!

"They are miserable, there is no doubt about it, all these whisperers and counterfeiters in the corners, although they try to get warm by crouching close to each other, but they tell me that their misery is a favour and distinction given to them by God, just as one beats the dogs one likes best; that perhaps this misery is also a preparation, a probation, a training; that perhaps it is still more something which will one day be compensated and paid back with a tremendous interest in gold, nay in happiness. This they call 'Blessedness.'"

Further!

"They are now giving me to understand, that not only are they better men than the mighty, the lords of the earth, whose spittle they have got to lick (not out of fear, not at all out of fear! But because God ordains that one should honour all authority)—not only are they better men, but that they also have a 'better time,' at any rate, will one day have a 'better time.' But enough! Enough! I can endure it no longer. Bad air! Bad air!

These workshops where ideals are manufactured—verily they reek with the crassest lies."

Nay. Just one minute! You are saying nothing about the masterpieces of these virtuosos of black magic, who can produce whiteness, milk, and innocence out of any black you like: have you not noticed what a pitch of refinement is attained by their chef d'œuvre, their most audacious, subtle, ingenious, and lying artist-trick? Take care! These cellar-beasts, full of revenge and hate—what do they make, forsooth, out of their revenge and hate? Do you hear these words? Would you suspect, if you trusted only their words, that you are among men of resentment and nothing else?

"I understand, I prick my ears up again (ah! ah! ah! and I hold my nose). Now do I hear for the first time that which they have said so often: 'We good, we are the righteous'— what they demand they call not revenge but 'the triumph of righteousness'; what they hate is not their enemy, no, they hate 'unrighteousness,' 'godlessness'; what they believe in and hope is not the hope of revenge, the intoxication of sweet revenge (—"sweeter than honey," did Homer call it?), but the victory of God, of the righteous God over the 'godless'; what is left for them to love in this world is not their brothers in hate, but their 'brothers in love,' as they say, all the good and righteous on the earth."

And how do they name that which serves them as a solace against all the troubles of life—their phantasmagoria of their anticipated future blessedness?

"How? Do I hear right? They call it 'the last judgment,' the advent of their kingdom, 'the kingdom of God'—but in the meanwhile they live 'in faith,' 'in love,' 'in hope.'"

Enough! Enough! 15.

In the faith in what? In the love for what? In the hope of what? These weaklings!—they also, forsooth, wish to be the strong some time; there is no doubt about it, some time their kingdom also must come—"the kingdom of God" is their name for it, as has been mentioned: they are so meek in everything! Yet in order to experience that kingdom it is necessary to live long, to live beyond death,—yes, eternal life is necessary so that one can make up for ever for that earthly life "in faith," "in love," "in hope." Make up for what? Make up by what? Dante, as it seems to me, made a crass mistake when with awe-inspiring ingenuity he placed that inscription over the gate of his hell, "Me too made eternal love": at any rate the following inscription would have a much better right to stand over the gate of the Christian Paradise and its "eternal blessedness"—"Me too made eternal hate"—granted of course that a truth may rightly stand over the gate to a lie! For what is the blessedness of that Paradise? Possibly we could quickly surmise it; but it is better that it should be explicitly attested by an authority who in such matters is not to be disparaged, Thomas of Aquinas, the great teacher and saint. "Beati in regno celesti" says he, as gently as a lamb, "videbunt pœnas damnatorum, ut beatitudo illis magis complaceat." Or if we wish to hear a stronger tone, a word from the mouth of a triumphant father of the Church, who warned his disciples against the cruel ecstasies of the public spectacles—But why? Faith offers us much more,—says he, de Spectac., c. 29 ss.,—something much stronger; thanks to the redemption, joys of quite another kind stand at our disposal; instead of athletes we have our martyrs; we wish for blood, well, we have the blood of Christ—but what then awaits us on the day of his return, of his triumph. And then does he proceed, does this enraptured visionary: "at enim supersunt alia spectacula, ille ultimas et perpetuus judicii dies, ille nationibus insperatus, ille derisus, cum tanta sæculi vetustas et tot ejus nativitates uno igne haurientur. Quæ tunc spectaculi latitudo! Quid admirer! quid rideam! Ubigaudeam! Ubi exultem, spectans tot et tantos reges, qui in cœlum recepti nuntiabantur, cum ipso Jove et ipsis suis testibus in imis tenebris congemescentes! Item præsides" (the provincial governors) "persecutores dominici nominis sævioribus quam ipsi flammis sævierunt insultantibus contra Christianos liquescentes! Quos præterea sapientes illos philosophos coram discipulis suis una conflagrantibus erubescentes, quibus nihil ad deum pertinere suadebant, quibus animas aut nullas aut non in pristina corpora redituras affirmabant! Etiam poetas non ad Rhadamanti nec ad Minois, sed ad inopinati Christi tribunal palpitantes! Tunc magis tragœdi audiendi, magis scilicet vocales" (with louder tones and more violent shrieks) "in sua propria calamitate; tunc histriones cognoscendi, solutiores multo per ignem; tunc spectandus auriga in flammea rota totus rubens, tunc xystici contemplandi non in gymnasiis, sed in igne jaculati, nisi quod ne tunc quidem illos velim vivos, ut qui malim ad eos potius conspectum insatiabilem conferre, qui in dominum scevierunt. Hic est ille, dicam fabri aut quæstuariæ filius" (as is shown by the whole of the following, and in particular by this well-known description of the mother of Jesus from the Talmud, Tertullian is henceforth referring to the Jews), "sabbati destructor, Samarites et dæmonium habens. Hic est quem a

Juda redemistis, hic est ille arundine et colaphis diverberatus, sputamentis de decoratus, felle et acete potatus. Hic est, quem clam discentes subripuerunt, ut resurrexisse dicatur vel hortulanus detraxit, ne lactucæ suæ frequentia commeantium laderentur. Ut talia species, ut talibus exultes, quis tibi prætor aut consul aut sacerdos de sua liberalitate prastabit? Et tamen hæc jam habemus quodammodo per fidem spiritu imaginante repræsentata. Ceterum qualia illa sunt, quæ nec oculus vidit nec auris audivit nec in cor hominis ascenderunt?" (I Cor. ii. 9.) "Credo circo et utraque cavea" (first and fourth row, or, according to others, the comic and the tragic stage) "et omni studio gratiora." Per fidem: so stands it written.

16.

Let us come to a conclusion. The two opposing values, "good and bad," "good and evil," have fought a dreadful, thousand-year fight in the world, and though indubitably the second value has been for a long time in the preponderance, there are not wanting places where the fortune of the fight is still undecisive. It can almost be said that in the meanwhile the fight reaches a higher and higher level, and that in the meanwhile it has become more and more intense, and always more and more psychological; so that nowadays there is perhaps no more decisive mark of the higher nature, of the more psychological nature, than to be in that sense self-contradictory, and to be actually still a battleground for those two opposites. The symbol of this fight, written in a writing which has remained worthy of perusal throughout the course of history up to the present time, is called "Rome against Judæa, Judæa against Rome."

Hitherto there has been no greater event than that fight, the putting of that question, that deadly antagonism. Rome found in the Jew the incarnation of the unnatural, as though it were its diametrically opposed monstrosity, and in Rome the Jew was held to be convicted of hatred of the whole human race: and rightly so, in so far as it is right to link the well-being and the future of the human race to the unconditional mastery of the aristocratic values, of the Roman values. What, conversely, did the Jews feel against Rome? One can surmise it from a thousand symptoms, but it is sufficient to carry one's mind back to the Johannian Apocalypse, that most obscene of all the written outbursts, which has revenge on its conscience. (One should also appraise at its full value the profound logic of the Christian instinct, when over this very book of hate it wrote the name of the Disciple of Love, that self-same disciple to whom it attributed that impassioned and ecstatic Gospel— therein lurks a portion of truth, however much literary forging may have been necessary for this purpose.) The Romans were the strong and aristocratic; a nation stronger and more aristocratic has never existed in the world, has never even been dreamed of; every relic of them, every inscription enraptures, granted that one can divine what it is that writes the inscription. The Jews, conversely, were that priestly nation of resentment par excellence, possessed by a unique genius for popular morals: just compare with the Jews the nations with analogous gifts, such as the Chinese or the Germans, so as to realise afterwards what is first rate, and what is fifth rate.

Which of them has been provisionally victorious, Rome or Judæa? but there is not a shadow of doubt; just consider to whom in Rome itself nowadays you bow down, as though before the quintessence of all the highest values—and not only in Rome, but almost over half the world, everywhere where man has been tamed or is about to be tamed—to three Jews, as we know, and one Jewess (to Jesus of Nazareth, to Peter the fisher, to Paul the tent-maker, and to the mother of the aforesaid Jesus, named Mary). This is very remarkable: Rome is undoubtedly defeated.

At any rate there took place in the Renaissance a brilliantly sinister revival of the classical ideal, of the aristocratic valuation of all things: Rome herself, like a man waking up from a trance, stirred beneath the burden of the new Judaised Rome that had been built over her, which presented the appearance of an œcumenical synagogue and was called the "Church": but immediately Judæa triumphed again, thanks to that fundamentally popular (German and English) movement of revenge, which is called the Reformation, and taking also into account its inevitable corollary, the restoration of the Church—the restoration also of the ancient graveyard peace of classical Rome. Judæa proved yet once more victorious over the classical ideal in the French Revolution, and in a sense which was even more crucial and even more profound: the last political aristocracy that existed in Europe, that of the French seventeenth and eighteenth centuries, broke into pieces beneath the instincts of a resentful populace—never had the world heard a greater jubilation, a more uproarious enthusiasm: indeed, there took place in the midst of it the most monstrous and unexpected phenomenon; the ancient ideal itself swept before the eyes and conscience of humanity with all its life and with unheard-of splendour, and in opposition to resentment's lying war-cry of the prerogative of the most, in opposition to the will to lowliness, abasement, and equalisation, the will to a retrogression and twilight of humanity, there rang out once again, stronger, simpler, more penetrating than ever, the terrible and enchanting counter-warcry of the prerogative of the few! Like a final signpost to other ways, there appeared Napoleon, the most unique and violent anachronism that ever existed, and in him the incarnate problem of the aristocratic ideal in itself—consider well what a problem it is:—Napoleon, that synthesis of Monster and Superman.

17.

Was it therewith over? Was that greatest of all antitheses of ideals thereby relegated ad acta for all time? Or only postponed, postponed for a long time? May there not take place at some time or other a much more awful, much more carefully prepared flaring up of the old conflagration? Further! Should not one wish that consummation with all one's strength?—will it one's self? demand it one's self? He who at this juncture begins, like my readers, to reflect, to think further, will have difficulty in coming quickly to a conclusion,—ground enough for me to come myself to a conclusion, taking it for granted that for some time past what I mean has been sufficiently clear, what I exactly mean by that dangerous motto which is inscribed on the body of my last book: Beyond Good and Evil—at any rate that is not the same as "Beyond Good and Bad."

Note.—I avail myself of the opportunity offered by this treatise to express, openly and formally, a wish which up to the present has only been expressed in occasional conversations with scholars, namely, that some Faculty of philosophy should, by means of a series of prize essays, gain the glory of having promoted the further study of the history of morals— perhaps this book may serve to give forcible impetus in such a direction. With regard to a possibility of this character, the following question deserves consideration. It merits quite as much the attention of philologists and historians as of actual professional philosophers.

"What indication of the history of the evolution of the moral ideas is afforded by philology, and especially by etymological investigation?"

On the other hand, it is of course equally necessary to induce physiologists and doctors to be interested in these problems (of the value of the valuations which have prevailed up to the present): in this connection the professional philosophers may be trusted to act as the spokesmen and intermediaries in these particular instances, after, of course, they have quite succeeded in transforming the relationship between philosophy and physiology and medicine, which is originally one of coldness and suspicion, into the most friendly and fruitful reciprocity. In point of fact, all tables of values, all the "thou shalts" known to history and ethnology, need primarily a physiological, at any rate in preference to a psychological, elucidation and interpretation; all equally require a critique from medical science. The question, "What is the value of this or that table of 'values' and morality?" will be asked from the most varied standpoints. For instance, the question of "valuable for what" can never be analysed with sufficient nicety. That, for instance, which would evidently have value with regard to promoting in a race the greatest possible powers of endurance (or with regard to increasing its adaptability to a specific climate, or with regard to the preservation of the greatest number) would have nothing like the same value, if it were a question of evolving a stronger species. In gauging values, the good of the majority and the good of the minority are opposed standpoints: we leave it to the naïveté of English biologists to regard the former standpoint as intrinsically superior. All the sciences have now to pave the way for the future task of the philosopher; this task being understood to mean, that he must solve the problem of value, that he has to fix the hierarchy of values.

SECOND ESSAY. "GUILT," "BAD CONSCIENCE," AND THE LIKE.

1.

The breeding of an animal that can promise—is not this just that very paradox of a task which nature has set itself in regard to man? Is not this the very problem of man? The fact that this problem has been to a great extent solved, must appear all the more phenomenal to one who can estimate at its full value that force of forgetfulness which works in opposition to it. Forgetfulness is no mere vis inertiæ, as the superficial believe, rather is it a power of obstruction, active and, in the strictest sense of the word, positive—a power responsible for the fact that what we have lived, experienced, taken into ourselves, no more enters into consciousness during the process of digestion (it might be called psychic absorption) than all the whole manifold process by which our physical nutrition, the so-called "incorporation," is carried on. The temporary shutting of the doors and windows of consciousness, the relief from the clamant alarums and excursions, with which our subconscious world of servant organs works in mutual co-operation and antagonism; a little quietude, a little tabula rasa of the consciousness, so as to make room again for the new, and above all for the more noble functions and functionaries, room for government, foresight, predetermination (for our organism is on an oligarchic model)—this is the utility, as I have said, of the active forgetfulness, which is a very sentinel and nurse of psychic order, repose, etiquette; and this shows at once why it is that there can exist no happiness, no gladness, no hope, no pride, no real present, without forgetfulness. The man in whom this preventative apparatus is damaged and discarded, is to be compared to a dyspeptic, and it is something more than a comparison—he can "get rid of" nothing. But this very animal who finds it necessary to be forgetful, in whom, in fact, forgetfulness represents a force and a form of robust health, has reared for himself an opposition-power, a memory, with whose help forgetfulness is, in certain instances, kept in check—in the cases, namely, where promises have to be made;—so that it is by no means a mere passive inability to get rid of a once indented impression, not merely the indigestion occasioned by a once pledged word, which one cannot dispose of, but an active refusal to get rid of it, a continuing and a wish to continue what has once been willed, an actual memory of the will; so that between the original "I will," "I shall do," and the actual discharge of the will, its act, we can easily interpose a world of new strange phenomena, circumstances, veritable volitions, without the snapping of this long chain of the will. But what is the underlying hypothesis of all this? How thoroughly, in order to be able to regulate the future in this way, must man have first learnt to distinguish between necessitated and accidental phenomena, to think causally, to see the distant as present and to anticipate it, to fix with certainty what is the end, and what is the means to that end; above all, to reckon, to have power to calculate—how thoroughly must man have first become calculable, disciplined, necessitated even for himself and his own conception of himself, that, like a man entering into a promise, he could guarantee himself as a future.

2.

This is simply the long history of the origin of responsibility. That task of breeding an animal which can make promises, includes, as we have already grasped, as its condition and preliminary, the more immediate task of first making man to a certain extent, necessitated, uniform, like among his like, regular, and consequently calculable. The immense work of what I have called, "morality of custom"1 (cp. Dawn of Day, Aphs. 9, 14, and 16), the actual work of man on himself during the longest period of the human race, his whole prehistoric work, finds its meaning, its great justification (in spite of all its innate hardness, despotism, stupidity, and idiocy) in this fact: man, with the help of the morality of customs and of social strait-waistcoats, was made genuinely calculable.

If, however, we place ourselves at the end of this colossal process, at the point where the tree finally matures its fruits, when society and its morality of custom finally bring to light that to which it was only the means, then do we find as the ripest fruit on its tree the sovereign individual, that resembles only himself, that has got loose from the morality of custom, the autonomous "super-moral" individual (for "autonomous" and "moral" are mutually-exclusive terms),—in short, the man of the personal, long, and independent will, competent to promise, and we find in him a proud consciousness (vibrating in every fibre), of what has been at last achieved and become vivified in him, a genuine consciousness of power and freedom, a feeling of human perfection in general. And this man who has grown to freedom, who is really competent to promise, this lord of the free will, this sovereign— how is it possible for him not to know how great is his superiority over everything incapable of binding itself by promises, or of being its own security, how great is the trust, the awe, the reverence that he awakes— he "deserves" all three—not to know that with this mastery over himself he is necessarily also given the mastery over circumstances, over nature, over all creatures with shorter wills, less reliable characters? The "free" man, the owner of a long unbreakable will, finds in this possessionhis standard of value: looking out from himself upon the others, he honours or he despises, and just as necessarily as he honours his peers, the strong and the reliable (those who can bind themselves by promises),—that is, every one who promises like a sovereign, with difficulty, rarely and slowly, who is sparing with his trusts but confers honour by the very fact of trusting, who gives his word as something that can be relied on, because he knows himself strong enough to keep it even in the teeth of disasters, even in the "teeth of fate,"—so with equal necessity will he have the heel of his foot ready for the lean and empty jackasses, who promise when they have no business to do so, and his rod of chastisement ready for the liar, who already breaks his word at the very minute when it is on his lips. The proud knowledge of the extraordinary privilege of responsibility, the consciousness of this rare freedom, of this power over himself and over fate, has sunk right down to his innermost depths, and has become an instinct, a dominating instinct—what name will he give to it, to this dominating instinct, if he needs to have a word for it? But there is no doubt about it—the sovereign man calls it his conscience.

3.

His conscience?—One apprehends at once that the idea "conscience," which is here seen in its supreme manifestation, supreme in fact to almost the point of strangeness, should already have behind it a long history and evolution. The ability to guarantee one's self with all due pride, and also at the same time to say yes to one's self—that is, as has been said, a ripe fruit, but also a late fruit:—How long must needs this fruit hang sour and bitter on the tree! And for an even longer period there was not a glimpse of such a fruit to to be had—no one had taken it on himself to promise it, although everything on the tree was quite ready for it, and everything was maturing for that very consummation. "How is a memory to be made for the man-animal? How is an impression to be so deeply fixed upon this ephemeral understanding, half dense, and half silly, upon this incarnate forgetfulness, that it will be permanently present?" As one may imagine, this primeval problem was not solved by exactly gentle answers and gentle means; perhaps there is nothing more awful and more sinister in the early history of man than his system of mnemonics. "Something is burnt in so as to remain in his memory: only that which never stops hurting remains in his memory." This is an axiom of the oldest (unfortunately also the longest) psychology in the world. It might even be said that wherever solemnity, seriousness, mystery, and gloomy colours are now found in the life of the men and of nations of the world, there is some survival of that horror which was once the universal concomitant of all promises, pledges, and obligations. The past, the past with all its length, depth, and hardness, wafts to us its breath, and bubbles up in us again, when we become "serious." When man thinks it necessary to make for himself a memory, he never accomplishes it without blood, tortures, and sacrifice; the most dreadful sacrifices and forfeitures (among them the sacrifice of the first-born), the most loathsome mutilation (for instance, castration), the most cruel rituals of all the religious cults (for all religions are really at bottom systems of cruelty)—all these things originate from that instinct which found in pain its most potent mnemonic. In a certain sense the whole of asceticism is to be ascribed to this: certain ideas have got to be made inextinguishable, omnipresent, "fixed," with the object of hypnotising the whole nervous and intellectual system through these "fixed ideas"—and the ascetic methods and modes of life are the means of freeing those ideas from the competition of all other ideas so as to make them "unforgettable." The worse memory man had, the ghastlier the signs presented by his customs; the severity of the penal laws affords in particular a gauge of the extent of man's difficulty in conquering forgetfulness, and in keeping a few primal postulates of social intercourse ever present to the minds of those who were the slaves of every momentary emotion and every momentary desire. We Germans do certainly not regard ourselves as an especially cruel and hard-hearted nation, still less as an especially casual and happy-go-lucky one; but one has only to look at our old penal ordinances in order to realise what a lot of trouble it takes in the world to evolve a "nation of thinkers" (I

mean: the European nation which exhibits at this very day the maximum of reliability, seriousness, bad taste, and positiveness, which has on the strength of these qualities a right to train every kind of European mandarin). These Germans employed terrible means to make for themselves a memory, to enable them to master their rooted plebeian instincts and the brutal crudity of those instincts: think of the old German punishments, for instance, stoning (as far back as the legend, the millstone falls on the head of the guilty man), breaking on the wheel (the most original invention and speciality of the German genius in the sphere of punishment), dart-throwing, tearing, or trampling by horses ("quartering"), boiling the criminal in oil or wine (still prevalent in the fourteenth and fifteenth centuries), the highly popular flaying ("slicing into strips"), cutting the flesh out of the breast; think also of the evil-doer being besmeared with honey, and then exposed to the flies in a blazing sun. It was by the help of such images and precedents that man eventually kept in his memory five or six "I will nots" with regard to which he had already given his promise, so as to be able to enjoy the advantages of society— and verily with the help of this kind of memory man eventually attained "reason"! Alas! reason, seriousness, mastery over the emotions, all these gloomy, dismal things which are called reflection, all these privileges and pageantries of humanity: how dear is the price that they have exacted! How much blood and cruelty is the foundation of all "good things"!

4.

But how is it that that other melancholy object, the

consciousness of sin, the whole "bad conscience," came into the world? And it is here that we turn back to our genealogists of morals. For the second time I say—or have I not said it yet?—that they are worth nothing. Just their own five- spans-long limited modern experience; no knowledge of the past, and no wish to know it; still less a historic instinct, a power of "second sight" (which is what is really required in this case)—and despite this to go in for the history of morals. It stands to reason that this must needs produce results which are removed from the truth by something more than a respectful distance.

Have these current genealogists of morals ever allowed themselves to have even the vaguest notion, for instance, that the cardinal moral idea of "ought"2 originates from the very material idea of "owe"? Or that punishment developed as a retaliation absolutely independently of any preliminary hypothesis of the freedom or determination of the will?—And this to such an extent, that a high degree of civilisation was always first necessary for the animal man to begin to make those much more primitive distinctions of "intentional," "negligent," "accidental," "responsible," and their contraries, and apply them in the assessing of punishment. That idea—"the wrong-doer deserves punishment because he might have acted otherwise," in spite of the fact that it is nowadays so cheap, obvious, natural, and inevitable, and that it has had to serve as an illustration of the way in which the sentiment of justice appeared on earth, is in point of fact an exceedingly late, and even refined form of human judgment and inference; the placing of this idea back at the beginning of the world is simply a clumsy violation of the principles of primitive psychology. Throughout the longest period of human history punishment was never based on the responsibility of the evil-doer for his action, and was consequently not based on the hypothesis that only the guilty should be punished;—on the contrary, punishment was inflicted in those days for the same reason that parents punish their children even nowadays, out of anger at an injury that they have suffered, an anger which vents itself mechanically on the author of the injury—but this anger is kept in bounds and modified through the idea that every injury has somewhere or other its equivalent price, and can really be paid off, even though it be by means of pain to the author.

Whence is it that this ancient deep-rooted and now perhaps ineradicable idea has drawn its strength, this idea of an equivalency between injury and pain? I have already revealed its origin, in the contractual relationship between creditor and ower, that is as old as the existence of legal rights at all, and in its turn points back to the primary forms of purchase, sale, barter, and trade.

5.

The German world "schuld" means both debt and guilt. Cp. the English "owe" and "ought," by which I occasionally render the double meaning.—H. B. S.

The realisation of these contractual relations excites, of course (as would be already expected from our previous observations), a great deal of suspicion and opposition towards the primitive society which made or sanctioned them. In this society promises will be made; in this society the object is to provide the promiser with a memory; in this society, so may we suspect, there will be full scope for hardness, cruelty, and pain: the "ower," in order to induce credit in his promise of repayment, in order to give a guarantee of the earnestness and sanctity of his promise, in order to drill into his own conscience the duty, the solemn duty, of repayment, will, by virtue of a contract with his creditor to meet the contingency of his not paying, pledge something that he still possesses, something that he still has in his power, for instance, his life or his wife, or his freedom or his body (or under certain religious conditions even his salvation, his soul's welfare, even his peace in the grave; so in Egypt, where the corpse of the ower found even in the grave no rest from the creditor—of course, from the Egyptian standpoint, this peace was a matter of particular importance). But especially has the creditor the power of inflicting on the body of the ower all kinds of pain and torture— the power, for instance, of cutting off from it an amount that appeared proportionate to the greatness of the debt;—this point of view resulted in the universal prevalence at an early date of precise schemes of valuation, frequently horrible in the minuteness and meticulosity of their application, legally sanctioned schemes of valuation for individual limbs and parts of the body. I consider it as already a progress, as a proof of a freer, less petty, and more Roman conception of law, when the Roman Code of the Twelve Tables decreed that it was immaterial how much or how little the creditors in such a contingency cut off, "si plus minusve secuerunt, ne fraude esto." Let us make the logic of the whole of this equalisation process clear; it is strange enough. The equivalence consists in this: instead of an advantage directly compensatory of his injury (that is, instead of an equalisation in money, lands, or some kind of chattel), the creditor is granted by way of repayment and compensation a certain sensation of satisfaction—the satisfaction of being able to vent, without any trouble, his power on one who is powerless, the delight "de faire le mal pour le plaisir de le faire," the joy in sheer violence: and this joy will be relished in proportion to the lowness and humbleness of the creditor in the social scale, and is quite apt to have the effect of the most delicious dainty, and even seem the foretaste of a higher social position.

Thanks to the punishment of the "ower," the creditor participates in the rights of the masters. At last he too, for once in a way, attains the edifying consciousness of being able to despise and ill-treat a creature— as an "inferior"—or at any rate of seeing him being despised and ill- treated, in case the actual power of punishment, the administration of punishment, has already become transferred to the "authorities." The compensation consequently consists in a claim on cruelty and a right to draw thereon.

6.

It is then in this sphere of the law of contract that we find the cradle of the whole moral world of the ideas of "guilt," "conscience," "duty," the "sacredness of duty,"—their commencement, like the commencement of all great things in the world, is thoroughly and continuously saturated with blood. And should we not add that this world has never really lost a certain savour of blood and torture (not even in old Kant; the categorical imperative reeks of cruelty). It was in this sphere likewise that there first became formed that sinister and perhaps now indissoluble association of the ideas of "guilt" and "suffering." To put the question yet again, why can suffering be a compensation for "owing"?—Because the infliction of suffering produces the highest degree of happiness, because the injured party will get in exchange for his loss (including his vexation at his loss) an extraordinary counter-pleasure: the infliction of suffering—a real feast, something that, as I have said, was all the more appreciated the greater the paradox created by the rank and social status of the creditor. These observations are purely conjectural; for, apart from the painful nature of the task, it is hard to plumb such profound depths: the clumsy introduction of the idea of "revenge" as a connecting-link simply hides and obscures the view instead of rendering it clearer (revenge itself simply leads back again to the identical problem—"How can the infliction of suffering be a satisfaction?"). In my opinion it is repugnant to the delicacy, and still more to the hypocrisy of tame domestic animals (that is, modern men; that is, ourselves), to realise with all their energy the extent to which cruelty constituted the great joy and delight of ancient man, was an ingredient which seasoned nearly all his pleasures, and conversely the extent of the naïveté and innocence with which he manifested his need for cruelty, when he actually made as a matter of principle "disinterested malice" (or, to use Spinoza's expression, the *sympathia malevolens*) into a normal characteristic of man— as consequently something to which the conscience says a hearty yes. The more profound observer has perhaps already had sufficient opportunity for noticing this most ancient and radical joy and delight of mankind; in Beyond Good and Evil, Aph. 188 (and even earlier, in The Dawn of Day, Aphs. 18, 77, 113), I have cautiously indicated the continually growing spiritualisation and "deification" of cruelty, which pervades the whole history of the higher civilisation (and in the larger sense even constitutes it). At any rate the time is not so long past when it was impossible to conceive of royal weddings and national festivals on a grand scale, without executions, tortures, or perhaps an auto-da-fé", or similarly to conceive of an aristocratic household, without a creature to serve as a butt for the cruel and malicious baiting of the inmates. (The reader will perhaps remember Don Quixote at the court of the Duchess: we read nowadays the whole of Don Quixote with a bitter taste in the mouth, almost with a sensation of torture, a fact which would appear very strange and very incomprehensible to the author and his contemporaries—they read it with the best conscience in the world as the gayest of books; they almost died with laughing at it.) The sight of suffering does one good, the infliction of suffering does one more good— this is a hard maxim, but none the less a fundamental maxim, old, powerful, and "human, all-too-human"; one, moreover, to which perhaps even the apes as well would subscribe: for it is said that in inventing bizarre cruelties they are giving abundant proof of their future humanity, to which, as it were, they are playing the prelude. Without cruelty, no feast: so teaches the oldest and longest history of man—and in punishment too is there so much of the festive.

7.

Entertaining, as I do, these thoughts, I am, let me say in parenthesis, fundamentally opposed to helping our pessimists to new water for the discordant and groaning mills of their disgust with life; on the contrary, it should be shown specifically that, at the time when mankind was not yet ashamed of its cruelty, life in the world was brighter than it is nowadays when there are pessimists. The darkening of the heavens over man has always increased in proportion to the growth of man's shame before man. The tired pessimistic outlook, the mistrust of the riddle of life, the icy negation of disgusted ennui, all those are not the signs of the most evil age of the human race: much rather do they come first to the light of day, as the swamp-flowers, which they are, when the swamp to which they belong, comes into existence—I mean the diseased refinement and moralisation, thanks to which the "animal man" has at last learnt to be ashamed of all his instincts. On the road to angelhood (not to use in this context a harder word) man has developed that dyspeptic stomach and coated tongue, which have made not only the joy and innocence of the animal repulsive to him, but also life itself:—so that sometimes he stands with stopped nostrils before his own self, and, like Pope Innocent the Third, makes a black list of his own horrors ("unclean generation, loathsome nutrition when in the maternal body, badness of the matter out of which man develops, awful stench, secretion of saliva, urine, and excrement"). Nowadays, when suffering is always trotted out as the first argument against existence, as its most sinister query, it is well to remember the times when men judged on converse principles because they could not dispense with the infliction of suffering, and saw therein a magic of the first order, a veritable bait of seduction to life.

Perhaps in those days (this is to solace the weaklings) pain did not hurt so much as it does nowadays: any physician who has treated negroes (granted that these are taken as representative of the prehistoric man) suffering from severe internal inflammations which would bring a European, even though he had the soundest constitution, almost to despair, would be in a position to come to this conclusion. Pain has not the same effect with negroes. (The curve of human sensibilities to pain seems indeed to sink in an extraordinary and almost sudden fashion, as soon as one has passed the upper ten thousand or ten millions of over-civilised humanity, and I personally have no doubt that, by comparison with one painful night passed by one single hysterical chit of a cultured woman, the suffering of all the animals taken together who have been put to the question of the knife, so as to give scientific answers, are simply negligible.) We may perhaps be allowed to admit the possibility of the craving for cruelty not necessarily having become really extinct: it only requires, in view of the fact that pain hurts more nowadays, a certain sublimation and subtilisation, it must especially be translated to the imaginative and psychic plane, and be adorned with such smug euphemisms, that even the most fastidious and hypocritical conscience could never grow suspicious of their real nature ("Tragic pity" is one of these euphemisms: another is "les nostalgies de la croix"). What really raises one's indignation against suffering is not suffering intrinsically, but the senselessness of suffering; such a senselessness, however, existed neither in Christianity, which interpreted suffering into a whole mysterious salvation-apparatus, nor in the beliefs of the naive ancient man, who only knew how to find a meaning in suffering from the standpoint of the spectator, or the inflictor of the suffering. In order to get the secret, undiscovered, and unwitnessed suffering out of the world it was almost compulsory to invent gods and a hierarchy of intermediate beings, in short, something which wanders even among secret places, sees even in the dark, and makes a point of never missing an interesting and painful spectacle. It was with the help of such inventions that life got to learn the tour de force, which has become part of its stock-in-trade, the tour de force of self-justification, of the justification of evil; nowadays this would perhaps require other auxiliary devices (for instance, life as a riddle, life as a problem of knowledge). "Every evil is justified in the sight of which a god finds edification," so rang the logic of primitive sentiment—and, indeed, was it only of primitive? The gods conceived as friends of spectacles of cruelty—oh how far does this primeval conception extend even nowadays into our European civilisation! One would perhaps like in this context to consult Luther and Calvin. It is at any rate certain that even the Greeks knew no more piquant seasoning for the happiness of their gods than the joys of cruelty. What, do you think, was the mood with which Homer makes his gods look down upon the fates of men? What final meaning have at bottom the Trojan War and similar tragic horrors? It is impossible to entertain any doubt on the point: they were intended as festival games for the gods, and, in so far as the poet is of a more godlike breed than other men, as festival games also for the poets. It was in just this spirit and no other, that at a later date the moral philosophers of Greece conceived the eyes of God as still looking down on the moral struggle, the heroism, and the self-torture of the virtuous; the Heracles of duty was on a stage, and was conscious of the fact; virtue without witnesses was something quite unthinkable for this nation of actors. Must not that philosophic invention, so audacious and so fatal, which was then absolutely new to Europe, the invention of "free will," of the absolute spontaneity of man in good and evil, simply have been made for the specific purpose of justifying the idea, that the interest of the gods in humanity and human virtue was inexhaustible?

There would never on the stage of this free-will world be a dearth of really new, really novel and exciting situations, plots, catastrophes. A world thought out on completely deterministic lines would be easily guessed by the gods, and would consequently soon bore them—sufficient reason for these friends of the gods, the philosophers, not to ascribe to their gods such a deterministic world. The whole of ancient humanity is full of delicate consideration for the spectator, being as it is a world of thorough publicity and theatricality, which could not conceive of happiness without spectacles and festivals.—And, as has already been said, even in great punishment there is so much which is festive.

8.

The feeling of "ought," of personal obligation (to take up again the train of our inquiry), has had, as we saw, its origin in the oldest and most original personal relationship that there is, the relationship between buyer and seller, creditor and ower: here it was that individual confronted individual, and that individual matched himself against individual. There has not yet been found a grade of civilisation so low, as not to manifest some trace of this relationship. Making prices, assessing values, thinking out equivalents, exchanging—all this preoccupied the primal thoughts of man to such an extent that in a certain sense it constituted thinking itself: it was here that was trained the oldest form of sagacity, it was here in this sphere that we can perhaps trace the first commencement of man's pride, of his feeling of superiority over other animals. Perhaps our word "Mensch" (manas) still expresses just something of this self-pride: man denoted himself as the being who measures values, who values and measures, as the "assessing" animal par excellence. Sale and purchase, together with their psychological concomitants, are older than the origins of any form of social organisation and union: it is rather from the most rudimentary form of individual right that the budding consciousness of exchange, commerce, debt, right, obligation, compensation was first transferred to the rudest and most elementary of the social complexes (in their relation to similar complexes), the habit of comparing force with force, together with that of measuring, of calculating. His eye was now focussed to this perspective; and with that ponderous consistency characteristic of ancient thought, which, though set in motion with difficulty, yet proceeds inflexibly along the line on which it has started, man soon arrived at the great generalisation, "everything has its price, all can be paid for," the oldest and most naive moral canon of justice, the beginning of all "kindness," of all "equity," of all "goodwill," of all "objectivity" in the world. Justice in this initial phase is the goodwill among people of about equal power to come to terms with each other, to come to an understanding again by means of a settlement, and with regard to the less powerful, to compel them to agree among themselves to a settlement.

9.

Measured always by the standard of antiquity (this antiquity, moreover, is present or again possible at all periods), the community stands to its members in that important and radical relationship of creditor to his "owers." Man lives in a community, man enjoys the advantages of a community (and what advantages! we occasionally underestimate them nowadays), man lives protected, spared, in peace and trust, secure from certain injuries and enmities, to which the man outside the community, the "peaceless" man, is exposed,—a German understands the original meaning of "Elend" (êlend),—secure because he has entered into pledges and obligations to the community in respect of these very injuries and enmities. What happens when this is not the case? The community, the defrauded creditor, will get itself paid, as well as it can, one can reckon on that. In this case the question of the direct damage done by the offender is quite subsidiary: quite apart from this the criminal3 is above all a breaker, a breaker of word and covenant to the whole, as regards all the advantages and amenities of the communal life in which up to that time he had participated. The criminal is an "ower" who not only fails to repay the advances and advantages that have been given to him, but even sets out to attack his creditor: consequently he is in the future not only, as is fair, deprived of all these advantages and amenities—he is in addition reminded of the importance of those advantages. The wrath of the injured creditor, of the community, puts him back in the wild and outlawed status from which he was previously protected: the community repudiates him—and now every kind of enmity can vent itself on him. Punishment is in this stage of civilisation simply the copy, the mimic, of the normal treatment of the hated, disdained, and conquered enemy, who is not only deprived of every right and protection but of every mercy; so we have the martial law and triumphant festival of the væ victis! in all its mercilessness and cruelty. This shows why war itself (counting the sacrificial cult of war) has produced all the forms under which punishment has manifested itself in history.

10.

As it grows more powerful, the community tends to take the offences of the individual less seriously, because they are now regarded as being much less revolutionary and dangerous to the corporate existence: the evil-doer is no more outlawed and put outside the pale, the common wrath can no longer vent itself upon him with its old licence,—on the contrary, from this very time it is against this wrath, and particularly against the wrath of those directly injured, that the evil-doer is carefully shielded and protected by the community. As, in fact, the penal law develops, the following characteristics become more and more clearly marked: compromise with the wrath of those directly affected by the misdeed; a consequent endeavour to localise the matter and to prevent a further, or indeed a general spread of the disturbance; attempts to find equivalents and to settle the whole matter (compositio); above all, the will, which manifests itself with increasing definiteness, to treat every offence as in a certain degree capable of being paid off, and consequently, at any rate up to a certain point, to isolate the offender from his act. As the power and the self-consciousness of a community increases, so proportionately does the penal law become mitigated; conversely every weakening and jeopardising of the community revives the harshest forms of that law. The creditor has always grown more humane proportionately as he has grown more rich; finally the amount of injury he can endure without really suffering becomes the criterion of his wealth. It is possible to conceive of a society blessed with so great a consciousness of its own power as to indulge in the most aristocratic luxury of letting its wrong-doers go scot-free.—"What do my parasites matter to me?" might society say. "Let them live and flourish! I am strong enough for it."—The justice which began with the maxim, "Everything can be paid off, everything must be paid off," ends with connivance at the escape of those who cannot pay to escape—it ends, like every good thing on earth, by destroying itself.—The self-destruction of Justice! we know the pretty name it calls itself—Grace! it remains, as is obvious, the privilege of the strongest, better still, their super-law.

11.

A deprecatory word here against the attempts, that have

lately been made, to find the origin of justice on quite another basis—namely, on that of resentment. Let me whisper a word in the ear of the psychologists, if they would fain study revenge itself at close quarters: this plant blooms its prettiest at present among Anarchists and anti- Semites, a hidden flower, as it has ever been, like the violet, though, forsooth, with another perfume. And as like must necessarily emanate from like, it will not be a matter for surprise that it is just in such circles that we see the birth of endeavours (it is their old birthplace— compare above, First Essay, paragraph 14), to sanctify revenge under the name of justice (as though Justice were at bottom merely a development of the consciousness of injury), and thus with the rehabilitation of revenge to reinstate generally and collectively all the reactive emotions. I object to this last point least of all. It even seems meritorious when regarded from the standpoint of the whole problem of biology (from which standpoint the value of these emotions has up to the present been underestimated). And that to which I alone call attention, is the circumstance that it is the spirit of revenge itself, from which develops this new nuance of scientific equity (for the benefit of hate, envy, mistrust, jealousy, suspicion, rancour, revenge). This scientific "equity" stops immediately and makes way for the accents of deadly enmity and prejudice, so soon as another group of emotions comes on the scene, which in my opinion are of a much higher biological value than these reactions, and consequently have a paramount claim to the valuation and appreciation of science: I mean the really active emotions, such as personal and material ambition, and so forth. (E. Dühring, Value of Life; Course of Philosophy, and passim.) So much against this tendency in general: but as for the particular maxim of Dühring's, that the home of Justice is to be found in the sphere of the reactive feelings, our love of truth compels us drastically to invert his own proposition and to oppose to him this other maxim: the last sphere conquered by the spirit of justice is the sphere of the feeling of reaction! When it really comes about that the just man remains just even as regards his injurer (and not merely cold, moderate, reserved, indifferent: being just is always a positive state); when, in spite of the strong provocation of personal insult, contempt, and calumny, the lofty and clear objectivity of the just and judging eye (whose glance is as profound as it is gentle) is untroubled, why then we have a piece of perfection, a past master of the world—something, in fact, which it would not be wise to expect, and which should not at any rate be too easily believed. Speaking generally, there is no doubt but that even the justest individual only requires a little dose of hostility, malice, or innuendo to drive the blood into his brain and the fairness from it. The active man, the attacking, aggressive man is always a hundred degrees nearer to justice than the man who merely reacts; he certainly has no need to adopt the tactics, necessary in the case of the reacting man, of making false and biassed valuations of his object. It is, in point of fact, for this reason that the aggressive man has at all times enjoyed the stronger, bolder, more aristocratic, and also freer outlook, the better conscience. On the other hand, we already surmise who it really is that has on his conscience the invention of the "bad conscience,"—the resentful man! Finally, let man look at himself in history. In what sphere up to the present has the whole administration of law, the actual need of law, found its earthly home? Perchance in the sphere of the reacting man? Not for a minute: rather in that of the active, strong, spontaneous, aggressive man? I deliberately defy the above- mentioned agitator (who himself makes this self-confession, "the creed of revenge has run through all my works and endeavours like the red thread of Justice"), and say, that judged historically law in the world represents the very war against the reactive feelings, the very war waged on those feelings by the powers of activity and aggression, which devote some of their strength to damming and keeping within bounds this effervescence of hysterical reactivity, and to forcing it to some compromise. Everywhere where justice is practised and justice is maintained, it is to be observed that the stronger power, when confronted with the weaker powers which are inferior to it (whether they be groups, or individuals), searches for weapons to put an end to the senseless fury of resentment, while it carries on its object, partly by taking the victim of resentment out of the clutches of revenge, partly by substituting for revenge a campaign of its own against the enemies of peace and order, partly by finding, suggesting, and occasionally enforcing settlements, partly by standardising certain equivalents for injuries, to which equivalents the element of resentment is henceforth finally referred. The most drastic measure, however, taken and effectuated by the supreme power, to combat the preponderance of the feelings of spite and vindictiveness—it takes this measure as soon as it is at all strong enough to do so—is the foundation of law, the imperative declaration of what in its eyes is to be regarded as just and lawful, and what unjust and unlawful: and while, after the foundation of law, the supreme power treats the aggressive and arbitrary acts of individuals, or of whole groups, as a violation of law, and a revolt against itself, it distracts the feelings of its subjects from the immediate injury inflicted by such a violation, and thus eventually attains the very opposite result to that always desired by revenge, which sees and recognises nothing but the standpoint of the injured party. From henceforth the eye becomes trained to a more and more impersonal valuation of the deed, even the eye of the injured party himself (though this is in the final stage of all, as has been previously remarked)—on this principle "right" and "wrong" first manifest themselves after the foundation of law (and not, as Dühring maintains, only after the act of violation).

To talk of intrinsic right and intrinsic wrong is absolutely nonsensical; intrinsically, an injury, an oppression, an exploitation, an annihilation can be nothing wrong, inasmuch as life is essentially (that is, in its cardinal functions) something which functions by injuring, oppressing, exploiting, and annihilating, and is absolutely inconceivable without such a character. It is necessary to make an even more serious confession:—viewed from the most advanced biological standpoint, conditions of legality can be only exceptional conditions, in that they are partial restrictions of the real life-will, which makes for power, and in that they are subordinated to the life-will's general end as particular means, that is, as means to create larger units of strength. A legal organisation, conceived of as sovereign and universal, not as a weapon in a fight of complexes of power, but as a weapon against fighting, generally something after the style of Dühring's communistic model of treating every will as equal with every other will, would be a principle hostile to life, a destroyer and dissolver of man, an outrage on the future of man, a symptom of fatigue, a secret cut to Nothingness.—

12.

A word more on the origin and end of punishment—two problems which are or ought to be kept distinct, but which unfortunately are usually lumped into one. And what tactics have our moral genealogists employed up to the present in these cases? Their inveterate naïveté. They find out some "end" in the punishment, for instance, revenge and deterrence, and then in all their innocence set this end at the beginning, as the causa fiendi of the punishment, and—they have done the trick. But the patching up of a history of the origin of law is the last use to which the "End in Law"4 ought to be put. Perhaps there is no more pregnant principle for any kind of history than the following, which, difficult though it is to master, should none the less be mastered in every detail.— The origin of the existence of a thing and its final utility, its practical application and incorporation in a system of ends, are toto cœlo opposed to each other—everything, anything, which exists and which prevails anywhere, will always be put to new purposes by a force superior to itself, will be commandeered afresh, will be turned and transformed to new uses; all "happening" in the organic world consists of overpowering and dominating, and again all overpowering and domination is a new interpretation and adjustment, which must necessarily obscure or absolutely extinguish the subsisting "meaning" and "end." The most perfect comprehension of the utility of any physiological organ (or also of a legal institution, social custom, political habit, form in art or in religious worship) does not for a minute imply any simultaneous comprehension of its origin: this may seem uncomfortable and unpalatable to the older men,—for it has been the immemorial belief that understanding the final cause or the utility of a thing, a form, an institution, means also understanding the reason for its origin: to give an example of this logic, the eye was made to see, the hand was made to grasp. So even punishment was conceived as invented with a view to punishing. But all ends and all utilities are only signs that a Will to Power has mastered a less powerful force, has impressed thereon out of its own self the meaning of a function; and the whole history of a "Thing," an organ, a custom, can on the same principle be regarded as a continuous "sign-chain" of perpetually new interpretations and adjustments, whose causes, so far from needing to have even a mutual connection, sometimes follow and alternate with each other absolutely haphazard. Similarly, the evolution of a "thing," of a custom, is anything but its progressus to an end, still less a logical and direct progressus attained with the minimum expenditure of energy and cost: it is rather the succession of processes of subjugation, more or less profound, more or less mutually independent, which operate on the thing itself; it is, further, the resistance which in each case invariably displayed this subjugation, the Protean wriggles by way of defence and reaction, and, further, the results of successful counter-efforts. The form is fluid, but the meaning is even more so—even inside every individual organism the case is the same: with every genuine growth of the whole, the "function" of the individual organs becomes shifted,—in certain cases a partial perishing of these organs, a diminution of their numbers (for instance, through annihilation of the connecting members), can be a symptom of growing strength and perfection. What I mean is this: even partial loss of utility, decay, and degeneration, loss of function and purpose, in a word, death, appertain to the conditions of the genuine progressus; which always appears in the shape of a will and way to greater power, and is always realised at the expense of innumerable smaller powers. The magnitude of a "progress" is gauged by the greatness of the sacrifice that it requires: humanity as a mass sacrificed to the prosperity of the one stronger species of Man—that would be a progress. I emphasise all the more this cardinal characteristic of the historic method, for the reason that in its essence it runs counter to predominant instincts and prevailing taste, which much prefer to put up with absolute casualness, even with the mechanical senselessness of all phenomena, than with the theory of a power-will, in exhaustive play throughout all phenomena. The democratic idiosyncrasy against everything which rules and wishes to rule, the modern misarchism (to coin a bad word for a bad thing), has gradually but so thoroughly transformed itself into the guise of intellectualism, the most abstract intellectualism, that even nowadays it penetrates and has the right to penetrate step by step into the most exact and apparently the most objective sciences: this tendency has, in fact, in my view already dominated the whole of physiology and biology, and to their detriment, as is obvious, in so far as it has spirited away a radical idea, the idea of true activity.

The tyranny of this idiosyncrasy, however, results in the theory of "adaptation" being pushed forward into the van of the argument, exploited; adaptation—that means to say, a second-class activity, a mere capacity for "reacting"; in fact, life itself has been defined (by Herbert Spencer) as an increasingly effective internal adaptation to external circumstances. This definition, however, fails to realise the real essence of life, its will to power. It fails to appreciate the paramount superiority enjoyed by those plastic forces of spontaneity, aggression, and encroachment with their new interpretations and tendencies, to the operation of which adaptation is only a natural corollary: consequently the sovereign office of the highest functionaries in the organism itself (among which the life-will appears as an active and formative principle) is repudiated. One remembers Huxley's reproach to Spencer of his "administrative Nihilism": but it is a case of something much more than "administration."

13.

To return to our subject, namely punishment, we must make consequently a double distinction: first, the relatively permanent element, the custom, the act, the "drama," a certain rigid sequence of methods of procedure; on the other hand, the fluid element, the meaning, the end, the expectation which is attached to the operation of such procedure. At this point we immediately assume, per analogiam (in accordance with the theory of the historic method, which we have elaborated above), that the procedure itself is something older and earlier than its utilisation in punishment, that this utilisation was introduced and interpreted into the procedure (which had existed for a long time, but whose employment had another meaning), in short, that the case is different from that hitherto supposed by our naïf genealogists of morals and of law, who thought that the procedure was invented for the purpose of punishment, in the same way that the hand had been previously thought to have been invented for the purpose of grasping. With regard to the other element in punishment, its fluid element, its meaning, the idea of punishment in a very late stage of civilisation (for instance, contemporary Europe) is not content with manifesting merely one meaning, but manifests a whole synthesis "of meanings." The past general history of punishment, the history of its employment for the most diverse ends, crystallises eventually into a kind of unity, which is difficult to analyse into its parts, and which, it is necessary to emphasise, absolutely defies definition. (It is nowadays impossible to say definitely the precise reason for punishment: all ideas, in which a whole process is promiscuously comprehended, elude definition; it is only that which has no history, which can be defined.) At an earlier stage, on the contrary, that synthesis of meanings appears much less rigid and much more elastic; we can realise how in each individual case the elements of the synthesis change their value and their position, so that now one element and now another stands out and predominates over the others, nay, in certain cases one element (perhaps the end of deterrence) seems to eliminate all the rest. At any rate, so as to give some idea of the uncertain, supplementary, and accidental nature of the meaning of punishment and of the manner in which one identical procedure can be employed and adapted for the most diametrically opposed objects, I will at this point give a scheme that has suggested itself to me, a scheme itself based on comparatively small and accidental material.—Punishment, as rendering the criminal harmless and incapable of further injury.—Punishment, as compensation for the injury sustained by the injured party, in any form whatsoever (including the form of sentimental compensation).—Punishment, as an isolation of that which disturbs the equilibrium, so as to prevent the further spreading of the disturbance.—Punishment as a means of inspiring fear of those who determine and execute the punishment.—Punishment as a kind of compensation for advantages which the wrong-doer has up to that time enjoyed (for example, when he is utilised as a slave in the mines).— Punishment, as the elimination of an element of decay (sometimes of a whole branch, as according to the Chinese laws, consequently as a means to the purification of the race, or the preservation of a social type).—- Punishment as a festival, as the violent oppression and humiliation of an enemy that has at last been subdued.—Punishment as a mnemonic, whether for him who suffers the punishment—the so-called "correction," or for the witnesses of its administration. Punishment, as the payment of a fee stipulated for by the power which protects the evil-doer from the excesses of revenge.—Punishment, as a compromise with the natural phenomenon of revenge, in so far as revenge is still maintained and claimed as a privilege by the stronger races.—Punishment as a declaration and measure of war against an enemy of peace, of law, of order, of authority, who is fought by society with the weapons which war provides, as a spirit dangerous to the community, as a breaker of the contract on which the community is based, as a rebel, a traitor, and a breaker of the peace.

14.

This list is certainly not complete; it is obvious that punishment is overloaded with utilities of all kinds. This makes it all the more permissible to eliminate one supposed utility, which passes, at any rate in the popular mind, for its most essential utility, and which is just what even now provides the strongest support for that faith in punishment which is nowadays for many reasons tottering. Punishment is supposed to have the value of exciting in the guilty the consciousness of guilt; in punishment is sought the proper instrumentum of that psychic reaction which becomes known as a "bad conscience," "remorse." But this theory is even, from the point of view of the present, a violation of reality and psychology: and how much more so is the case when we have to deal with the longest period of man's history, his primitive history! Genuine remorse is certainly extremely rare among wrong-doers and the victims of punishment; prisons and houses of correction are not the soil on which this worm of remorse pullulates for choice— this is the unanimous opinion of all conscientious observers, who in many cases arrive at such a judgment with enough reluctance and against their own personal wishes. Speaking generally, punishment hardens and numbs, it produces concentration, it sharpens the consciousness of alienation, it strengthens the power of resistance. When it happens that it breaks the man's energy and brings about a piteous prostration and abjectness, such a result is certainly even less salutary than the average effect of punishment, which is characterised by a harsh and sinister doggedness. The thought of those prehistoric millennia brings us to the unhesitating conclusion, that it was simply through punishment that the evolution of the consciousness of guilt was most forcibly retarded—at any rate in the victims of the punishing power. In particular, let us not underestimate the extent to which, by the very sight of the judicial and executive procedure, the wrong-doer is himself prevented from feeling that his deed, the character of his act, is intrinsically reprehensible: for he sees clearly the same kind of acts practised in the service of justice, and then called good, and practised with a good conscience; acts such as espionage, trickery, bribery, trapping, the whole intriguing and insidious art of the policeman and the informer—the whole system, in fact, manifested in the different kinds of punishment (a system not excused by passion, but based on principle), of robbing, oppressing, insulting, imprisoning, racking, murdering.—All this he sees treated by his judges, not as acts meriting censure and condemnation in themselves, but only in a particular context and application. It was not on this soil that grew the "bad conscience," that most sinister and interesting plant of our earthly vegetation— in point of fact, throughout a most lengthy period, no suggestion of having to do with a "guilty man" manifested itself in the consciousness of the man who judged and punished. One had merely to deal with an author of an injury, an irresponsible piece of fate. And the man himself, on whom the punishment subsequently fell like a piece of fate, was occasioned no more of an "inner pain" than would be occasioned by the sudden approach of some uncalculated event, some terrible natural catastrophe, a rushing, crushing avalanche against which there is no resistance.

15.

This truth came insidiously enough to the consciousness of Spinoza (to the disgust of his commentators, who (like Kuno Fischer, for instance) give themselves no end of trouble to misunderstand him on this point), when one afternoon (as he sat raking up who knows what memory) he indulged in the question of what was really left for him personally of the celebrated morsus conscientiæ—Spinoza, who had relegated "good and evil" to the sphere of human imagination, and indignantly defended the honour of his "free" God against those blasphemers who affirmed that God did everything sub ratione boni ("but this was tantamount to subordinating God to fate, and would really be the greatest of all absurdities"). For Spinoza the world had returned again to that innocence in which it lay before the discovery of the bad conscience: what, then, had happened to the morsus conscientiæ? "The antithesis of gaudium," said he at last to himself,—"A sadness accompanied by the recollection of a past event which has turned out contrary to all expectation" (Eth. III., Propos. XVIII. Schol. i. ii.). Evil-doers have throughout thousands of years felt when overtaken by punishment exactly like Spinoza, on the subject of their "offence": "here is something which went wrong contrary to my anticipation," not "I ought not to have done this."—They submitted themselves to punishment, just as one submits one's self to a disease, to a misfortune, or to death, with that stubborn and resigned fatalism which gives the Russians, for instance, even nowadays, the advantage over us Westerners, in the handling of life. If at that period there was a critique of action, the criterion was prudence: the real effect of punishment is unquestionably chiefly to be found in a sharpening of the sense of prudence, in a lengthening of the memory, in a will to adopt more of a policy of caution, suspicion, and secrecy; in the recognition that there are many things which are unquestionably beyond one's capacity; in a kind of improvement in self-criticism. The broad effects which can be obtained by punishment in man and beast, are the increase of fear, the sharpening of the sense of cunning, the mastery of the desires: so it is that punishment tames man, but does not make him "better"—it would be more correct even to go so far as to assert the contrary ("Injury makes a man cunning," says a popular proverb: so far as it makes him cunning, it makes him also bad. Fortunately, it often enough makes him stupid).

16.

At this juncture I cannot avoid trying to give a tentative and provisional expression to my own hypothesis concerning the origin of the bad conscience: it is difficult to make it fully appreciated, and it requires continuous meditation, attention, and digestion. I regard the bad conscience as the serious illness which man was bound to contract under the stress of the most radical change which he has ever experienced— that change, when he found himself finally imprisoned within the pale of society and of peace.

Just like the plight of the water-animals, when they were

compelled either to become land-animals or to perish, so was the plight of these half-animals, perfectly adapted as they were to the savage life of war, prowling, and adventure— suddenly all their instincts were rendered worthless and "switched off." Henceforward they had to walk on their feet—"carry themselves," whereas heretofore they had been carried by the water: a terrible heaviness oppressed them. They found themselves clumsy in obeying the simplest directions, confronted with this new and unknown world they had no longer their old guides—the regulative instincts that had led them unconsciously to safety—they were reduced, were those unhappy creatures, to thinking, inferring, calculating, putting together causes and results, reduced to that poorest and most erratic organ of theirs, their "consciousness." I do not believe there was ever in the world such a feeling of misery, such a leaden discomfort—further, those old instincts had not immediately ceased their demands! Only it was difficult and rarely possible to gratify them: speaking broadly, they were compelled to satisfy themselves by new and, as it were, hole-and- corner methods. All instincts which do not find a vent without, turn inwards—this is what I mean by the growing "internalisation" of man: consequently we have the first growth in man, of what subsequently was called his soul. The whole inner world, originally as thin as if it had been stretched between two layers of skin, burst apart and expanded proportionately, and obtained depth, breadth, and height, when man's external outlet became obstructed. These terrible bulwarks, with which the social organisation protected itself against the old instincts of freedom (punishments belong pre-eminently to these bulwarks), brought it about that all those instincts of wild, free, prowling man became turned backwards against man himself. Enmity, cruelty, the delight in persecution, in surprises, change, destruction—the turning all these instincts against their own possessors: this is the origin of the "bad conscience." It was man, who, lacking external enemies and obstacles, and imprisoned as he was in the oppressive narrowness and monotony of custom, in his own impatience lacerated, persecuted, gnawed, frightened, and ill-treated himself; it was this animal in the hands of the tamer, which beat itself against the bars of its cage; it was this being who, pining and yearning for that desert home of which it had been deprived, was compelled to create out of its own self, an adventure, a torture- chamber, a hazardous and perilous desert—it was this fool, this homesick and desperate prisoner—who invented the "bad conscience." But thereby he introduced that most grave and sinister illness, from which mankind has not yet recovered, the suffering of man from the disease called man, as the result of a violent breaking from his animal past, the result, as it were, of a spasmodic plunge into a new environment and new conditions of existence, the result of a declaration of war against the old instincts, which up to that time had been the staple of his power, his joy, his formidableness. Let us immediately add that this fact of an animal ego turning against itself, taking part against itself, produced in the world so novel, profound, unheard-of, problematic, inconsistent, and pregnant a phenomenon, that the aspect of the world was radically altered thereby. In sooth, only divine spectators could have appreciated the drama that then began, and whose end baffles conjecture as yet—a drama too subtle, too wonderful, too paradoxical to warrant its undergoing a non-sensical and unheeded performance on some random grotesque planet! Henceforth man is to be counted as one of the most unexpected and sensational lucky shots in the game of the "big baby" of Heracleitus, whether he be called Zeus or Chance—he awakens on his behalf the interest, excitement, hope, almost the confidence, of his being the harbinger and forerunner of something, of man being no end, but only a stage, an interlude, a bridge, a great promise.

17.

It is primarily involved in this hypothesis of the origin of the bad conscience, that that alteration was no gradual and no voluntary alteration, and that it did not manifest itself as an organic adaptation to new conditions, but as a break, a jump, a necessity, an inevitable fate, against which there was no resistance and never a spark of resentment. And secondarily, that the fitting of a hitherto unchecked and amorphous population into a fixed form, starting as it had done in an act of violence, could only be accomplished by acts of violence and nothing else—that the oldest "State" appeared consequently as a ghastly tyranny, a grinding ruthless piece of machinery, which went on working, till this raw material of a semi-animal populace was not only thoroughly kneaded and elastic, but also moulded. I used the word "State": my meaning is self-evident, namely, a herd of blonde beasts of prey, a race of conquerors and masters, which with all its warlike organisation and all its organising power pounces with its terrible claws on a population, in numbers possibly tremendously superior, but as yet formless, as yet nomad. Such is the origin of the "State." That fantastic theory that makes it begin with a contract is, I think, disposed of. He who can command, he who is a master by "nature," he who comes on the scene forceful in deed and gesture—what has he to do with contracts? Such beings defy calculation, they come like fate, without cause, reason, notice, excuse, they are there like the lightning is there, too terrible, too sudden, too convincing, too "different," to be personally even hated. Their work is an instinctive creating and impressing of forms, they are the most involuntary, unconscious artists that there are:—their appearance produces instantaneously a scheme of sovereignty which is live, in which the functions are partitioned and apportioned, in which above all no part is received or finds a place, until pregnant with a "meaning" in regard to the whole. They are ignorant of the meaning of guilt, responsibility, consideration, are these born organisers; in them predominates that terrible artist-egoism, that gleams like brass, and that knows itself justified to all eternity, in its work, even as a mother in her child. It is not in them that there grew the bad conscience, that is elementary—but it would not have grown without them, repulsive growth as it was, it would be missing, had not a tremendous quantity of freedom been expelled from the world by the stress of their hammer-strokes, their artist violence, or been at any rate made invisible and, as it were, latent.

This instinct of freedom forced into being latent—it is already clear—this instinct of freedom forced back, trodden back, imprisoned within itself, and finally only able to find vent and relief in itself; this, only this, is the beginning of the "bad conscience."

18.

Beware of thinking lightly of this phenomenon, by reason of its initial painful ugliness. At bottom it is the same active force which is at work on a more grandiose scale in those potent artists and organisers, and builds states, which here, internally, on a smaller and pettier scale and with a retrogressive tendency, makes itself a bad science in the "labyrinth of the breast," to use Goethe's phrase, and which builds negative ideals; it is, I repeat, that identical instinct of freedom(to use my own language, the will to power): only the material, on which this force with all its constructive and tyrannous nature is let loose, is here man himself, his whole old animal self— and not as in the case of that more grandiose and sensational phenomenon, the other man, other men. This secret self-tyranny, this cruelty of the artist, this delight in giving a form to one's self as a piece of difficult, refractory, and suffering material, in burning in a will, a critique, a contradiction, a contempt, a negation; this sinister and ghastly labour of love on the part of a soul, whose will is cloven in two within itself, which makes itself suffer from delight in the infliction of suffering; this wholly active bad conscience has finally (as one already anticipates)—true fountainhead as it is of idealism and imagination— produced an abundance of novel and amazing beauty and affirmation, and perhaps has really been the first to give birth to beauty at all. What would beauty be, forsooth, if its contradiction had not first been presented to consciousness, if the ugly had not first said to itself, "I am ugly"? At any rate, after this hint the problem of how far idealism and beauty can be traced in such opposite ideas as "selflessness," self- denial, self-sacrifice, becomes less problematical; and indubitably in future we shall certainly know the real and original character of the delight experienced by the self-less, the self-denying, the self- sacrificing: this delight is a phase of cruelty.—So much provisionally for the origin of "altruism" as a moral value, and the marking out the ground from which this value has grown: it is only the bad conscience, only the will for self-abuse, that provides the necessary conditions for the existence of altruism as a value.

19.

Undoubtedly the bad conscience is an illness, but an illness like pregnancy is an illness. If we search out the conditions under which this illness reaches its most terrible and sublime zenith, we shall see what really first brought about its entry into the world. But to do this we must take a long breath, and we must first of all go back once again to an earlier point of view. The relation at civil law of the ower to his creditor (which has already been discussed in detail), has been interpreted once again (and indeed in a manner which historically is exceedingly remarkable and suspicious) into a relationship, which is perhaps more incomprehensible to us moderns than to any other era;

that is, into the relationship of the existing generation to its ancestors. Within the original tribal association—we are talking of primitive times—each living generation recognises a legal obligation towards the earlier generation, and particularly towards the earliest, which founded the family (and this is something much more than a mere sentimental obligation, the existence of which, during the longest period of man's history, is by no means indisputable). There prevails in them the conviction that it is only thanks to sacrifices and efforts of their ancestors, that the race persists at all—and that this has to be paid back to them by sacrifices and services. Thus is recognised the owing of a debt, which accumulates continually by reason of these ancestors never ceasing in their subsequent life as potent spirits to secure by their power new privileges and advantages to the race. Gratis, perchance? But there is no gratis for that raw and "mean-souled" age. What return can be made?—Sacrifice (at first, nourishment, in its crudest sense), festivals, temples, tributes of veneration, above all, obedience—since all customs are, quâ works of the ancestors, equally their precepts and commands—are the ancestors evergiven enough? This suspicion remains and grows: from time to time it extorts a great wholesale ransom, something monstrous in the way of repayment of the creditor (the notorious sacrifice of the first-born, for example, blood, human blood in any case). The fear of ancestors and their power, the consciousness of owing debts to them, necessarily increases, according to this kind of logic, in the exact proportion that the race itself increases, that the race itself becomes more victorious, more independent, more honoured, more feared. This, and not the contrary, is the fact. Each step towards race decay, all disastrous events, all symptoms of degeneration, of approaching disintegration, always diminish the fear of the founders' spirit, and whittle away the idea of his sagacity, providence, and potent presence.

Conceive this crude kind of logic carried to its climax: it follows that the ancestors of the most powerful races must, through the growing fear that they exercise on the imaginations, grow themselves into monstrous dimensions, and become relegated to the gloom of a divine mystery that transcends imagination—the ancestor becomes at last necessarily transfigured into a god. Perhaps this is the very origin of the gods, that is, an origin from fear! And those who feel bound to add, "but from piety also," will have difficulty in maintaining this theory, with regard to the primeval and longest period of the human race. And of course this is even more the case as regards the middle period, the formative period of the aristocratic races—the aristocratic races which have given back with interest to their founders, the ancestors (heroes, gods), all those qualities which in the meanwhile have appeared in themselves, that is, the aristocratic qualities. We will later on glance again at the ennobling and promotion of the gods (which of course is totally distinct from their "sanctification"): let us now provisionally follow to its end the course of the whole of this development of the consciousness of "owing."

20.

According to the teaching of history, the consciousness of owing debts to the deity by no means came to an end with the decay of the clan organisation of society; just as mankind has inherited the ideas of "good" and "bad" from the race-nobility (together with its fundamental tendency towards establishing social distinctions), so with the heritage of the racial and tribal gods it has also inherited the incubus of debts as yet unpaid and the desire to discharge them. The transition is effected by those large populations of slaves and bondsmen, who, whether through compulsion or through submission and "mimicry," have accommodated themselves to the religion of their masters; through this channel these inherited tendencies inundate the world. The feeling of owing a debt to the deity has grown continuously for several centuries, always in the same proportion in which the idea of God and the consciousness of God have grown and become exalted among mankind. (The whole history of ethnic fights, victories, reconciliations, amalgamations, everything, in fact, which precedes the eventual classing of all the social elements in each great race-synthesis, are mirrored in the hotch-potch genealogy of their gods, in the legends of their fights, victories, and reconciliations. Progress towards universal empires invariably means progress towards universal deities; despotism, with its subjugation of the independent nobility, always paves the way for some system or other of monotheism.) The appearance of the Christian god, as the record god up to this time, has for that very reason brought equally into the world the record amount of guilt consciousness. Granted that we have gradually started on the reverse movement, there is no little probability in the deduction, based on the continuous decay in the belief in the Christian god, to the effect that there also already exists a considerable decay in the human consciousness of owing (ought); in fact, we cannot shut our eyes to the prospect of the complete and eventual triumph of atheism freeing mankind from all this feeling of obligation to their origin, their causa prima. Atheism and a kind of second innocence complement and supplement each other.

21.

So much for my rough and preliminary sketch of the interrelation of the ideas "ought" (owe) and "duty" with the postulates of religion. I have intentionally shelved up to the present the actual moralisation of these ideas (their being pushed back into the conscience, or more precisely the interweaving of the bad conscience with the idea of God), and at the end of the last paragraph used language to the effect that this moralisation did not exist, and that consequently these ideas had necessarily come to an end, by reason of what had happened to their hypothesis, the credence in our "creditor," in God. The actual facts differ terribly from this theory. It is with the moralisation of the ideas "ought" and "duty," and with their being pushed back into the bad conscience, that comes the first actual attempt to reverse the direction of the development we have just described, or at any rate to arrest its evolution; it is just at this juncture that the very hope of an eventual redemption has to put itself once for all into the prison of pessimism, it is at this juncture that the eye has to recoil and rebound in despair from off an adamantine impossibility, it is at this juncture that the ideas "guilt" and "duty" have to turn backwards—turn backwards against whom? There is no doubt about it; primarily against the "ower," in whom the bad conscience now establishes itself, eats, extends, and grows like a polypus throughout its length and breadth, all with such virulence, that at last, with the impossibility of paying the debt, there becomes conceived the idea of the impossibility of paying the penalty, the thought of its inexpiability (the idea of "eternal punishment")—finally, too, it turns against the "creditor," whether found in the causa prima of man, the origin of the human race, its sire, who henceforth becomes burdened with a curse ("Adam," "original sin," "determination of the will"), or in Nature from whose womb man springs, and on whom the responsibility for the principle of evil is now cast ("Diabolisation of Nature"), or in existence generally, on this logic an absolute white elephant, with which mankind is landed (the Nihilistic flight from life, the demand for Nothingness, or for the opposite of existence, for some other existence, Buddhism and the like)—till suddenly we stand before that paradoxical and awful expedient, through which a tortured humanity has found a temporary alleviation, that stroke of genius called Christianity:—God personally immolating himself for the debt of man, God paying himself personally out of a pound of his own flesh, God as the one being who can deliver man from what man had become unable to deliver himself—the creditor playing scapegoat for his debtor, from love (can you believe it?), from love of his debtor!...

22.

The reader will already have conjectured what took place on the stage and behind the scenes of this drama. That will for self-torture, that inverted cruelty of the animal man, who, turned subjective and scared into introspection (encaged as he was in "the State," as part of his taming process), invented the bad conscience so as to hurt himself, after the natural outlet for this will to hurt, became blocked—in other words, this man of the bad conscience exploited the religious hypothesis so as to carry his martyrdom to the ghastliest pitch of agonised intensity. Owing something to God: this thought becomes his instrument of torture. He apprehends in God the most extreme antitheses that he can find to his own characteristic and ineradicable animal instincts, he himself gives a new interpretation to these animal instincts as being against what he "owes" to God (as enmity, rebellion, and revolt against the "Lord," the "Father," the "Sire," the "Beginning of the world"), he places himself between the horns of the dilemma, "God" and "Devil." Every negation which he is inclined to utter to himself, to the nature, naturalness, and reality of his being, he whips into an ejaculation of "yes," uttering it as something existing, living, efficient, as being God, as the holiness of God, the judgment of God, as the hangmanship of God, as transcendence, as eternity, as unending torment, as hell, as infinity of punishment and guilt. This is a kind of madness of the will in the sphere of psychological cruelty which is absolutely unparalleled:—man's will to find himself guilty and blameworthy to the point of inexpiability, his will to think of himself as punished, without the punishment ever being able to balance the guilt, his will to infect and to poison the fundamental basis of the universe with the problem of punishment and guilt, in order to cut off once and for all any escape out of this labyrinth of "fixed ideas," his will for rearing an ideal—that of the "holy God"—face to face with which he can have tangible proof of his own un-worthiness. Alas for this mad melancholy beast man! What phantasies invade it, what paroxysms of perversity, hysterical senselessness, and mental bestiality break out immediately, at the very slightest check on its being the beast of action.

All this is excessively interesting, but at the same time tainted with a black, gloomy, enervating melancholy, so that a forcible veto must be invoked against looking too long into these abysses. Here is disease, undubitably, the most ghastly disease that has as yet played havoc among men: and he who can still hear (but man turns now deaf ears to such sounds), how in this night of torment and nonsense there has rung out the cry of love, the cry of the most passionate ecstasy, of redemption in love, he turns away gripped by an invincible horror—in man there is so much that is ghastly—too long has the world been a mad-house.

23.

Let this suffice once for all concerning the origin of the "holy God." The fact that in itself the conception of gods is not bound to lead necessarily to this degradation of the imagination (a temporary representation of whose vagaries we felt bound give), the fact that there exist nobler methods of utilising the invention of gods than in this self- crucifixion and self-degradation of man, in which the last two thousand years of Europe have been past masters—these facts can fortunately be still perceived from every glance that we cast at the Grecian gods, these mirrors of noble and grandiose men, in which the animal in man felt itself deified, and did not devour itself in subjective frenzy. These Greeks long utilised their gods as simple buffers against the "bad conscience"— so that they could continue to enjoy their freedom of soul: this, of course, is diametrically opposed to Christianity's theory of its god. They went very far on this principle, did these splendid and lion-hearted children; and there is no lesser authority than that of the Homeric Zeus for making them realise occasionally that they are taking life too casually. "Wonderful," says he on one occasion—it has to do with the case of Ægistheus, a very bad case indeed—

"Wonderful how they grumble, the mortals against the immortals, Only from us, they presume, comes evil, but in their folly, Fashion they, spite of fate, the doom of their own disaster."

Yet the reader will note and observe that this Olympian spectator and judge is far from being angry with them and thinking evil of them on this score. "How foolish they are," so thinks he of the misdeeds of mortals— and "folly," "imprudence," "a little brain disturbance," and nothing more, are what the Greeks, even of the strongest, bravest period, have admitted to be the ground of much that is evil and fatal.—Folly, not sin, do you understand?... But even this brain disturbance was a problem—"Come, how is it even possible? How could it have really got in brains like ours, the brains of men of aristocratic ancestry, of men of fortune, of men of good natural endowments, of men of the best society, of men of nobility and virtue?" This was the question that for century on century the aristocratic Greek put to himself when confronted with every (to him incomprehensible) outrage and sacrilege with which one of his peers had polluted himself. "It must be that a god had infatuated him," he would say at last, nodding his head.—This solution is typical of the Greeks, ... accordingly the gods in those times subserved the functions of justifying man to a certain extent even in evil—in those days they took upon themselves not the punishment, but, what is more noble, the guilt.

24.

I conclude with three queries, as you will see. "Is an ideal actually set up here, or is one pulled down?" I am perhaps asked. But have ye sufficiently asked yourselves how dear a payment has the setting up of every ideal in the world exacted? To achieve that consummation how much truth must always be traduced and misunderstood, how many lies must be sanctified, how much conscience has got to be disturbed, how many pounds of "God" have got to be sacrificed every time? To enable a sanctuary to be set up a sanctuary has got to be destroyed: that is a law—show me an instance where it has not been fulfilled! We modern men, we inherit the immemorial tradition of vivisecting the conscience, and practising cruelty to our animal selves. That is the sphere of our most protracted training, perhaps of our artistic prowess, at any rate of our dilettantism and our perverted taste. Man has for too long regarded his natural proclivities with an "evil eye," so that eventually they have become in his system affiliated to a bad conscience. A converse endeavour would be intrinsically feasible—but who is strong enough to attempt it?—namely, to affiliate to the "bad conscience" all those unnatural proclivities, all those transcendental aspirations, contrary to sense, instinct, nature, and animalism—in short, all past and present ideals, which are all ideals opposed to life, and traducing the world. To whom is one to turn nowadays with such hopes and pretensions?—It is just the good men that we should thus bring about our ears; and in addition, as stands to reason, the indolent, the hedgers, the vain, the hysterical, the tired W h a t is more offensive or more thoroughly calculated to alienate, than giving any hint of the exalted severity with which we treat ourselves? And again how conciliatory, how full of love does all the world show itself towards us so soon as we do as all the world docs, and "let ourselves go" like all the world. For such a consummation we need spirits of different calibre than seems really feasible in this age; spirits rendered potent through wars and victories, to whom conquest, adventure, danger, even pain, have become a need; for such a consummation we need habituation to sharp, rare air, to winter wanderings, to literal and metaphorical ice and mountains; we even need a kind of sublime malice, a supreme and most self-conscious insolence of knowledge, which is the appanage of great health; we need (to summarise the awful truth) just this great health!

Is this even feasible to-day?... But some day, in a stronger age than this rotting and introspective present, must he in sooth come to us, even the redeemer of great love and scorn, the creative spirit, rebounding by the impetus of his own force back again away from every transcendental plane and dimension, he whose solitude is misunderstanded (sic) of the people, as though it were a flight from reality;—while actually it is only his diving, burrowing, and penetrating into reality, so that when he comes again to the light he can at once bring about by these means the redemption of this reality; its redemption from the curse which the old ideal has laid upon it. This man of the future, who in this wise will redeem us from the old ideal, as he will from that ideal's necessary corollary of great nausea, will to nothingness, and Nihilism; this tocsin of noon and of the great verdict, which renders the will again free, who gives back to the world its goal and to man his hope, this Antichrist and Antinihilist, this conqueror of God and of Nothingness—he must one day come.

25.

But what am I talking of? Enough! Enough? At this juncture

I have only one proper course, silence: otherwise tresspass on a domain open alone to one who is younger than I, one stronger, more "future" than I—open alone to Zarathustra, Zarathustra the godless.

THIRD ESSAY. WHAT IS THE MEANING OF ASCETIC IDEALS?

"Careless, mocking, forceful—so does wisdom wish us: she is a woman, and never loves any one but a warrior."

Thus Spake Zarathustra.

1.

What is the meaning of ascetic ideals? In artists, nothing, or too much; in philosophers and scholars, a kind of "flair" and instinct for the conditions most favourable to advanced intellectualism; in women, at best an additional seductive fascination, a little morbidezza on a fine piece of flesh, the angelhood of a fat, pretty animal; in physiological failures and whiners (in the majority of mortals), an attempt to pose as "too good" for this world, a holy form of debauchery, their chief weapon in the battle with lingering pain and ennui; in priests, the actual priestly faith, their best engine of power, and also the supreme authority for power; in saints, finally a pretext for hibernation, their novissima gloriæ cupido, their peace in nothingness ("God"), their form of madness.

But in the very fact that the ascetic ideal has meant so much to man, lies expressed the fundamental feature of man's will, his horror vacui: he needs a goal—and he will sooner will nothingness than not will at all.— Am I not understood?— Have I not been understood?—"Certainly not, sir?"—Well, let us begin at the beginning.

2.

What is the meaning of ascetic ideals? Or, to take an individual case in regard to which I have often been consulted, what is the meaning, for example, of an artist like Richard

Wagner paying homage to chastity in his old age? He had always done so, of course, in a certain sense, but it was not till quite the end, that he did so in an ascetic sense. What is the meaning of this "change of attitude," this radical revolution in his attitude—for that was what it was? Wagner veered thereby straight round into his own opposite. What is the meaning of an artist veering round into his own opposite? At this point (granted that we do not mind stopping a little over this question), we immediately call to mind the best, strongest, gayest, and boldest period, that there perhaps ever was in Wagner's life: that was the period, when he was genuinely and deeply occupied with the idea of "Luther's Wedding." Who knows what chance is responsible for our now having the Meistersingers instead of this wedding music? And how much in the latter is perhaps just an echo of the former? But there is no doubt but that the theme would have dealt with the praise of chastity. And certainly it would also have dealt with the praise of sensuality, and even so, it would seem quite in order, and even so, it would have been equally Wagnerian. For there is no necessary antithesis between chastity and sensuality: every good marriage, every authentic heart-felt love transcends this antithesis. Wagner would, it seems to me, have done well to have brought this pleasing reality home once again to his Germans, by means of a bold and graceful "Luther Comedy," for there were and are among the Germans many revilers of sensuality; and perhaps Luther's greatest merit lies just in the fact of his having had the courage of his sensuality (it used to be called, prettily enough, "evangelistic freedom "). But even in those cases where that antithesis between chastity and sensuality does exist, there has fortunately been for some time no necessity for it to be in any way a tragic antithesis. This should, at any rate, be the case with all beings who are sound in mind and body, who are far from reckoning their delicate balance between "animal" and "angel," as being on the face of it one of the principles opposed to existence—the most subtle and brilliant spirits, such as Goethe, such as Hafiz, have even seen in this a further charm of life. Such "conflicts" actually allure one to life. On the other hand, it is only too clear that when once these ruined swine are reduced to worshipping chastity—and there are such swine—they only see and worship in it the antithesis to themselves, the antithesis to ruined swine. Oh what a tragic grunting and eagerness! You can just think of it—they worship that painful and superfluous contrast, which Richard Wagner in his latter days undoubtedly wished to set to music, and to place on the stage! "For what purpose, forsooth?" as we may reasonably ask. What did the swine matter to him; what do they matter to us?

3.

At this point it is impossible to beg the further question of what he really had to do with that manly (ah, so unmanly) country bumpkin, that poor devil and natural, Parsifal, whom he eventually made a Catholic by such fraudulent devices. What? Was this Parsifal really meant seriously? One might be tempted to suppose the contrary, even to wish it—that the Wagnerian Parsifal was meant joyously, like a concluding play of a trilogy or satyric drama, in which Wagner the tragedian wished to take farewell of us, of himself, above all of tragedy, and to do so in a manner that should be quite fitting and worthy, that is, with an excess of the most extreme and flippant parody of the tragic itself, of the ghastly earthly seriousness and earthly woe of old—a parody of that most crude phase in the unnaturalness of the ascetic ideal, that had at length been overcome. That, as I have said, would have been quite worthy of a great tragedian; who like every artist first attains the supreme pinnacle of his greatness when he can look down into himself and his art, when he can laugh at himself. Is Wagner's Parsifal his secret laugh of superiority over himself, the triumph of that supreme artistic freedom and artistic transcendency which he has at length attained. We might, I repeat, wish it were so, for what can Parsifal, taken seriously, amount to? Is it really necessary to see in it (according to an expression once used against me) the product of an insane hate of knowledge, mind, and flesh? A curse on flesh and spirit in one breath of hate? An apostasy and reversion to the morbid Christian and obscurantist ideals? And finally a self-negation and self-elimination on the part of an artist, who till then had devoted all the strength of his will to the contrary, namely, the highest artistic expression of soul and body. And not only of his art; of his life as well.

Just remember with what enthusiasm Wagner followed in the footsteps of Feuerbach. Feuerbach's motto of "healthy sensuality" rang in the ears of Wagner during the thirties and forties of the century, as it did in the ears of many Germans (they dubbed themselves "Young Germans"), like the word of redemption. Did he eventually change his mind on the subject? For it seems at any rate that he eventually wished to change his teaching on that subject ... and not only is that the case with the Parsifal trumpets on the stage: in the melancholy, cramped, and embarrassed lucubrations of his later years, there are a hundred places in which there are manifestations of a secret wish and will, a despondent, uncertain, unavowed will to preach actual retrogression, conversion, Christianity, mediævalism, and to say to his disciples, "All is vanity! Seek salvation elsewhere!" Even the "blood of the Redeemer" is once invoked.

4.

Let me speak out my mind in a case like this, which has many painful elements—and it is a typical case: it is certainly best to separate an artist from his work so completely that he cannot be taken as seriously as his work. He is after all merely the presupposition of his work, the womb, the soil, in certain cases the dung and manure, on which and out of which it grows—and consequently, in most cases, something that must be forgotten if the work itself is to be enjoyed. The insight into the origin of a work is a matter for psychologists and vivisectors, but never either in the present or the future for the æsthetes, the artists. The author and creator of Parsifal was as little spared the necessity of sinking and living himself into the terrible depths and foundations of mediæval soul-contrasts, the necessity of a malignant abstraction from all intellectual elevation, severity, and discipline, the necessity of a kind of mental perversity (if the reader will pardon me such a word), as little as a pregnant woman is spared the horrors and marvels of pregnancy, which, as I have said, must be forgotten if the child is to be enjoyed. We must guard ourselves against the confusion, into which an artist himself would fall only too easily (to employ the English terminology) out of psychological "contiguity"; as though the artist himself actually were the object which he is able to represent, imagine, and express. In point of fact, the position is that even if he conceived he were such an object, he would certainly not represent, conceive, express it. Homer would not have created an Achilles, nor Goethe a Faust, if Homer had been an Achilles or if Goethe had been a Faust. A complete and perfect artist is to all eternity separated from the "real," from the actual; on the other hand, it will be appreciated that he can at times get tired to the point of despair of this eternal "unreality" and falseness of his innermost being— and that he then sometimes attempts to trespass on to the most forbidden ground, on reality, and attempts to have real existence. With what success? The success will be guessed—it is the typical velleity of the artist; the same velleity to which Wagner fell a victim in his old age, and for which he had to pay so dearly and so fatally (he lost thereby his most valuable friends). But after all, quite apart from this velleity, who would not wish emphatically for Wagner's own sake that he had taken farewell of us and of his art in a different manner, not with a Parsifal, but in more victorious, more self-confident, more Wagnerian style—a style less misleading, a style less ambiguous with regard to his whole meaning, less Schopenhauerian, less Nihilistic?...

5.

What, then, is the meaning of ascetic ideals? In the case of an artist we are getting to understand their meaning: Nothing at all ... or so much that it is as good as nothing at all. Indeed, what is the use of them? Our artists have for a long time past not taken up a sufficiently independent attitude, either in the world or against it, to warrant their valuations and the changes in these valuations exciting interest. At all times they have played the valet of some morality, philosophy, or religion, quite apart from the fact that unfortunately they have often enough been the inordinately supple courtiers of their clients and patrons, and the inquisitive toadies of the powers that are existing, or even of the new powers to come. To put it at the lowest, they always need a rampart, a support, an already constituted authority: artists never stand by themselves, standing alone is opposed to their deepest instincts. So, for example, did Richard Wagner take, "when the time had come," the philosopher Schopenhauer for his covering man in front, for his rampart.

Who would consider it even thinkable, that he would have had the courage for an ascetic ideal, without the support afforded him by the philosophy of Schopenhauer, without the authority of Schopenhauer, which dominated Europe in the seventies? (This is without consideration of the question whether an artist without the milk1 of an orthodoxy would have been possible at all.) This brings us to the more serious question: What is the meaning of a real philosopher paying homage to the ascetic ideal, a really self-dependent intellect like Schopenhauer, a man and knight with a glance of bronze, who has the courage to be himself, who knows how to stand alone without first waiting for men who cover him in front, and the nods of his superiors? Let us now consider at once the remarkable attitude of Schopenhauer towards art, an attitude which has even a fascination for certain types. For that is obviously the reason why Richard Wagner all at once went over to Schopenhauer (persuaded thereto, as one knows, by a poet, Herwegh), went over so completely that there ensued the cleavage of a complete theoretic contradiction between his earlier and his later æsthetic faiths the earlier, for example, being expressed in Opera and Drama, the later in the writings which he published from 1870 onwards. In particular, Wagner from that time onwards (and this is the volte-face which alienates us the most) had no scruples about changing his judgment concerning the value and position of music itself. What did he care if up to that time he had made of music a means, a medium, a "woman," that in order to thrive needed an end, a man—that is, the drama? He suddenly realised that more could be effected by the novelty of the Schopenhauerian theory in majorem musicæ gloriam—that is to say, by means of the sovereignty of music, as Schopenhauer understood it; music abstracted from and opposed to all the other arts, music as the independent art-in-itself, not like the other arts, affording reflections of the phenomenal world, but rather the language of the will itself, speaking straight out of the "abyss" as its most personal, original, and direct manifestation. This extraordinary rise in the value of music (a rise which seemed to grow out of the Schopenhauerian philosophy) was at once accompanied by an unprecedented rise in the estimation in which the musician himself was held: he became now an oracle, a priest, nay, more than a priest, a kind of mouthpiece for the "intrinsic essence of things," a telephone from the other world—from henceforward he talked not only music, did this ventriloquist of God, he talked metaphysic; what wonder that one day he eventually talked ascetic ideals.

6.

Schopenhauer has made use of the Kantian treatment of the æsthetic problem—though he certainly did not regard it with the Kantian eyes. Kant thought that he showed honour to art when he favoured and placed in the foreground those of the predicates of the beautiful, which constitute the honour of knowledge: impersonality and universality. This is not the place to discuss whether this was not a complete mistake; all that I wish to emphasise is that Kant, just like other philosophers, instead of envisaging the æsthetic problem from the standpoint of the experiences of the artist (the creator), has only considered art and beauty from the standpoint of the spectator, and has thereby imperceptibly imported the spectator himself into the idea of the "beautiful"! But if only the philosophers of the beautiful had sufficient knowledge of this "spectator"!— Knowledge of him as a great fact of personality, as a great experience, as a wealth of strong and most individual events, desires, surprises, and raptures in the sphere of beauty! But, as I feared, the contrary was always the case. And so we get from our philosophers, from the very beginning, definitions on which the lack of a subtler personal experience squats like a fat worm of crass error, as it does on Kant's famous definition of the beautiful. "That is beautiful," says Kant, "which pleases without interesting." Without interesting! Compare this definition with this other one, made by a real "spectator" and "artist"—by Stendhal, who once called the beautiful une promesse de bonheur. Here, at any rate, the one point which Kant makes prominent in the æsthetic position is repudiated and eliminated—le désintéressement. Who is right, Kant or Stendhal? When, forsooth, our æsthetes never get tired of throwing into the scales in Kant's favour the fact that under the magic of beauty men can look at even naked female statues "without interest," we can certainly laugh a little at their expense:—in regard to this ticklish point the experiences of artists are more "interesting," and at any rate Pygmalion was not necessarily an "unæsthetic man." Let us think all the better of the innocence of our æsthetes, reflected as it is in such arguments; let us, for instance, count to Kant's honour the country- parson naïveté of his doctrine concerning the peculiar character of the sense of touch! And here we come back to Schopenhauer, who stood in much closer neighbourhood to the arts than did Kant, and yet never escaped outside the pale of the Kantian definition; how was that? The circumstance is marvellous enough: he interprets the expression, "without interest," in the most personal fashion, out of an experience which must in his case have been part and parcel of his regular routine.

On few subjects does Schopenhauer speak with such certainty as on the working of æsthetic contemplation: he says of it that it simply counteracts sexual interest, like lupulin and camphor; he never gets tired of glorifying this escape from the "Life-will" as the great advantage and utility of the æsthetic state. In fact, one is tempted to ask if his fundamental conception of Will and Idea, the thought that there can only exist freedom from the "will" by means of "idea," did not originate in a generalisation from this sexual experience. (In all questions concerning the Schopenhauerian philosophy, one should, by the bye, never lose sight of the consideration that it is the conception of a youth of twenty-six, so that it participates not only in what is peculiar to Schopenhauer's life, but in what is peculiar to that special period of his life.) Let us listen, for instance, to one of the most expressive among the countless passages which he has written in honour of the æsthetic state (World as Will and Idea, i. 231); let us listen to the tone, the suffering, the happiness, the gratitude, with which such words are uttered: "This is the painless state which Epicurus praised as the highest good and as the state of the gods; we are during that moment freed from the vile pressure of the will, we celebrate the Sabbath of the will's hard labour, the wheel of Ixion stands still." What vehemence of language! What images of anguish and protracted revulsion! How almost pathological is that temporal antithesis between "that moment" and everything else, the "wheel of Ixion," "the hard labour of the will," "the vile pressure of the will." But granted that Schopenhauer was a hundred times right for

himself personally, how does that help our insight into the nature of the beautiful? Schopenhauer has described one effect of the beautiful,—the calming of the will,—but is this effect really normal? As has been mentioned, Stendhal, an equally sensual but more happily constituted nature than Schopenhauer, gives prominence to another effect of the "beautiful." "The beautiful promises happiness." To him it is just the excitement of the "will" (the "interest") by the beauty that seems the essential fact. And does not Schopenhauer ultimately lay himself open to the objection, that he is quite wrong in regarding himself as a Kantian on this point, that he has absolutely failed to understand in a Kantian sense the Kantian definition of the beautiful—;that the beautiful pleased him as well by means of an interest, by means, in fact, of the strongest and most personal interest of all, that: of the victim of torture who escapes from his torture?—And to come back again to our first question, "What is the meaning of a philosopher paying homage to ascetic ideals?" We get now, at any rate, a first hint; he wishes to escape from a torture.

7.

Let us beware of making dismal faces at the word "torture"—there is certainly in this case enough to deduct, enough to discount—there is even something to laugh at. For we must certainly not underestimate the fact that Schopenhauer, who in practice treated sexuality as a personal enemy (including its tool, woman, that "instrumentum diaboli"), needed enemies to keep him in a good humour; that he loved grim, bitter, blackish-green words; that he raged for the sake of raging, out of passion; that he would have grown ill, would have become a pessimist (for he was not a pessimist, however much he wished to be), without his enemies, without Hegel, woman, sensuality, and the whole "will for existence" "keeping on." Without them Schopenhauer would not have "kept on," that is a safe wager; he would have run away: but his enemies held him fast, his enemies always enticed him back again to existence, his wrath was just as theirs' was to the ancient Cynics, his balm, his recreation, his recompense, his remedium against disgust, his happiness. So much with regard to what is most personal in the case of Schopenhauer; on the other hand, there is still much which is typical in him—and only now we come back to our problem. It is an accepted and indisputable fact, so long as there are philosophers in the world and wherever philosophers have existed (from India to England, to take the opposite poles of philosophic ability), that there exists a real irritation and rancour on the part of philosophers towards sensuality.

Schopenhauer is merely the most eloquent, and if one has the ear for it, also the most fascinating and enchanting outburst. There similarly exists a real philosophic bias and affection for the whole ascetic ideal; there should be no illusions on this score. Both these feelings, as has been said, belong to the type; if a philosopher lacks both of them, then he is—you may be certain of it—never anything but a "pseudo." What does this mean? For this state of affairs must first be, interpreted: in itself it stands there stupid, to all eternity, like any "Thing-in-itself." Every animal, including la bête philosophe, strives instinctively after an optimum of favourable conditions, under which he can let his whole strength have play, and achieves his maximum consciousness of power; with equal instinctiveness, and with a fine perceptive flair which is superior to any reason, every animal shudders mortally at every kind of disturbance and hindrance which obstructs or could obstruct his way to that optimum (it is not his way to happiness of which I am talking, but his way to power, to action, the most powerful action, and in point of fact in many cases his way to unhappiness). Similarly, the philosopher shudders mortally at marriage, together with all that could persuade him to it—marriage as a fatal hindrance on the way to the optimum. Up to the present what great philosophers have been married? Heracleitus, Plato, Descartes, Spinoza, Leibnitz, Kant, Schopenhauer—they were not married, and, further, one cannot imagine them as married. A married philosopher belongs to comedy, that is my rule; as for that exception of a Socrates—the malicious Socrates married himself, it seems, ironice, just to prove this very rule. Every philosopher would say, as Buddha said, when the birth of a son was announced to him: "Râhoula has been born to me, a fetter has been forged for me" (Râhoula means here "a little demon"); there must come an hour of reflection to every "free spirit" (granted that he has had previously an hour of thoughtlessness), just as one came once to the same Buddha: "Narrowly cramped," he reflected, "is life in the house; it is a place of uncleanness; freedom is found in leaving the house." Because he thought like this, he left the house. So many bridges to independence are shown in the ascetic ideal, that the philosopher cannot refrain from exultation and clapping of hands when he hears the history of all those resolute ones, who on one day uttered a nay to all servitude and went into some desert; even granting that they were only strong asses, and the absolute opposite of strong minds. What, then, does the ascetic ideal mean in a philosopher? This is my answer—it will have been guessed long ago: when he sees this ideal the philosopher smiles because he sees therein an optimum of the conditions of the highest and boldest intellectuality; he does not thereby deny "existence," he rather affirms thereby his existence and only his existence, and this perhaps to the point of not being far off the blasphemous wish, pereat mundus, fiat philosophia, fiat philosophus, fiam!

8.

These philosophers, you see, are by no means uncorrupted witnesses and judges of the value of the ascetic ideal. They think of themselves —what is the "saint" to them? They think of that which to them personally is most indispensable; of freedom from compulsion, disturbance, noise: freedom from business, duties, cares; of clear head; of the dance, spring, and flight of thoughts; of good air—rare, clear, free, dry, as is the air on the heights, in which every animal creature becomes more intellectual and gains wings; they think of peace in every cellar; all the hounds neatly chained; no baying of enmity and uncouth rancour; no remorse of wounded ambition; quiet and submissive internal organs, busy as mills, but unnoticed; the heart alien, transcendent, future, posthumous—to summarise, they mean by the ascetic ideal the joyous asceticism of a deified and newly fledged animal, sweeping over life rather than resting. We know what are the three great catch-words of the ascetic ideal: poverty, humility, chastity; and now just look closely at the life of all the great fruitful inventive spirits— you will always find again and again these three qualities up to a certain extent. Not for a minute, as is self- evident, as though, perchance, they were part of their virtues—what has this type of man to do with virtues?—but as the most essential and natural conditions of their best existence, their finest fruitfulness. In this connection it is quite possible that their predominant intellectualism had first to curb an unruly and irritable pride, or an insolent sensualism, or that it had all its work cut out to maintain its wish for the "desert" against perhaps an inclination to luxury and dilettantism, or similarly against an extravagant liberality of heart and hand. But their intellect did effect all this, simply because it was the dominant instinct, which carried through its orders in the case of all the other instincts. It effects it still; if it ceased to do so, it would simply not be dominant. But there is not one iota of "virtue" in all this. Further, the desert, of which I just spoke, in which the strong, independent, and well-equipped spirits retreat into their hermitage—oh, how different is it from the cultured classes' dream of a desert! In certain cases, in fact, the cultured classes themselves are the desert. And it is certain that all the actors of the intellect would not endure this desert for a minute. It is nothing like romantic and Syrian enough for them, nothing like enough of a stage desert! Here as well there are plenty of asses, but at this point the resemblance ceases. But a desert nowadays is something like this—perhaps a deliberate obscurity; a getting-out-of the way of one's self; a fear of noise, admiration, papers, influence; a little office, a daily task, something that hides rather than brings to light; sometimes associating with harmless, cheerful beasts and fowls, the sight of which refreshes; a mountain for company, but not a dead one, one with eyes (that is, with lakes); in certain cases even a room in a crowded hotel where one can reckon on not being recognised, and on being able to talk with impunity to every one: here is the desert—oh, it is lonely enough, believe me! I grant that when Heracleitus retreated to the courts and cloisters of the colossal temple of Artemis, that "wilderness" was worthier; why do we lack such temples? (perchance we do not lack them: I just think of my splendid study in the Piazza di San Marco, in spring, of course, and in the morning, between ten and twelve). But that which Heracleitus shunned is still just what we too avoid nowadays: the noise and democratic babble of the Ephesians, their politics, their news from the "empire" (I mean, of course, Persia), their market-trade in "the things of to-day "—for there is one thing from which we philosophers especially need a rest—from the things of "to-day." We honour the silent, the cold, the noble, the far, the past, everything, in fact, at the sight of which the soul is not bound to brace itself up and defend itself—something with which one can speak without speaking aloud. Just listen now to the tone a spirit has when it speaks; every spirit has its own tone and loves its own tone. That thing yonder, for instance, is bound to be an agitator, that is, a hollow head, a hollow mug: whatever may go into him, everything comes back from him dull and thick, heavy with the echo of the great void. That spirit yonder nearly always speaks hoarse: has he, perchance, thought himself hoarse? It may be so—ask the physiologists—but he who thinks in words, thinks as a speaker and not as a thinker (it shows that he does not think of objects or think objectively, but only of his relations with objects—that, in point of fact, he only thinks of himself and his audience). This third one speaks aggressively, he comes too near our body, his breath blows on us—we shut our mouth involuntarily, although he speaks to us through a book: the tone of his style supplies the reason—he has no time, he has small faith in himself, he finds expression now or never. But a spirit who is sure of himself speaks softly; he seeks secrecy, he lets himself be awaited, A philosopher is recognised by the fact that he shuns three brilliant and noisy things—fame, princes, and women: which is not to say that they do not come to him. He shuns every glaring light: therefore he shuns his time and its "daylight." Therein he is as a shadow; the deeper sinks the sun, the greater grows the shadow. As for his humility, he endures, as he endures darkness, a certain dependence and obscurity: further, he is afraid of the shock of lightning, he shudders at the insecurity of a tree which is too isolated and too exposed, on which every storm vents its temper, every temper its storm. His "maternal" instinct, his secret love for that which grows in him, guides him into states where he is relieved from the necessity of taking care of himself, in the same way in which the "mother" instinct in woman has thoroughly maintained up to the present woman's dependent position. After all, they demand little enough, do these philosophers, their favourite motto is, "He who possesses is possessed." All this is not, as I must say again and again, to be attributed to a virtue, to a meritorious wish for moderation and simplicity; but because their supreme lord so demands of them, demands wisely and inexorably; their lord who is eager only for one thing, for which alone he musters, and for which alone he hoards everything— time, strength, love, interest. This kind of man likes not to be disturbed by enmity, he likes not to be disturbed by friendship, it is a type which forgets or despises easily. It strikes him as bad form to play the martyr, "to suffer for truth"—he leaves all that to the ambitious and to the stage-heroes of the intellect, and to all those, in fact, who have time enough for such luxuries (they themselves, the philosophers, have something to do for truth).

They make a sparing use of big words; they are said to be adverse to the word "truth" itself: it has a "high falutin'" ring. Finally, as far as the chastity of philosophers is concerned, the fruitfulness of this type of mind is manifestly in another sphere than that of children; perchance in some other sphere, too, they have the survival of their name, their little immortality (philosophers in ancient India would express themselves with still greater boldness: "Of what use is posterity to him whose soul is the world?"). In this attitude there is not a trace of chastity, by reason of any ascetic scruple or hatred of the flesh, any more than it is chastity for an athlete or a jockey to abstain from women; it is rather the will of the dominant instinct, at any rate, during the period of their advanced philosophic pregnancy. Every artist knows the harm done by sexual intercourse on occasions of great mental strain and preparation; as far as the strongest artists and those with the surest instincts are concerned, this is not necessarily a case of experience—hard experience—but it is simply their "maternal" instinct which, in order to benefit the growing work, disposes recklessly (beyond all its normal stocks and supplies) of the vigour of its animal life; the greater power then absorbs the lesser.

Let us now apply this interpretation to gauge correctly the case of Schopenhauer, which we have already mentioned: in his case, the sight of the beautiful acted manifestly like a resolving irritant on the chief power of his nature (the power of contemplation and of intense penetration); so that this strength exploded and became suddenly master of his consciousness. But this by no means excludes the possibility of that particular sweetness and fulness, which is peculiar to the æsthetic state, springing directly from the ingredient of sensuality (just as that "idealism" which is peculiar to girls at puberty originates in the same source)—it may be, consequently, that sensuality is not removed by the approach of the æsthetic state, as Schopenhauer believed, but merely becomes transfigured, and ceases to enter into the consciousness as sexual excitement. (I shall return once again to this point in connection with the more delicate problems of the physiology of the æsthetic, a subject which up to the present has been singularly untouched and unelucidated.)

9.

A certain asceticism, a grimly gay whole-hearted renunciation, is, as we have seen, one of the most favourable conditions for the highest intellectualism, and, consequently, for the most natural corollaries of such intellectualism: we shall therefore be proof against any surprise at the philosophers in particular always treating the ascetic ideal with a certain amount of predilection. A serious historical investigation shows the bond between the ascetic ideal and philosophy to be still much tighter and still much stronger. It may be said that it was only in the leading strings of this ideal that philosophy really learnt to make its first steps and baby paces—alas how clumsily, alas how crossly, alas how ready to tumble down and lie on its stomach was this shy little darling of a brat with its bandy legs! The early history of philosophy is like that of all good things;—for a long time they had not the courage to be themselves, they kept always looking round to see if no one would come to their help; further, they were afraid of all who looked at them. Just enumerate in order the particular tendencies and virtues of the philosopher—his tendency to doubt, his tendency to deny, his tendency to wait (to be "ephectic"), his tendency to analyse, search, explore, dare, his tendency to compare and to equalise, his will to be neutral and objective, his will for everything which is "sine ira et studio":— has it yet been realised that for quite a lengthy period these tendencies went counter to the first claims of morality and conscience? (To say nothing at all of Reason, which even Luther chose to call Frau Klüglin,2 the sly whore.) Has it been yet appreciated that a philosopher, in the event of his arriving at self-consciousness, must needs feel himself an incarnate "nitimur in vetitum"—and consequently guard himself against "his own sensations," against self-consciousness? It is, I repeat, just the same with all good things, on which we now pride ourselves; even judged by the standard of the ancient Greeks, our whole modern life, in so far as it is not weakness, but power and the consciousness of power, appears pure "Hybris" and godlessness: for the things which are the very reverse of those which we honour to-day, have had for a long time conscience on their side, and God as their guardian. "Hybris" is our whole attitude to nature nowadays, our violation of nature with the help of machinery, and all the unscrupulous ingenuity of our scientists and engineers. "Hybris" is our attitude to God, that is, to some alleged teleological and ethical spider behind the meshes of the great trap of the causal web. Like Charles the Bold in his war with Louis the Eleventh, we may say, "je combats l'universelle araignée"; "Hybris" is our attitude to ourselves— for we experiment with ourselves in a way that we would not allow with any animal, and with pleasure and curiosity open our soul in our living body: what matters now to us the "salvation" of the soul? We heal ourselves afterwards: being ill is instructive, we doubt it not, even more instructive than being well—inoculators of disease seem to us to-day even more necessary than any medicine-men and "saviours." There is no doubt we do violence to ourselves nowadays, we crackers of the soul's kernel, we incarnate riddles, who are ever asking riddles, as though life were naught else than the cracking of a nut; and even thereby must we necessarily become day by day more and more worthy to be asked questions and worthy to ask them, even thereby do we perchance also become worthier to—live?

... All good things were once bad things; from every original sin has grown an original virtue. Marriage, for example, seemed for a long time a sin against the rights of the community; a man formerly paid a fine for the insolence of claiming one woman to himself (to this phase belongs, for instance, the jus primæ noctis, to-day still in Cambodia the privilege of the priest, that guardian of the "good old customs").

The soft, benevolent, yielding, sympathetic feelings— eventually valued so highly that they almost became "intrinsic values," were for a very long time actually despised by their possessors: gentleness was then a subject for shame, just as hardness is now (compare Beyond Good and Evil, Aph. 260).

The submission to law: oh, with what qualms of conscience was it that the noble races throughout the world renounced the vendetta and gave the law power over themselves! Law was long a vetitum, a blasphemy, an innovation; it was introduced with force, like a force, to which men only submitted with a sense of personal shame. Every tiny step forward in the world was formerly made at the cost of mental and physical torture. Nowadays the whole of this point of view—"that not only stepping forward, nay, stepping at all, movement, change, all needed their countless martyrs," rings in our ears quite strangely. I have put it forward in the Dawn of Day, Aph. 18. "Nothing is purchased more dearly," says the same book a little later, "than the modicum of human reason and freedom which is now our pride. But that pride is the reason why it is now almost impossible for us to feel in sympathy with those immense periods of the 'Morality of Custom,' which lie at the beginning of the 'world's history,' constituting as they do the real decisive historical principle which has fixed the character of humanity; those periods, I repeat, when throughout the world suffering passed for virtue, cruelty for virtue, deceit for virtue, revenge for virtue, repudiation of the reason for virtue; and when, conversely, well-being passed current for danger, the desire for knowledge for danger, pity for danger, peace for danger, being pitied for shame, work for shame, madness for divinity, and change for immorality and incarnate corruption!"

10.

There is in the same book, Aph. 12, an explanation of the burden of unpopularity under which the earliest race of contemplative men had to live—despised almost as widely as they were first feared! Contemplation first appeared on earth in a disguised shape, in an ambiguous form, with an evil heart and often with an uneasy head: there is no doubt about it.

The inactive, brooding, unwarlike element in the instincts

of contemplative men long invested them with a cloud of suspicion: the only way to combat this was to excite a definite fear. And the old Brahmans, for example, knew to a nicety how to do this! The oldest philosophers were well versed in giving to their very existence and appearance, meaning, firmness, background, by reason whereof men learnt to fear them; considered more precisely, they did this from an even more fundamental need, the need of inspiring in themselves fear and self-reverence. For they found even in their own souls all the valuations turned against themselves; they had to fight down every kind of suspicion and antagonism against "the philosophic element in themselves." Being men of a terrible age, they did this with terrible means: cruelty to themselves, ingenious self-mortification—this was the chief method of these ambitious hermits and intellectual revolutionaries, who were obliged to force down the gods and the traditions of their own soul, so as to enable themselves to believe in their own revolution. I remember the famous story of the King Vicvamitra, who, as the result of a thousand years of self-martyrdom, reached such a consciousness of power and such a confidence in himself that he undertook to build a new heaven: the sinister symbol of the oldest and newest history of philosophy in the whole world. Every one who has ever built anywhere a "new heaven" first found the power thereto in his own hell Let us compress the facts into a short formula. The philosophic spirit had, in order to be possible to any extent at all, to masquerade and disguise itself as one of the previously fixed types of the contemplative man, to disguise itself as priest, wizard, soothsayer, as a religious man generally: the ascetic ideal has for a long time served the philosopher as a superficial form, as a condition which enabled him to exist To be able to be a philosopher he had to exemplify the ideal; to exemplify it, he was bound to believe in it. The peculiarly etherealised abstraction of philosophers, with their negation of the world, their enmity to life, their disbelief in the senses, which has been maintained up to the most recent time, and has almost thereby come to be accepted as the ideal philosophic attitude—this abstraction is the result of those enforced conditions under which philosophy came into existence, and continued to exist; inasmuch as for quite a very long time philosophy would have been absolutely impossible in the world without an ascetic cloak and dress, without an ascetic self-misunderstanding. Expressed plainly and palpably, the ascetic priest has taken the repulsive and sinister form of the caterpillar, beneath which and behind which alone philosophy could live and slink about....

Has all that really changed? Has that flamboyant and dangerous winged creature, that "spirit" which that caterpillar concealed within itself, has it, I say, thanks to a sunnier, warmer, lighter world, really and finally flung off its hood and escaped into the light? Can we to-day point to enough pride, enough daring, enough courage, enough self-confidence, enough mental will, enough will for responsibility, enough freedom of the will, to enable the philosopher to be now in the world really— possible?

11.

And now, after we have caught sight of the ascetic priest, let us tackle our problem. What is the meaning of the ascetic ideal? It now first becomes serious—vitally serious. We are now confronted with the real representatives of the serious. "What is the meaning of all seriousness?" This even more radical question is perchance already on the tip of our tongue: a question, fairly, for physiologists, but which we for the time being skip. In that ideal the ascetic priest finds not only his faith, but also his will, his power, his interest. His right to existence stands and falls with that ideal. What wonder that we here run up against a terrible opponent (on the supposition, of course, that we are the opponents of that ideal), an opponent fighting for his life against those who repudiate that ideal!. .. On the other hand, it is from the outset improbable that such a biased attitude towards our problem will do him any particular good; the ascetic priest himself will scarcely prove the happiest champion of his own ideal (on the same principle on which a woman usually fails when she wishes to champion "woman")—let alone proving the most objective critic and judge of the controversy now raised. We shall therefore—so much is already obvious—rather have actually to help him to defend himself properly against ourselves, than we shall have to fear being too well beaten by him. The idea, which is the subject of this dispute, is the value of our life from the standpoint of the ascetic priests: this life, then (together with the whole of which it is a part, "Nature," "the world," the whole sphere of becoming and passing away), is placed by them in relation to an existence of quite another character, which it excludes and to which it is opposed, unless it deny its own self: in this case, the case of an ascetic life, life is taken as a bridge to another existence. The ascetic treats life as a maze, in which one must walk backwards till one comes to the place where it starts; or he treats it as an error which one may, nay must, refute by action: for he demands that he should be followed; he enforces, where he can, his valuation of existence. What does this mean? Such a monstrous valuation is not an exceptional case, or a curiosity recorded in human history: it is one of the most general and persistent facts that there are. The reading from the vantage of a distant star of the capital letters of our earthly life, would perchance lead to the conclusion that the earth was the especially ascetic planet, a den of discontented, arrogant, and repulsive creatures, who never got rid of a deep disgust of themselves, of the world, of all life, and did themselves as much hurt as possible out of pleasure in hurting— presumably their one and only pleasure.

Let us consider how regularly, how universally, how practically at every single period the ascetic priest puts in his appearance: he belongs to no particular race; he thrives everywhere; he grows out of all classes. Not that he perhaps bred this valuation by heredity and propagated it—the contrary is the case. It must be a necessity of the first order which makes this species, hostile, as it is, to life, always grow again and always thrive again.—Life itself must certainly have an interest in the continuance of such a type of self- contradiction. For an ascetic life is a self-contradiction: here rules resentment without parallel, the resentment of an insatiate instinct and ambition, that would be master, not over some element in life, but over life itself, over life's deepest, strongest, innermost conditions; here is an attempt made to utilise power to dam the sources of power; here does the green eye of jealousy turn even against physiological well-being, especially against the expression of such well-being, beauty, joy; while a sense of pleasure is experienced and sought in abortion, in decay, in pain, in misfortune, in ugliness, in voluntary punishment, in the exercising, flagellation, and sacrifice of the self. All this is in the highest degree paradoxical: we are here confronted with a rift that wills itself to be a rift, which enjoys itself in this very suffering, and even becomes more and more certain of itself, more and more triumphant, in proportion as its own presupposition, physiological vitality, decreases. "The triumph just in the supreme agony:" under this extravagant emblem did the ascetic ideal fight from of old; in this mystery of seduction, in this picture of rapture and torture, it recognised its brightest light, its salvation, its final victory. Crux, nux, lux—it has all these three in one.

12.

Granted that such an incarnate will for contradiction and unnaturalness is induced to philosophise; on what will it vent its pet caprice? On that which has been felt with the greatest certainty to be true, to be real; it will look for error in those very places where the life instinct fixes truth with the greatest positiveness. It will, for instance, after the example of the ascetics of the Vedanta Philosophy, reduce matter to an illusion, and similarly treat pain, multiplicity, the whole logical contrast of "Subject" and "Object"—errors, nothing but errors! To renounce the belief in one's own ego, to deny to one's self one's own "reality"—what a triumph! and here already we have a much higher kind of triumph, which is not merely a triumph over the senses, over the palpable, but an infliction of violence and cruelty on reason; and this ecstasy culminates in the ascetic self- contempt, the ascetic scorn of one's own reason making this decree: there is a domain of truth and of life, but reason is specially excluded therefrom By the bye, even in the Kantian idea of "the intellegible character of things" there remains a trace of that schism, so dear to the heart of the ascetic, that schism which likes to turn reason against reason; in fact, "intelligible character" means in Kant a kind of quality in things of which the intellect comprehends this much, that for it, the intellect, it is absolutely incomprehensible. After all, let us, in our character of knowers, not be ungrateful towards such determined reversals of the ordinary perspectives and values, with which the mind had for too long raged against itself with an apparently futile sacrilege!

In the same way the very seeing of another vista, the very wishing to see another vista, is no little training and preparation of the intellect for its eternal "Objectivity"—objectivity being understood not as "contemplation without interest" (for that is inconceivable and non- sensical), but as the ability to have the pros and cons in one's power and to switch them on and off, so as to get to know how to utilise, for the advancement of knowledge, the difference in the perspective and in the emotional interpretations. But let us, forsooth, my philosophic colleagues, henceforward guard ourselves more carefully against this mythology of dangerous ancient ideas, which has set up a "pure, will- less, painless, timeless subject of knowledge"; let us guard ourselves from the tentacles of such contradictory ideas as "pure reason," "absolute spirituality," "knowledge-in-itself":—in these theories an eye that cannot be thought of is required to think, an eye which ex hypothesi has no direction at all, an eye in which the active and interpreting functions are cramped, are absent; those functions, I say, by means of which "abstract" seeing first became seeing something; in these theories consequently the absurd and the non-sensical is always demanded of the eye. There is only a seeing from a perspective, only a "knowing" from a perspective, and the more emotions we express over a thing, the more eyes, different eyes, we train on the same thing, the more complete will be our "idea" of that thing, our "objectivity." But the elimination of the will altogether, the switching off of the emotions all and sundry, granted that we could do so, what! would not that be called intellectual castration?

13.

But let us turn back. Such a self-contradiction, as apparently manifests itself among the ascetics, "Life turned against Life," is—this much is absolutely obvious—from the physiological and not now from the psychological standpoint, simply nonsense. It can only be an apparent contradiction; it must be a kind of provisional expression, an explanation, a formula, an adjustment, a psychological misunderstanding of something, whose real nature could not be understood for a long time, and whose real essence could not be described; a mere word jammed into an old gap of human knowledge. To put briefly the facts against its being real: the ascetic ideal springs from the prophylactic and self-preservative instincts which mark a decadent life, which seeks by every means in its power to maintain its position and fight for its existence; it points to a partial physiological depression and exhaustion, against which the most profound and intact life-instincts fight ceaselessly with new weapons and discoveries. The ascetic ideal is such a weapon: its position is consequently exactly the reverse of that which the worshippers of the ideal imagine—life struggles in it and through it with death and against death; the ascetic ideal is a dodge for the preservation of life. An important fact is brought out in the extent to which, as history teaches, this ideal could rule and exercise power over man, especially in all those places where the civilisation and taming of man was completed: that fact is, the diseased state of man up to the present, at any rate, of the man who has been tamed, the physiological struggle of man with death (more precisely, with the disgust with life, with exhaustion, with the wish for the "end"). The ascetic priest is the incarnate wish for an existence of another kind, an existence on another plane,—he is, in fact, the highest point of this wish, its official ecstasy and passion: but it is the very power of this wish which is the fetter that binds him here; it is just that which makes him into a tool that must labour to create more favourable conditions for earthly existence, for existence on the human plane—it is with this very power that he keeps the whole herd of failures, distortions, abortions, unfortunates, sufferers from themselves of every kind, fast to existence, while he as the herdsman goes instinctively on in front. You understand me already: this ascetic priest, this apparent enemy of life, this denier—he actually belongs to the really great conservative and affirmative forces of life

What does it come from, this diseased state? For man is more diseased, more uncertain, more changeable, more unstable than any other animal, there is no doubt of it—he is the diseased animal: what does it spring from?

Certainly he has also dared, innovated, braved more,

challenged fate more than all the other animals put together; he, the great experimenter with himself, the unsatisfied, the insatiate, who struggles for the supreme mastery with beast, Nature, and gods, he, the as yet ever uncompelled, the ever future, who finds no more any rest from his own aggressive strength, goaded inexorably on by the spur of the future dug into the flesh of the present:—how should not so brave and rich an animal also be the most endangered, the animal with the longest and deepest sickness among all sick animals?... Man is sick of it, oft enough there are whole epidemics of this satiety (as about 1348, the time of the Dance of Death): but even this very nausea, this tiredness, this disgust with himself, all this is discharged from him with such force that it is immediately made into a new fetter. His "nay," which he utters to life, brings to light as though by magic an abundance of graceful "yeas"; even when he wounds himself, this master of destruction, of self-destruction, it is subsequently the wound itself that forces him to live.

14.

The more normal is this sickliness in man—and we cannot dispute this normality—the higher honour should be paid to the rare cases of psychical and physical powerfulness, the windfalls of humanity, and the more strictly should the sound be guarded from that worst of air, the air of the sick-room. Is that done? The sick are the greatest danger for the healthy; it is not from the strongest that harm comes to the strong, but from the weakest. Is that known? Broadly considered, it is not for a minute the fear of man, whose diminution should be wished for; for this fear forces the strong to be strong, to be at times terrible—it preserves in its integrity the sound type of man. What is to be feared, what does work with a fatality found in no other fate, is not the great fear of, but the great nausea with, man; and equally so the great pity for man.

Supposing that both these things were one day to espouse each other, then inevitably the maximum of monstrousness would immediately come into the world—the "last will" of man, his will for nothingness, Nihilism. And, in sooth, the way is well paved thereto. He who not only has his nose to smell with, but also has eyes and ears, he sniffs almost wherever he goes to-day an air something like that of a mad-house, the air of a hospital—I am speaking, as stands to reason, of the cultured areas of mankind, of every kind of "Europe" that there is in fact in the world. The sick are the great danger of man, not the evil, not the "beasts of prey." They who are from the outset botched, oppressed, broken, those are they, the weakest are they, who most undermine the life beneath the feet of man, who instil the most dangerous venom and scepticism into our trust in life, in man, in ourselves. Where shall we escape from it, from that covert look (from which we carry away a deep sadness), from that averted look of him who is misborn from the beginning, that look which betrays what such a man says to himself—that look which is a groan?" Would that I were something else," so groans this look, "but there is no hope. I am what I am: how could I get away from myself? And, verily—I am sick of myself!" On such a soil of self-contempt, a veritable swamp soil, grows that weed, that poisonous growth, and all so tiny, so hidden, so ignoble, so sugary. Here teem the worms of revenge and vindictiveness; here the air reeks of things secret and unmentionable; here is ever spun the net of the most malignant conspiracy—the conspiracy of the sufferers against the sound and the victorious; here is the sight of the victorious hated.

And what lying so as not to acknowledge this hate as hate! What a show of big words and attitudes, what an art of "righteous" calumniation!

These abortions! what a noble eloquence gushes from their

lips! What an amount of sugary, slimy, humble submission oozes in their eyes! What do they really want? At any rate to represent righteousness ness, love, wisdom, superiority, that is the ambition of these "lowest ones," these sick ones! And how clever does such an ambition make them! You cannot, in fact, but admire the counterfeiter dexterity with which the stamp of virtue, even the ring, the golden ring of virtue, is here imitated. They have taken a lease of virtue absolutely for themselves, have these weaklings and wretched invalids, there is no doubt of it; "We alone are the good, the righteous," so do they speak, "we alone are the homines bonæ voluntatis." They stalk about in our midst as living reproaches, as warnings to us—as though health, fitness, strength, pride, the sensation of power, were really vicious things in themselves, for which one would have some day to do penance, bitter penance. Oh, how they themselves are ready in their hearts to exact penance, how they thirst after being hangmen!

Among them is an abundance of revengeful ones disguised as judges, who ever mouth the word righteousness like a venomous spittle— with mouth, I say, always pursed, always ready to spit at everything, which does not wear a discontented look, but is of good cheer as it goes on its way. Among them, again, is that most loathsome species of the vain, the lying abortions, who make a point of representing "beautiful souls," and perchance of bringing to the market as "purity of heart" their distorted sensualism swathed in verses and other bandages; the species of "self-comforters" and masturbators of their own souls. The sick man's will to represent some form or other of superiority, his instinct for crooked paths, which lead to a tyranny over the healthy—where can it not be found, this will to power of the very weakest? The sick woman especially: no one surpasses her in refinements for ruling, oppressing, tyrannising. The sick woman, moreover, spares nothing living, nothing dead; she grubs up again the most buried things (the Bogos say, "Woman is a hyena"). Look into the background of every family, of every body, of every community: everywhere the fight of the sick against the healthy—a silent fight for the most part with minute poisoned powders, with pin- pricks, with spiteful grimaces of patience, but also at times with that diseased pharisaism of pure pantomime, which plays for choice the rôle of "righteous indignation." Right into the hallowed chambers of knowledge can it make itself heard, can this hoarse yelping of sick hounds, this rabid lying and frenzy of such "noble" Pharisees (I remind readers, who have ears, once more of that Berlin apostle of revenge, Eugen Dühring, who makes the most disreputable and revolting use in all present-day Germany of moral refuse; Dühring, the paramount moral blusterer that there is to-day, even among his own kidney, the Anti- Semites). They are all men of resentment, are these physiological distortions and worm-riddled objects, a whole quivering kingdom of burrowing revenge, indefatigable and insatiable in its outbursts against the happy, and equally so in disguises for revenge, in pretexts for revenge: when will they really reach their final, fondest, most sublime triumph of revenge? At that time, doubtless, when they succeed in pushing their own misery, in fact, all misery, into the consciousness of the happy; so that the latter begin one day to be ashamed of their happiness, and perchance say to themselves when they meet, "It is a shame to be happy! there is too much misery!" ... But there could not possibly be a greater and more fatal misunderstanding than that of the happy, the fit, the strong in body and soul, beginning in this way to doubt their right to happiness. Away with this "perverse world"! Away with this shameful soddenness of sentiment! Preventing the sick making the healthy sick—for that is what such a soddenness comes to— this ought to be our supreme object in the world—but for this it is above all essential that the healthy should remain separated from the sick, that they should even guard themselves from the look of the sick, that they should not even associate with the sick. Or may it, perchance, be their mission to be nurses or doctors? But they could not mistake and disown their mission more grossly—the higher must not degrade itself to be the tool of the lower, the pathos of distance must to all eternity keep their missions also separate. The right of the happy to existence, the right of bells with a full tone over the discordant cracked bells, is verily a thousand times greater: they alone are the sureties of the future, they alone are bound to man's future. What they can, what they must do, that can the sick never do, should never do! but if they are to be enabled to do what only they must do, how can they possibly be free to play the doctor, the comforter, the "Saviour" of the sick?... And therefore good air! good air! and away, at any rate, from the neighbourhood of all the madhouses and hospitals of civilisation! And therefore good company, our own company, or solitude, if it must be so! but away, at any rate, from the evil fumes of internal corruption and the secret worm-eaten state of the sick! that, forsooth, my friends, we may defend ourselves, at any rate for still a time, against the two worst plagues that could have been reserved for us—against the great nausea with man! against the great pity for man!

15.

If you have understood in all their depths—and I demand that you should grasp them profoundly and understand them profoundly—the reasons for the impossibility of its being the business of the healthy to nurse the sick, to make the sick healthy, it follows that you have grasped this further necessity— the necessity of doctors and nurses who themselves are sick. And now we have and hold with both our hands the essence of the ascetic priest. The ascetic priest must be accepted by us as the predestined saviour, herdsman, and champion of the sick herd: thereby do we first understand his awful historic mission. The lordship over sufferers is his kingdom, to that points his instinct, in that he finds his own special art, his master-skill, his kind of happiness. He must himself be sick, he must be kith and kin to the sick and the abortions so as to understand them, so as to arrive at an understanding with them; but he must also be strong, even more master of himself than of others, impregnable, forsooth, in his will for power, so as to acquire the trust and the awe of the weak, so that he can be their hold, bulwark, prop, compulsion, overseer, tyrant, god. He has to protect them, protect his herds—against whom? Against the healthy, doubtless also against the envy towards the healthy. He must be the natural adversary and scorner of every rough, stormy, reinless, hard, violently-predatory health and power. The priest is the first form of the more delicate animal that scorns more easily than it hates. He will not be spared the waging of war with the beasts of prey, a war of guile (of "spirit") rather than of force, as is self-evident— he will in certain cases find it necessary to conjure up out of himself, or at any rate to represent practically a new type of the beast of prey—a new animal monstrosity in which the polar bear, the supple, cold, crouching panther, and, not least important, the fox, are joined together in a trinity as fascinating as it is fearsome. If necessity exacts it, then will he come on the scene with bearish seriousness, venerable, wise, cold, full of treacherous superiority, as the herald and mouthpiece of mysterious powers, sometimes going among even the other kind of beasts of prey, determined as he is to sow on their soil, wherever he can, suffering, discord, self-contradiction, and only too sure of his art, always to be lord of sufferers at all times. He brings with him, doubtless, salve and balsam; but before he can play the physician he must first wound; so, while he soothes the pain which the wound makes, he at the same time poisons the wound. Well versed is he in this above all things, is this wizard and wild beast tamer, in whose vicinity everything healthy must needs become ill, and everything ill must needs become tame. He protects, in sooth, his sick herd well enough, does this strange herdsman; he protects them also against themselves, against the sparks (even in the centre of the herd) of wickedness, knavery, malice, and all the other ills that the plaguey and the sick are heir to; he fights with cunning, hardness, and stealth against anarchy and against the ever imminent break-up inside the herd, where resentment, that most dangerous blasting-stuff and explosive, ever accumulates and accumulates. Getting rid of this blasting-stuff in such a way that it does not blow up the herd and the herdsman, that is his real feat, his supreme utility; if you wish to comprise in the shortest formula the value of the priestly life, it would be correct to say the priest is the diverter of the course of resentment. Every sufferer, in fact, searches instinctively for a cause of his suffering; to put it more exactly, a doer,—to put it still more precisely, a sentient responsible doer,—in brief, something living, on which, either actually or in effigie, he can on any pretext vent his emotions. For the venting of emotions is the sufferer's greatest attempt at alleviation, that is to say, stupefaction, his mechanically desired narcotic against pain of any kind. It is in this phenomenon alone that is found, according to my judgment, the real physiological cause of resentment, revenge, and their family is to be found—that is, in a demand for the deadening of pain through emotion: this cause is generally, but in my view very erroneously, looked for in the defensive parry of a bare protective principle of reaction, of a "reflex movement" in the case of any sudden hurt and danger, after the manner that a decapitated frog still moves in order to get away from a corrosive acid.

But the difference is fundamental. In one case the object is to prevent being hurt any more; in the other case the object is to deaden a racking, insidious, nearly unbearable pain by a more violent emotion of any kind whatsoever, and at any rate for the time being to drive it out of the consciousness— for this purpose an emotion is needed, as wild an emotion as possible, and to excite that emotion some excuse or other is needed. "It must be somebody's fault that I feel bad"—this kind of reasoning is peculiar to all invalids, and is but the more pronounced, the more ignorant they remain of the real cause of their feeling bad, the physiological cause (the cause may lie in a disease of the nervus sympathicus, or in an excessive secretion of bile, or in a want of sulphate and phosphate of potash in the blood, or in pressure in the bowels which stops the circulation of the blood, or in degeneration of the ovaries, and so forth). Ail sufferers have an awful resourcefulness and ingenuity in finding excuses for painful emotions; they even enjoy their jealousy, their broodings over base actions and apparent injuries, they burrow through the intestines of their past and present in their search for obscure mysteries, wherein they will be at liberty to wallow in a torturing suspicion and get drunk on the venom of their own malice—they tear open the oldest wounds, they make themselves bleed from the scars which have long been healed, they make evil-doers out of friends, wife, child, and everything which is nearest to them. "I suffer: it must be somebody's fault"—so thinks every sick sheep. But his herdsman, the ascetic priest, says to him, "Quite so, my sheep, it must be the fault of some one; but thou thyself art that some one, it is all the fault of thyself alone—it is the fault of thyself alone against thyself": that is bold enough, false enough, but one thing is at least attained; thereby, as I have said, the course of resentment is—diverted.

16.

You can see now what the remedial instinct of life has at least tried to effect, according to my conception, through the ascetic priest, and the purpose for which he had to employ a temporary tyranny of such paradoxical and anomalous ideas as "guilt," "sin," "sinfulness," "corruption," "damnation." What was done was to make the sick harmless up to a certain point, to destroy the incurable by means of themselves, to turn the milder cases severely on to themselves, to give their resentment a backward direction ("man needs but one thing"), and to exploit similarly the bad instincts of all sufferers with a view to self- discipline, self-surveillance, self-mastery. It is obvious that there can be no question at all in the case of a "medication" of this kind, a mere emotional medication, of any real healing of the sick in the physiological sense; it cannot even for a moment be asserted that in this connection the instinct of life has taken healing as its goal and purpose. On the one hand, a kind of congestion and organisation of the sick (the word "Church" is the most popular name for it): on the other, a kind of provisional safeguarding of the comparatively healthy, the more perfect specimens, the cleavage of a rift between healthy and sick—for a long time that was all! and it was much! it was very much!

I am proceeding, as you see, in this essay, from an hypothesis which, as far as such readers as I want are concerned, does not require to be proved; the hypothesis that "sinfulness" in man is not an actual fact, but rather merely the interpretation of a fact, of a physiological discomfort,— a discomfort seen through a moral religious perspective which is no longer binding upon us. The fact, therefore, that any one feels "guilty," "sinful," is certainly not yet any proof that he is right in feeling so, any more than any one is healthy simply because he feels healthy. Remember the celebrated witch-ordeals: in those days the most acute and humane judges had no doubt but that in these cases they were confronted with guilt,—the "witches" themselves had no doubt on the point,—and yet the guilt was lacking. Let me elaborate this hypothesis: I do not for a minute accept the very "pain in the soul" as a real fact, but only as an explanation (a casual explanation) of facts that could not hitherto be precisely formulated; I regard it therefore as something as yet absolutely in the air and devoid of scientific cogency—just a nice fat word in the place of a lean note of interrogation. When any one fails to get rid of his "pain in the soul," the cause is, speaking crudely, to be found not in his "soul" but more probably in his stomach (speaking crudely, I repeat, but by no means wishing thereby that you should listen to me or understand me in a crude spirit). A strong and well-constituted man digests his experiences (deeds and misdeeds all included) just as he digests his meats, even when he has some tough morsels to swallow. If he fails to "relieve himself" of an experience, this kind of indigestion is quite as much physiological as the other indigestion—and indeed, in more ways than one, simply one of the results of the other. You can adopt such a theory, and yet entre nous be nevertheless the strongest opponent of all materialism.

17.

But is he really a physician, this ascetic priest? We already understand why we are scarcely allowed to call him a physician, however much he likes to feel a "saviour" and let himself be worshipped as a saviour.3 It is only the actual suffering, the discomfort of the sufferer, which he combats, not its cause, not the actual state of sickness—this needs must constitute our most radical objection to priestly medication. But just once put yourself into that point of view, of which the priests have a monopoly, you will find it hard to exhaust your amazement, at what from that standpoint he has completely seen, sought, and found.

The mitigation of suffering, every kind of "consoling"—all this manifests itself as his very genius: with what ingenuity has he interpreted his mission of consoler, with what aplomb and audacity has he chosen weapons necessary for the part. Christianity in particular should be dubbed a great treasure-chamber of ingenious consolations,—such a store of refreshing, soothing, deadening drugs has it accumulated within itself; so many of the most dangerous and daring expedients has it hazarded; with such subtlety, refinement, Oriental refinement, has it divined what emotional stimulants can conquer, at any rate for a time, the deep depression, the leaden fatigue, the black melancholy of physiological cripples—for, speaking generally, all religions are mainly In the German text "Heiland." This has the double meaning of "healer" and "saviour."—H. B. S. concerned with fighting a certain fatigue and heaviness that has infected everything. You can regard it as prima facie probable that in certain places in the world there was almost bound to prevail from time to time among large masses of the population a sense of physiological depression, which, however, owing to their lack of physiological knowledge, did not appear to their consciousness as such, so that consequently its "cause" and its cure can only be sought and essayed in the science of moral psychology (this, in fact, is my most general formula for what is generally called a "religion"). Such a feeling of depression can have the most diverse origins; it may be the result of the crossing of too heterogeneous races (or of classes—genealogical and racial differences are also brought out in the classes: the European "Weltschmerz," the "Pessimism" of the nineteenth century, is really the result of an absurd and sudden class-mixture); it may be brought about by a mistaken emigration—a race falling into a climate for which its power of adaptation is insufficient (the case of the Indians in India); it may be the effect of old age and fatigue (the Parisian pessimism from 1850 onwards); it may be a wrong diet (the alcoholism of the Middle Ages, the nonsense of vegetarianism—which, however, have in their favour the authority of Sir Christopher in Shakespeare); it may be blood-deterioration, malaria, syphilis, and the like (German depression after the Thirty Years' War, which infected half Germany with evil diseases, and thereby paved the way for German servility, for German pusillanimity). In such a case there is invariably recourse to a war on a grand scale with the feeling of depression; let us inform ourselves briefly on its most important practices and phases (I leave on one side, as stands to reason, the actual philosophic war against the feeling of depression which is usually simultaneous—it is interesting enough, but too absurd, too practically negligible, too full of cobwebs, too much of a hole-and-corner affair, especially when pain is proved to be a mistake, on the naïf hypothesis that pain must needs vanish when the mistake underlying it is recognised—but behold! it does anything but vanish ...).

That dominant depression is primarily fought by weapons which reduce the consciousness of life itself to the lowest degree. Wherever possible, no more wishes, no more wants; shun everything which produces emotion, which produces "blood" (eating no salt, the fakir hygiene); no love; no hate; equanimity; no revenge; no getting rich; no work; begging; as far as possible, no woman, or as little woman as possible; as far as the intellect is concerned, Pascal's principle, "il faut s'abêtir." To put the result in ethical and psychological language, "self-annihilation," "sanctification"; to put it in physiological language, "hypnotism"—the attempt to find some approximate human equivalent for what hibernation is for certain animals, for what æstivation is for many tropical plants, a minimum of assimilation and metabolism in which life just manages to subsist without really coming into the consciousness. An amazing amount of human energy has been devoted to this object— perhaps uselessly? There cannot be the slightest doubt but that such sportsmen of "saintliness," in whom at times nearly every nation has abounded, have really found a genuine relief from that which they have combated with such a rigorous training—in countless cases they really escaped by the help of their system of hypnotism away from deep physiological depression; their method is consequently counted among the most universal ethnological facts. Similarly it is improper to consider such a plan for starving the physical element and the desires, as in itself a symptom of insanity (as a clumsy species of roast-beef-eating "freethinkers" and Sir Christophers are fain to do); all the more certain is it that their method can and does pave the way to all kinds of mental disturbances, for instance, "inner lights" (as far as the case of the Hesychasts of Mount Athos), auditory and visual hallucinations, voluptuous ecstasies and effervescences of sensualism (the history of St. Theresa). The explanation of such events given by the victims is always the acme of fanatical falsehood; this is self-evident. Note well, however, the tone of implicit gratitude that rings in the very will for an explanation of such a character. The supreme state, salvation itself, that final goal of universal hypnosis and peace, is always regarded by them as the mystery of mysteries, which even the most supreme symbols are inadequate to express; it is regarded as an entry and homecoming to the essence of things, as a liberation from all illusions, as "knowledge," as "truth," as "being" as an escape from every end, every wish, every action, as something even beyond Good and Evil.

"Good and Evil," quoth the Buddhists, "both are fetters. The perfect man is master of them both."

"The done and the undone," quoth the disciple of the Vedânta, "do him no hurt; the good and the evil he shakes from off him, sage that he is; his kingdom suffers no more from any act; good and evil, he goes beyond them both."—An absolutely Indian conception, as much Brahmanist as Buddhist.

Neither in the Indian nor in the Christian doctrine is this "Redemption" regarded as attainable by means of virtue and moral improvement, however high they may place the value of the hypnotic efficiency of virtue: keep clear on this point—indeed it simply corresponds with the facts. The fact that they remained true on this point is perhaps to be regarded as the best specimen of realism in the three great religions, absolutely soaked as they are with morality, with this one exception. "For those who know, there is no duty." "Redemption is not attained by the acquisition of virtues; for redemption consists in being one with Brahman, who is incapable of acquiring any perfection; and equally little does it consist in the giving up of faults, for the Brahman, unity with whom is what constitutes redemption, is eternally pure" (these passages are from the Commentaries of the Cankara, quoted from the first real European expert of the Indian philosophy, my friend Paul Deussen). We wish, therefore, to pay honour to the idea of "redemption" in the great religions, but it is somewhat hard to remain serious in view of the appreciation meted out to the deep sleep by these exhausted pessimists who are too tired even to dream—to the deep sleep considered, that is, as already a fusing into Brahman, as the attainment of the unio mystica with God. "When he has completely gone to sleep," says on this point the oldest and most venerable "script," "and come to perfect rest, so that he sees no more any vision, then, oh dear one, is he united with Being, he has entered into his own self—encircled by the Self with its absolute knowledge, he has no more any consciousness of that which is without or of that which is within. Day and night cross not these bridges, nor age, nor death, nor suffering, nor good deeds, nor evil deeds." "In deep sleep," say similarly the believers in this deepest of the three great religions, "does the soul lift itself from out this body of ours, enters the supreme light and stands out therein in its true shape: therein is it the supreme spirit itself, which travels about, while it jests and plays and enjoys itself, whether with women, or chariots, or friends; there do its thoughts turn no more back to this appanage of a body, to which the 'prana' (the vital breath) is harnessed like a beast of burden to the cart." None the less we will take care to realise (as we did when discussing "redemption") that in spite of all its pomps of Oriental extravagance this simply expresses the same criticism on life as did the clear, cold, Greekly cold, but yet suffering Epicurus. The hypnotic sensation of nothingness, the peace of deepest sleep, anæsthesia in short—that is what passes with the sufferers and the absolutely depressed for, forsooth, their supreme good, their value of values; that is what must be treasured by them as something positive, be felt by them as the essence of the Positive (according to the same logic of the feelings, nothingness is in all pessimistic religions called God).

18.

Such a hypnotic deadening of sensibility and susceptibility to pain, which presupposes somewhat rare powers, especially courage, contempt of opinion, intellectual stoicism, is less frequent than another and certainly easier training which is tried against states of depression. I mean mechanical activity. It is indisputable that a suffering existence can be thereby considerably alleviated. This fact is called to-day by the somewhat ignoble title of the "Blessing of work." The alleviation consists in the attention of the sufferer being absolutely diverted from suffering, in the incessant monopoly of the consciousness by action, so that consequently there is little room left for suffering—for narrow is it, this chamber of human consciousness! Mechanical activity and its corollaries, such as absolute regularity, punctilious unreasoning obedience, the chronic routine of life, the complete occupation of time, a certain liberty to be impersonal, nay, a training in "impersonality," self- forgetfulness, "incuria sui"—with what thoroughness and expert subtlety have all these methods been exploited by the ascetic priest in his war with pain!

When he has to tackle sufferers of the lower orders, slaves, or prisoners (or women, who for the most part are a compound of labour-slave and prisoner), all he has to do is to juggle a little with the names, and to rechristen, so as to make them see henceforth a benefit, a comparative happiness, in objects which they hated—the slave's discontent with his lot was at any rate not invented by the priests. An even more popular means of fighting depression is the ordaining of a little joy, which is easily accessible and can be made into a rule; this medication is frequently used in conjunction with the former ones. The most frequent form in which joy is prescribed as a cure is the joy in producing joy (such as doing good, giving presents, alleviating, helping, exhorting, comforting, praising, treating with distinction); together with the prescription of "love your neighbour." The ascetic priest prescribes, though in the most cautious doses, what is practically a stimulation of the strongest and most life-assertive impulse—the Will for Power. The happiness involved in the "smallest superiority" which is the concomitant of all benefiting, helping, extolling, making one's self useful, is the most ample consolation, of which, if they are well-advised, physiological distortions avail themselves: in other cases they hurt each other, and naturally in obedience to the same radical instinct. An investigation of the origin of Christianity in the Roman world shows that co-operative unions for poverty, sickness, and burial sprang up in the lowest stratum of contemporary society, amid which the chief antidote against depression, the little joy experienced in mutual benefits, was deliberately fostered. Perchance this was then a novelty, a real discovery? This conjuring up of the will for co-operation, for family organisation, for communal life, for "Cœnacula" necessarily brought the Will for Power, which had been already infinitesimally stimulated, to a new and much fuller manifestation. The herd organisation is a genuine advance and triumph in the fight with depression. With the growth of the community there matures even to individuals a new interest, which often enough takes him out of the more personal element in his discontent, his aversion to himself, the "despectus sui" of Geulincx. All sick and diseased people strive instinctively after a herd-organisation, out of a desire to shake off their sense of oppressive discomfort and weakness; the ascetic priest divines this instinct and promotes it; wherever a herd exists it is the instinct of weakness which has wished for the herd, and the cleverness of the priests which has organised it, for, mark this: by an equally natural necessity the strong strive as much for isolation as the weak for union: when the former bind themselves it is only with a view to an aggressive joint action and joint satisfaction of their Will for Power, much against the wishes of their individual consciences; the latter, on the contrary, range themselves together with positive delight in such a muster—their instincts are as much gratified thereby as the instincts of the "born master" (that is, the solitary beast-of-prey species of man) are disturbed and wounded to the quick by organisation. There is always lurking beneath every oligarchy—such is the universal lesson of history— the desire for tyranny. Every oligarchy is continually quivering with the tension of the effort required by each individual to keep mastering this desire. (Such, e.g., was the Greek; Plato shows it in a hundred places, Plato, who knew his contemporaries—and himself.)

19.

The methods employed by the ascetic priest, which we have already learnt to know—stifling of all vitality, mechanical energy, the little joy, and especially the method of "love your neighbour" herd-organisation, the awaking of the communal consciousness of power, to such a pitch that the individual's disgust with himself becomes eclipsed by his delight in the thriving of the community—these are, according to modern standards, the "innocent" methods employed in the fight with depression; let us turn now to the more interesting topic of the "guilty" methods. The guilty methods spell one thing: to produce emotional excess—which is used as the most efficacious anæsthetic against their depressing state of protracted pain; this is why priestly ingenuity has proved quite inexhaustible in thinking out this one question: "By what means can you produce an emotional excess?" This sounds harsh: it is manifest that it would sound nicer and would grate on one's ears less, if I were to say, forsooth: "The ascetic priest made use at all times of the enthusiasm contained in all strong emotions." But what is the good of still soothing the delicate ears of our modern effeminates? What is the good on our side of budging one single inch before their verbal Pecksniffianism. For us psychologists to do that would be at once practical Pecksniffianism, apart from the fact of its nauseating us. The good taste (others might say, the righteousness) of a psychologist nowadays consists, if at all, in combating the shamefully moralised language with which all modern judgments on men and things are smeared. For, do not deceive yourself: what constitutes the chief characteristic of modern souls and of modern books is not the lying, but the innocence which is part and parcel of their intellectual dishonesty.

The inevitable running up against this "innocence" everywhere constitutes the most distasteful feature of the somewhat dangerous business which a modern psychologist has to undertake: it is a part of our great danger—it is a road which perhaps leads us straight to the great nausea—I know quite well the purpose which all modern books will and can serve (granted that they last, which I am not afraid of, and granted equally that there is to be at some future day a generation with a more rigid, more severe, and healthier taste)—the function which all modernity generally will serve with posterity: that of an emetic,—and this by reason of its moral sugariness and falsity, its ingrained feminism, which it is pleased to call "Idealism," and at any rate believes to be idealism. Our cultured men of to-day, our "good" men, do not lie—that is true; but it does not redound to their honour! The real lie, the genuine, determined, "honest" lie (on whose value you can listen to Plato) would prove too tough and strong an article for them by a long way; it would be asking them to do what people have been forbidden to ask them to do, to open their eyes to their own selves, and to learn to distinguish between "true" and "false" in their own selves. The dishonest lie alone suits them: everything which feels a good man is perfectly incapable of any other attitude to anything than that of a dishonourable liar, an absolute liar, but none the less an innocent liar, a blue-eyed liar, a virtuous liar. These "good men," they are all now tainted with morality through and through, and as far as honour is concerned they are disgraced and corrupted for all eternity. Which of them could stand a further truth "about man"? or, put more tangibly, which of them could put up with a true biography?

One or two instances: Lord Byron composed a most personal autobiography, but Thomas Moore was "too good" for it; he burnt his friend's papers. Dr. Gwinner, Schopenhauer's executor, is said to have done the same; for Schopenhauer as well wrote much about himself, and perhaps also against himself: The virtuous American Thayer, Beethoven's biographer, suddenly stopped his work: he had come to a certain point in that honourable and simple life, and could stand it no longer. Moral: What sensible man nowadays writes one honest word about himself? He must already belong to the Order of Holy Foolhardiness. We are promised an autobiography of Richard Wagner; who doubts but that it would be a clever autobiography? Think, forsooth, of the grotesque horror which the Catholic priest Janssen aroused in Germany with his inconceivably square and harmless pictures of the German Reformation; what wouldn't people do if some real psychologist were to tell us about a genuine Luther, tell us, not with the moralist simplicity of a country priest or the sweet and cautious modesty of a Protestant historian, but say with the fearlessness of a Taine, that springs from force of character and not from a prudent toleration of force. (The Germans, by the bye, have already produced the classic specimen of this toleration—they may well be allowed to reckon him as one of their own, in Leopold Ranke, that born classical advocate of every causa fortior, that cleverest of all the clever opportunists.)

20.

But you will soon understand me.—Putting it shortly, there is reason enough, is there not, for us psychologists nowadays never getting from a certain mistrust of out own selves? Probably even we ourselves are still "too good" for our work, probably, whatever contempt we feel for this popular craze for morality, we ourselves are perhaps none the less its victims, prey, and slaves; probably it infects even us. Of what was that diplomat warning us, when he said to his colleagues: "Let us especially mistrust our first impulses, gentlemen! they are almost always good"? So should nowadays every psychologist talk to his colleagues. And thus we get back to our problem, which in point of fact does require from us a certain severity, a certain mistrust especially against "first impulses." The ascetic ideal in the service of projected emotional excess:—he who remembers the previous essay will already partially anticipate the essential meaning compressed into these above ten words. The thorough unswitching of the human soul, the plunging of it into terror, frost, ardour, rapture, so as to free it, as through some lightning shock, from all the smallness and pettiness of unhappiness, depression, and discomfort: what ways lead to this goal? And which of these ways does somost safely?... At bottom all great emotions have this power, provided that they find a sudden outlet—emotions such as rage, fear, lust, revenge, hope, triumph, despair, cruelty; and, in sooth, the ascetic priest has had no scruples in taking into his service the whole pack of hounds that rage in the human kennel, unleashing now these and now those, with the same constant object of waking man out of his protracted melancholy, of chasing away, at any rate for a time, his dull pain, his shrinking misery, but always under the sanction of a religious interpretation and justification. This emotional excess has subsequently to be paid for, this is self-evident—it makes the ill more ill—and therefore this kind of remedy for pain is according to modern standards a "guilty" kind.

The dictates of fairness, however, require that we should all the more emphasise the fact that this remedy is applied with a good conscience, that the ascetic priest has prescribed it in the most implicit belief in its utility and indispensability;—often enough almost collapsing in the presence of the pain which he created;—that we should similarly emphasise the fact that the violent physiological revenges of such excesses, even perhaps the mental disturbances, are not absolutely inconsistent with the general tenor of this kind of remedy; this remedy, which, as we have shown previously, is not for the purpose of healing diseases, but of fighting the unhappiness of that depression, the alleviation and deadening of which was its object. The object was consequently achieved. The keynote by which the ascetic priest was enabled to get every kind of agonising and ecstatic music to play on the fibres of the human soul—was, as every one knows, the exploitation of the feeling of "guilt." I have already indicated in the previous essay the origin of this feeling—as a piece of animal psychology and nothing else: we were thus confronted with the feeling of "guilt," in its crude state, as it were. It was first in the hands of the priest, real artist that he was in the feeling of guilt, that it took shape—oh, what a shape! "Sin"—for that is the name of the new priestly version of the animal "bad-conscience" (the inverted cruelty)—has up to the present been the greatest event in the history of the diseased soul: in "sin" we find the most perilous and fatal masterpiece of religious interpretation. Imagine man, suffering from himself, some way or other but at any rate physiologically, perhaps like an animal shut up in a cage, not clear as to the why and the wherefore! imagine him in his desire for reasons—reasons bring relief—in his desire again for remedies, narcotics at last, consulting one, who knows even the occult—and see, lo and behold, he gets a hint from his wizard, the ascetic priest, his first hint on the "cause" of his trouble: he must search for it in himself, in his guiltiness, in a piece of the past, he must understand his very suffering as a state of punishment. He has heard, he has understood, has the unfortunate: he is now in the plight of a hen round which a line has been drawn. He never gets out of the circle of lines. The sick man has been turned into "the sinner"—and now for a few thousand years we never get away from the sight of this new invalid, of "a sinner"— shall we ever get away from it?—wherever we just look, everywhere the hypnotic gaze of the sinner always moving in one direction (in the direction of guilt, the only cause of suffering); everywhere the evil conscience, this "greuliche thier,"4 to use Luther's language; everywhere rumination over the past, a distorted view of action, the gaze of the "green-eyed monster" turned on all action; everywhere the wilful misunderstanding of suffering, its transvaluation into feelings of guilt, fear of retribution; everywhere the scourge, the hairy shirt, the starving body, contrition; everywhere the sinner breaking himself on the ghastly wheel of a restless and morbidly eager conscience; everywhere mute pain, extreme fear, the agony of a tortured heart, the spasms of an unknown happiness, the shriek for "redemption." In point of fact, thanks to this system of procedure, the old depression, dullness, and fatigue were absolutely conquered, life itself became very interesting again, awake, eternally awake, sleepless, glowing, burnt away, exhausted and yet not tired—such was the figure cut by man, "the sinner," who was initiated into these mysteries. This grand old wizard of an ascetic priest fighting with depression—he had clearly triumphed, his kingdom had come: men no longer grumbled at pain, men panted after pain: "More pain! More pain!" So for centuries on end shrieked the demand of his acolytes and initiates. Every emotional excess which hurt; everything which broke, overthrew, crushed, transported, ravished; the mystery of torture-chambers, the ingenuity of hell itself—all this was now discovered, divined, exploited, all this was at the service of the wizard, all this served to promote the triumph of his ideal, the ascetic ideal. "My kingdom is not of this world," quoth he, both at the beginning and at the end: had he still the right to talk like that?—Goethe has maintained that there are only thirty-six tragic situations: we would infer from that, did we not know otherwise, that Goethe was no ascetic priest. He—knows more.

21.

So far as all this kind of priestly medicine-mongering, the "guilty" kind, is concerned, every word of criticism is superfluous. As for the suggestion that emotional excess of the type, which in these cases the ascetic priest is fain to order to his sick patients (under the most sacred euphemism, as is obvious, and equally impregnated with the sanctity of his purpose), has ever really been of use to any sick man, who, forsooth, would feel inclined to maintain a proposition of that character? At any rate, some understanding should be come to as to the expression "be of use." If you only wish to express that such a system of treatment has reformed man, I do not gainsay it: I merely add that "reformed" conveys to my mind as much as "tamed," "weakened," "discouraged," "refined," "daintified," "emasculated" (and thus it means almost as much as injured). But when you have to deal principally with sick, depressed, and oppressed creatures, such a system, even granted that it makes the ill "better," under any circumstances also makes them more ill: ask the mad-doctors the invariable result of a methodical application of penance-torture, contrition, and salvation ecstasies. Similarly ask history. In every body politic where the ascetic priest has established this treatment of the sick, disease has on every occasion spread with sinister speed throughout its length and breadth. What was always the "result"? A shattered nervous system, in addition to the existing malady, and this in the greatest as in the smallest, in the individuals as in masses. We find, in consequence of the penance and redemption-training, awful epileptic epidemics, the greatest known to history, such as the St. Vitus and St. John dances of the Middle Ages; we find, as another phase of its after-effect, frightful mutilations and chronic depressions, by means of which the temperament of a nation or a city (Geneva, Bale) is turned once for all into its opposite;—this training, again, is responsible for the witch-hysteria, a phenomenon analogous to somnambulism (eight great epidemic outbursts of this only between 1564 and 1605);—we find similarly in its train those delirious death-cravings of large masses, whose awful "shriek," "evviva la morte!" was heard over the whole of Europe, now interrupted by voluptuous variations and anon by a rage for destruction, just as the same emotional sequence with the same intermittencies and sudden changes is now universally observed in every case where the ascetic doctrine of sin scores once more a great success (religious neurosis appears as a manifestation of the devil, there is no doubt of it. What is it? Quæritur). Speaking generally, the ascetic ideal and its sublime-moral cult, this most ingenious, reckless, and perilous systematisation of all methods of emotional excess, is writ large in a dreadful and unforgettable fashion on the whole history of man, and unfortunately not only on history. I was scarcely able to put forward any other element which attacked the health and race efficiency of Europeans with more destructive power than did this ideal; it can be dubbed, without exaggeration, the real fatality in the history of the health of the European man. At the most you can merely draw a comparison with the specifically German influence: I mean the alcohol poisoning of Europe, which up to the present has kept pace exactly with the political and racial pre–dominance of the Germans (where they inoculated their blood, there too did they inoculate their vice). Third in the series comes syphilis—magno sed proximo intervallo.

22.

The ascetic priest has, wherever he has obtained the mastery, corrupted the health of the soul, he has consequently also corrupted taste in artibus et litteris—he corrupts it still. "Consequently?" I hope I shall be granted this "consequently "; at any rate, I am not going to prove it first. One solitary indication, it concerns the arch-book of Christian literature, their real model, their "book-in-itself." In the very midst of the Græco- Roman splendour, which was also a splendour of books, face to face with an ancient world of writings which had not yet fallen into decay and ruin, at a time when certain books were still to be read, to possess which we would give nowadays half our literature in exchange, at that time the simplicity and vanity of Christian agitators (they are generally called Fathers of the Church) dared to declare: "We too have our classical literature, we do not need that of the Greeks"—

and meanwhile they proudly pointed to their books of legends, their letters of apostles, and their apologetic tractlets, just in the same way that to-day the English "Salvation Army" wages its fight against Shakespeare and other "heathens" with an analogous literature. You already guess it, I do not like the "New Testament"; it almost upsets me that I stand so isolated in my taste so far as concerns this valued, this over-valued Scripture; the taste of two thousand years is against me; but what boots it! "Here I stand! I cannot help myself"5—I have the courage of my bad taste.

The Old Testament—yes, that is something quite different, all honour to the Old Testament! I find therein great men, an heroic landscape, and one of the rarest phenomena in the world, the incomparable naïveté of the strong heart; further still, I find a people. In the New, on the contrary, just a hostel of petty sects, pure rococo of the soul, twisting angles and fancy touches, nothing but conventicle air, not to forget an occasional whiff of bucolic sweetness which appertains to the epoch (and the Roman province) and is less Jewish than Hellenistic. Meekness and braggadocio cheek by jowl; an emotional garrulousness that almost deafens; passionate hysteria, but no passion; painful pantomime; here manifestly every one lacked good breeding. How dare any one make so "Here I stand! I cannot help myself. God help me! Amen"— were Luther's words before the Reichstag at Worms.—H. B. S. much fuss about their little failings as do these pious little fellows! No one cares a straw about it—let alone God. Finally they actually wish to have "the crown of eternal life," do all these little provincials! In return for what, in sooth? For what end? It is impossible to carry insolence any further. An immortal Peter! who could stand him! They have an ambition which makes one laugh: the thing dishes up cut and dried his most personal life, his melancholies, and common-or-garden troubles, as though the Universe itself were under an obligation to bother itself about them, for it never gets tired of wrapping up God Himself in the petty misery in which its troubles are involved. And how about the atrocious form of this chronic hobnobbing with God? This Jewish, and not merely Jewish, slobbering and clawing importunacy towards God!—There exist little despised "heathen nations" in East Asia, from whom these first Christians could have learnt something worth learning, a little tact in worshiping; these nations do not allow themselves to say aloud the name of their God. This seems to me delicate enough, it is certain that it is too delicate, and not only for primitive Christians; to take a contrast, just recollect Luther, the most "eloquent" and insolent peasant whom Germany has had, think of the Lutherian tone, in which he felt quite the most in his element during his tête-à-têtes with God. Luther's opposition to the mediæval saints of the Church (in particular, against "that devil's hog, the Pope"), was, there is no doubt, at bottom the opposition of a boor, who was offended at the good etiquette of the Church, that worship-etiquette of the sacerdotal code, which only admits to the holy of holies the initiated and the silent, and shuts the door against the boors. These definitely were not to be allowed a hearing in this planet— but Luther the peasant simply wished it otherwise; as it was, it was not German enough for him. He personally wished himself to talk direct, to talk personally, to talk "straight from the shoulder" with his God. Well, he's done it. The ascetic ideal, you will guess, was at no time and in no place, a school of good taste, still less of good manners— at the best it was a school for sacerdotal manners: that is, it contains in itself something which was a deadly enemy to all good manners. Lack of measure, opposition to measure, it is itself a "non plus ultra."

23.

The ascetic ideal has corrupted not only health and taste, there are also third, fourth, fifth, and sixth things which it has corrupted—I shall take care not to go through the catalogue (when should I get to the end?). I have here to expose not what this ideal effected; but rather only what it means, on what it is based, what lies lurking behind it and under it, that of which it is the provisional expression, an obscure expression bristling with queries and misunderstandings. And with this object only in view I presumed "not to spare" my readers a glance at the awfulness of its results, a glance at its fatal results; I did this to prepare them for the final and most awful aspect presented to me by the question of the significance of that ideal. What is the significance of the power of that ideal, the monstrousness of its power? Why is it given such an amount of scope? Why is not a better resistance offered against it? The ascetic ideal expresses one will: where is the opposition will, in which an opposition ideal expresses itself? The ascetic ideal has an aim— this goal is, putting it generally, that all the other interests of human life should, measured by its standard, appear petty and narrow; it explains epochs, nations, men, in reference to this one end; it forbids any other interpretation, any other end; it repudiates, denies, affirms, confirms, only in the sense of its own interpretation (and was there ever a more thoroughly elaborated system of interpretation?); it subjects itself to no power, rather does it believe in its own precedence over every power—it believes that nothing powerful exists in the world that has not first got to receive from "it" a meaning, a right to exist, a value, as being an instrument in its work, a way and means to its end, to one end. Where is the counterpart of this complete system of will, end, and interpretation? Why is the counterpart lacking? Where is the other "one aim"? But I am told it is not lacking, that not only has it fought a long and fortunate fight with that ideal, but that further it has already won the mastery over that ideal in all essentials: let our whole modern science attest this—that modern science, which, like the genuine reality-philosophy which it is, manifestly believes in itself alone, manifestly has the courage to be itself, the will to be itself, and has got on well enough without God, another world, and negative virtues.

With all their noisy agitator-babble, however, they effect nothing with me; these trumpeters of reality are bad musicians, their voices do not come from the deeps with sufficient audibility, they are not the mouthpiece for the abyss of scientific knowledge—for to-day scientific knowledge is an abyss—the word "science," in such trumpeter-mouths, is a prostitution, an abuse, an impertinence. The truth is just the opposite from what is maintained in the ascetic theory. Science has to-day absolutely no belief in itself, let alone in an ideal superior to itself, and wherever science still consists of passion, love, ardour, suffering, it is not the opposition to that ascetic ideal, but rather the incarnation of its latest and noblest form. Does that ring strange? There are enough brave and decent working people, even among the learned men of to-day, who like their little corner, and who, just because they are pleased so to do, become at times indecently loud with their demand, that people to-day should be quite content, especially in science—for in science there is so much useful work to do. I do not deny it—there is nothing I should like less than to spoil the delight of these honest workers in their handiwork; for I rejoice in their work. But the fact of science requiring hard work, the fact of its having contented workers, is absolutely no proof of science as a whole having to-day one end, one will, one ideal, one passion for a great faith; the contrary, as I have said, is the case. When science is not the latest manifestation of the ascetic ideal—but these are cases of such rarity, selectness, and exquisiteness, as to preclude the general judgment being affected thereby—science is a hiding-place for every kind of cowardice, disbelief, remorse, despectio sui, bad conscience—it is the very anxiety that springs from having no ideal, the suffering from the lack of a great love, the discontent with an enforced moderation. Oh, what does all science not cover to-day? How much, at any rate, does it not try to cover? The diligence of our best scholars, their senseless industry, their burning the candle of their brain at both ends— their very mastery in their handiwork—how often is the real meaning of all that to prevent themselves continuing to see a certain thing? Science as a self- anæsthetic: do you know that? You wound them—every one who consorts with scholars experiences this—you wound them sometimes to the quick through just a harmless word; when you think you are paying them a compliment you embitter them beyond all bounds, simply because you didn't have the finesse to infer the real kind of customers you had to tackle, the sufferer kind (who won't own up even to themselves what they really are), the dazed and unconscious kind who have only one fear—coming to consciousness.

24.

And now look at the other side, at those rare cases, of which I spoke, the most supreme idealists to be found nowadays among philosophers and scholars. Have we, perchance, found in them the sought- for opponents of the ascetic ideal, its anti-idealists? In fact, they believe themselves to be such, these "unbelievers" (for they are all of them that): it seems that this idea is their last remnant of faith, the idea of being opponents of this ideal, so earnest are they on this subject, so passionate in word and gesture;—but does it follow that what they believe must necessarily be true? We "knowers" have grown by degrees suspicious of all kinds of believers, our suspicion has step by step habituated us to draw just the opposite conclusions to what people have drawn before;

that is to say, wherever the strength of a belief is particularly prominent to draw the conclusion of the difficulty of proving what is believed, the conclusion of its actual improbability. We do not again deny that "faith produces salvation": for that very reason we do deny that faith proves anything,—a strong faith, which produces happiness, causes suspicion of the object of that faith, it does not establish its "truth," it does establish a certain probability of—illusion.

What is now the position in these cases? These solitaries and deniers of to-day; these fanatics in one thing, in their claim to intellectual cleanness; these hard, stern, continent, heroic spirits, who constitute the glory of our time; all these pale atheists, anti-Christians, immoralists, Nihilists; these sceptics, "ephectics," and "hectics" of the intellect (in a certain sense they are the latter, both collectively and individually); these supreme idealists of knowledge, in whom alone nowadays the intellectual conscience dwells and is alive—in point of fact they believe themselves as far away as possible from the ascetic ideal, do these "free, very free spirits": and yet, if I may reveal what they themselves cannot see—for they stand too near themselves: this ideal is simply their ideal, they represent it nowadays and perhaps no one else, they themselves are its most spiritualised product, its most advanced picket of skirmishers and scouts, its most insidious delicate and elusive form of seduction.—If I am in any way a reader of riddles, then I will be one with this sentence: for some time past there have been no free spirits; for they still believe in truth. When the Christian Crusaders in the East came into collision with that invincible order of assassins, that order of free spirits par excellence, whose lowest grade lives in a state of discipline such as no order of monks has ever attained, then in some way or other they managed to get an inkling of that symbol and tally-word, that was reserved for the highest grade alone as their secretum, "Nothing is true, everything is allowed,"—in sooth, that was freedom of thought, thereby was taking leave of the very belief in truth. Has indeed any European, any Christian freethinker, ever yet wandered into this proposition and its labyrinthine consequences? Does he know from experience the Minotauros of this den.—I doubt it—nay, I know otherwise. Nothing is more really alien to these "mono-fanatics," these so-called "free spirits," than freedom and unfettering in that sense; in no respect are they more closely tied, the absolute fanaticism of their belief in truth is unparalleled. I know all this perhaps too much from experience at close quarters— that dignified philosophic abstinence to which a belief like that binds its adherents, that stoicism of the intellect, which eventually vetoes negation as rigidly as it does affirmation, that wish for standing still in front of the actual, the factum brutum, that fatalism in "petits faits" (ce petit faitalism, as I call it), in which French Science now attempts a kind of moral superiority over German, this renunciation of interpretation generally (that is, of forcing, doctoring, abridging, omitting, suppressing, inventing, falsifying, and all the other essential attributes of interpretation)—all this, considered broadly, expresses the asceticism of virtue, quite as efficiently as does any repudiation of the senses (it is at bottom only a modus of that repudiation.) But what forces it into that unqualified will for truth is the faith in the ascetic ideal itself, even though it take the form of its unconscious imperatives,—make no mistake about it, it is the faith, I repeat, in a metaphysical value, an intrinsic value of truth, of a character which is only warranted and guaranteed in this ideal (it stands and falls with that ideal). Judged strictly, there does not exist a science without its "hypotheses," the thought of such a science is inconceivable, illogical: a philosophy, a faith, must always exist first to enable science to gain thereby a direction, a meaning, a limit and method, a right to existence. (He who holds a contrary opinion on the subject—he, for example, who takes it upon himself to establish philosophy "upon a strictly scientific basis"—has first got to "turn up-side-down" not only philosophy but also truth itself—the gravest insult which could possibly be offered to two such respectable females!) Yes, there is no doubt about it—and here I quote my Joyful Wisdom, cp. Book V. Aph. 344: "The man who is truthful in that daring and extreme fashion, which is the presupposition of the faith in science, asserts thereby a different world from that of life, nature, and history; and in so far as he asserts the existence of that different world, come, must he not similarly repudiate its counterpart, this world, our world? The belief on which our faith in science is based has remained to this day a metaphysical belief—even we knowers of to-day, we godless foes of metaphysics, we too take our fire from that conflagration which was kindled by a thousand-year-old faith, from that

Christian belief, which was also Plato's belief, the belief that God is truth, that truth is divine But what if this belief becomes more and more incredible, what if nothing proves itself to be divine, unless it be error, blindness, lies—what if God, Himself proved Himself to be our oldest lie?"—It is necessary to stop at this point and to consider the situation carefully. Science itself now needs a justification (which is not for a minute to say that there is such a justification). Turn in this context to the most ancient and the most modern philosophers: they all fail to realise the extent of the need of a justification on the part of the Will for Truth—here is a gap in every philosophy—what is it caused by? Because up to the present the ascetic ideal dominated all philosophy, because Truth was fixed as Being, as God, as the Supreme Court of Appeal, because Truth was not allowed to be a problem. Do you understand this "allowed"? From the minute that the belief in the God of the ascetic ideal is repudiated, there exists a new problem: the problem of the value of truth. The Will for

Truth needed a critique—let us define by these words our own task——the value of truth is tentatively to be called in question (If this seems too laconically expressed, I recommend the reader to peruse again that passage from the Joyful Wisdom which bears the title, "How far we also are still pious," Aph. 344, and best of all the whole fifth book of that work, as well as the Preface to The Dawn of Day.)

25.

No! You can't get round me with science, when I search for the natural antagonists of the ascetic ideal, when I put the question: "Where is the opposed will in which the opponent ideal expresses itself?" Science is not, by a long way, independent enough to fulfil this function; in every department science needs an ideal value, a power which creates values, and in whose service it can believe in itself —science itself never creates values. Its relation to the ascetic ideal is not in itself antagonistic; speaking roughly, it rather represents the progressive force in the inner evolution of that ideal. Tested more exactly, its opposition and antagonism are concerned not with the ideal itself, but only with that ideal's outworks, its outer garb, its masquerade, with its temporary hardening, stiffening, and dogmatising—it makes the life in the ideal free once more, while it repudiates its superficial elements. These two phenomena, science and the ascetic ideal, both rest on the same basis—I have already made this clear—the basis, I say, oft the same over- appreciation of truth (more accurately the same belief in the impossibility of valuing and of criticising truth), and consequently they are necessarily allies, so that, in the event of their being attacked, they must always be attacked and called into question together. A valuation of the ascetic ideal inevitably entails a valuation of science as well; lose no time in seeing this clearly, and be sharp to catch it! (Art, I am speaking provisionally, for I will treat it on some other occasion in greater detail,—art, I repeat, in which lying is sanctified and the will for deception has good conscience on its side, is much more fundamentally opposed to the ascetic ideal than is science: Plato's instinct felt this— Plato, the greatest enemy of art which Europe has produced up to the present. Plato versus Homer, that is the complete, the true antagonism— —on the one side, the whole-hearted "transcendental," the great defamer of life; on the other, its involuntary panegyrist, the golden nature. An artistic subservience to the service of the ascetic ideal is consequently the most absolute artistic corruption that there can be, though unfortunately it is one of the most frequent phases, for nothing is more corruptible than an artist.) Considered physiologically, moreover, science rests on the same, basis as does the ascetic ideal: a certain impoverishment of life is the presupposition of the latter as of the former— add, frigidity of the emotions, slackening of the tempo, the substitution of dialectic for instinct, seriousness impressed on mien and gesture (seriousness, that most unmistakable sign of strenuous metabolism, of struggling, toiling life). Consider the periods in a nation in which the learned man comes into prominence; they are the periods of exhaustion, often of sunset, of decay—the effervescing strength, the confidence in life, the confidence in the future are no more. The preponderance of the mandarins never signifies any good, any more than does the advent of democracy, or arbitration instead of war, equal rights for women, the religion of pity, and all the other symptoms of declining life. (Science handled as a problem! what is the meaning of science?—upon this point the Preface to the Birth of Tragedy.) No! this "modern science"—mark you this well—is at times the best ally for the ascetic ideal, and for the very reason that it is the ally which is most unconscious, most automatic, most secret, and most subterranean! They have been playing into each other's hands up to the present, have these "poor in spirit" and the scientific opponents of that ideal (take care, by the bye, not to think that these opponents are the antithesis of this ideal, that they are the rich in spirit—that they are not; I have called them the hectic in spirit). As for these celebrated victories of science; there is no doubt that they are victories—but victories over what? There was not for a single minute any victory among their list over the ascetic ideal, rather was it made stronger, that is to say, more elusive, more abstract, more insidious, from the fact that a wall, an outwork, that had got built on to the main fortress and disfigured its appearance, should from time to time be ruthlessly destroyed and broken down by science. Does any one seriously suggest that the downfall of the theological astronomy signified the downfall of that ideal?— Has, perchance, man grown less in need of a transcendental solution of his riddle of existence, because since that time this existence has become more random, casual, and superfluous in the visible order of the universe? Has there not been since the time of Copernicus an unbroken progress in the self-belittling of man and his will for belittling himself? Alas, his belief in his dignity, his uniquenesses irreplaceableness in the scheme of existence, is gone—he has become animal, literal, unqualified, and unmitigated animal, he who in his earlier belief was almost God ("child of God," "demi-God"). Since Copernicus man seems to have fallen on to a steep plane—he rolls faster and faster away from the centre—whither? into nothingness? into the "thrilling sensation of his own nothingness"—Well! this would be the straight way—to the old ideal?—All science (and by no means only astronomy, with regard to the humiliating and deteriorating effect of which Kant has made a remarkable confession, "it annihilates my own importance"), all science, natural as much as unnatural—by unnatural I mean the self-critique of reason—nowadays sets out to talk man out of his present opinion of himself, as though that opinion had been nothing but a bizarre piece of conceit; you might go so far as to say that science finds its peculiar pride, its peculiar bitter form of stoical ataraxia, in preserving man's contempt of himself, that state which it took so much trouble to bring about, as man's final and most serious claim to self- appreciation (rightly so, in point of fact, for he who despises is always "one who has not forgotten how to appreciate"). But does all this involve any real effort to counteract the ascetic ideal? Is it really seriously suggested that Kant's victory over the theological dogmatism about "God," "Soul," "Freedom," "Immortality," has damaged that ideal in any way (as the theologians have imagined to be the case for a long time past)?— And in this connection it does not concern us for a single minute, if Kant himself intended any such consummation. It is certain that from the time of Kant every type of transcendentalist is playing a winning game— they are emancipated from the theologians; what luck!— he has revealed to them that secret art, by which they can now pursue their "heart's desire" on their own responsibility, and with all the respectability of science. Similarly, who can grumble at the agnostics, reverers, as they are, of the unknown and the absolute mystery, if they now worship their very query as God? (Xaver Doudan talks somewhere of the ravages which l'habitude d'admirer l'inintelligible au lieu de rester tout simplement dans l'inconnu has produced—the ancients, he thinks, must have been exempt from those ravages.) Supposing that everything, "known" to man, fails to satisfy his desires, and on the contrary contradicts and horrifies them, what a divine way out of all this to be able to look for the responsibility, not in the "desiring" but in "knowing"!—"There is no knowledge. Consequently— there is a God"; what a novel elegantia syllogismi! what a triumph for the ascetic ideal!

26.

Or, perchance, does the whole of modern history show in its demeanour greater confidence in life, greater confidence in its ideals? Its loftiest pretension is now to be a mirror; it repudiates all teleology; it will have no more "proving"; it disdains to play the judge, and thereby shows its good taste—it asserts as little as it denies, it fixes, it "describes." All this is to a high degree ascetic, but at the same time it is to a much greater degree nihilistic; make no mistake about this! You see in the historian a gloomy, hard, but determined gaze,—an eye that looks out as an isolated North Pole explorer looks out (perhaps so as not to look within, so as not to look back?)—there is snow—here is life silenced, the last crows which caw here are called "whither?" "Vanity," "Nada"—here nothing more flourishes and grows, at the most the metapolitics of St. Petersburg and the "pity" of Tolstoi. But as for that other school of historians, a perhaps still more "modern" school, a voluptuous and lascivious school which ogles life and the ascetic ideal with equal fervour, which uses the word "artist" as a glove, and has nowadays established a "corner" for itself, in all the praise given to contemplation; oh, what a thirst do these sweet intellectuals excite even for ascetics and winter landscapes! Nay! The devil take these "contemplative" folk! How much liefer would I wander with those historical Nihilists through the gloomiest, grey, cold mist!—nay, I shall not mind listening (supposing I have to choose) to one who is completely unhistorical and anti-historical (a man, like Dühring for instance, over whose periods a hitherto shy and unavowed species of "beautiful souls" has grown intoxicated in contemporary Germany, the species anarchistica within the educated proletariate). The "contemplative" are a hundred times worse—I never knew anything which produced such intense nausea as one of those "objective" chairs,6 one of those scented mannikins-about-town of history, a thing half-priest, half-satyr (Renan parfum), which betrays by the high, shrill falsetto of his applause what he lacks and where he lacks it, who betrays where in this case the Fates have plied their ghastly shears, alas! in too surgeon-like a fashion! This is distasteful to me, and irritates my patience; let him keep patient at such sights who has nothing to lose thereby,—such a sight enrages me, such spectators embitter me against the "play," even more than does the play itself (history itself, you understand); Anacreontic moods imperceptibly come over me. This Nature, who gave to the steer its horn, to the lion its χάσμ' □ δοντων, for what purpose did Nature give me my foot?—To kick, by St. Anacreon, and not merely to run away! To trample on all the worm-eaten "chairs," the cowardly contemplators, the lascivious eunuchs of history, the flirters with ascetic ideals, the righteous hypocrites of impotence! All reverence on my part to the ascetic ideal, in so far as it is honourable! So long as it believes in itself and plays no pranks on us! But I like not all these coquettish bugs who have an insatiate ambition to smell of the infinite, until eventually the infinite smells of bugs; I like not the whited sepulchres with their stagey reproduction of life; I like not the tired and the used up who wrap themselves in wisdom and look "objective"; I like not the agitators dressed up as heroes, who hide their dummy-heads behind the stalking-horse of an ideal; I like not the ambitious artists who would fain play the ascetic and the priest, and are at bottom nothing but tragic clowns; I like not, again, these newest speculators in idealism, the Anti-Semites, who nowadays roll their eyes in the patent Christian- Aryan-man-of-honour fashion, and by an abuse of moralist attitudes and agitation dodges, so cheap as to exhaust any patience, strive to excite all the blockhead elements in the populace (the invariable success of every kind of intellectual charlatanism in present-day Germany hangs together with the almost indisputable and already quite palpable desolation of the German mind, whose cause I look for in a too exclusive diet, of papers, politics, beer, and Wagnerian music, not forgetting the condition precedent of this diet, the national exclusiveness and vanity, the strong but narrow principle, "Germany, Germany above everything,"7 and finally the paralysis agitans of "modern ideas").

Europe nowadays is, above all, wealthy and ingenious in means of excitement; it apparently has no more crying necessity than stimulantia and alcohol. Hence the enormous counterfeiting of ideals, those most fiery spirits of the mind; hence too the repulsive, evil- smelling, perjured, pseudo–alcoholic air everywhere. I should like to know how many cargoes of imitation idealism, of hero-costumes and high falutin' clap-trap, how many casks of sweetened pity liqueur (Firm: la religion de la souffrance), how many crutches of righteous indignation for the help of these flat-footed intellects, how many comedians of the Christian moral ideal would need to-day to be exported from Europe, to enable its air to smell pure again. It is obvious that, in regard to this over-production, a new trade possibility lies open; it is obvious that there is a new business to be done in little ideal idols and obedient "idealists"—don't pass over this tip! Who has sufficient courage? We have in our hands the possibility of idealising the whole earth. But what am I talking about courage? we only need one thing here—a hand, a free, a very free hand.

27.

Enough! enough! let us leave these curiosities and complexities of the modern spirit, which excite as much laughter as disgust. Our problem can certainly do without them, the problem of meaning of the ascetic ideal—what has it got to do with yesterday or to-day? those things shall be handled by me more thoroughly and severely in another connection (under the title "A Contribution to the History of European Nihilism," I refer for this to a work which I am preparing: The Will to Power, an Attempt at a Transvaluation of All Values). The only reason why I come to allude to it here is this: the ascetic ideal has at times, even in the most intellectual sphere, only one real kind of enemies and damagers: these are the comedians of this ideal—for they awake mistrust. Everywhere otherwise, where the mind is at work seriously, powerfully, and without counterfeiting, it dispenses altogether now with an ideal (the popular expression for this abstinence is "Atheism")—with the exception of the will for truth. But this will, this remnant of an ideal, is, if you will believe me, that ideal itself in its severest and cleverest formulation, esoteric through and through, stripped of all outworks, and consequently not so much its remnant as its kernel. Unqualified honest atheism (and its air only do we breathe, we, the most intellectual men of this age) is not opposed to that ideal, to the extent that it appears to be; it is rather one of the final phases of its evolution, one of its syllogisms and pieces of inherent logic—it is the awe-inspiring catastrophe of a two-thousand- year training in truth, which finally forbids itself the lie of the belief in God. (The same course of development in India—quite independently, and consequently of some demonstrative value—the same ideal driving to the same conclusion the decisive point reached five hundred years before the European era, or more precisely at the time of Buddha—it started in the Sankhyam philosophy, and then this was popularised through Buddha, and made into a religion.)

What, I put the question with all strictness, has really triumphed over the Christian God? The answer stands in my Joyful Wisdom, Aph. 357: "the Christian morality itself, the idea of truth, taken as it was with increasing seriousness, the confessor-subtlety of the Christian conscience translated and sublimated into the scientific conscience into intellectual cleanness at any price. Regarding Nature as though it were a proof of the goodness and guardianship of God; interpreting history in honour of a divine reason, as a constant proof of a moral order of the world and a moral teleology; explaining our own personal experiences, as pious men have for long enough explained them, as though every arrangement, every nod, every single thing were invented and sent out of love for the salvation of the soul; all this is now done away with, all this has the conscience against it, and is regarded by every subtler conscience as disreputable, dishonourable, as lying, feminism, weakness, cowardice—by means of this severity, if by means of anything at all, are we, in sooth, good Europeans and heirs of Europe's longest and bravest self-mastery."... All great things go to ruin by reason of themselves, by reason of an act of self-dissolution: so wills the law of life, the law of necessary "self-mastery" even in the essence of life—ever is the law- giver finally exposed to the cry, "patere legem quam ipse tulisti"; in thus wise did Christianity go to ruin as a dogma, through its own morality; in thus wise must Christianity go again to ruin to-day as a morality—we are standing on the threshold of this event. After Christian truthfulness has drawn one conclusion after the other, it finally draws its strongest conclusion, its conclusion against itself; this, however, happens, when it puts the question, "what is the meaning of every will for truth?" And here again do I touch on my problem, on our problem, my unknown friends (for as yet I know of no friends): what sense has our whole being, if it does not mean that in our own selves that will for truth has come to its own consciousness as a problem?——By reason of this attainment of self-consciousness on the part of the will for truth, morality from henceforward—there is no doubt about it—goes to pieces: this is that great hundred-act play that is reserved for the next two centuries of Europe, the most terrible, the most mysterious, and perhaps also the most hopeful of all plays.

28.

If you except the ascetic ideal, man, the animal man had no meaning. His existence on earth contained no end; "What is the purpose of man at all?" was a question without an answer; the will for man and the world was lacking; behind every great human destiny rang as a refrain a still greater "Vanity!" The ascetic ideal simply means this: that something was lacking, that a tremendous void encircled man—he did not know how to justify himself, to explain himself, to affirm himself, he suffered from the problem of his own meaning. He suffered also in other ways, he was in the main a diseased animal; but his problem was not suffering itself, but the lack of an answer to that crying question, "To what purpose do we suffer?" Man, the bravest animal and the one most inured to suffering, does not repudiate suffering in itself: he wills it, he even seeks it out, provided that he is shown a meaning for it, a purpose of suffering. Not suffering, but the senselessness of suffering was the curse which till then lay spread over humanity—and the ascetic ideal gave it a meaning! It was up till then the only meaning; but any meaning is better than no meaning; the ascetic ideal was in that connection the "faute de mieux" par excellence that existed at that time. In that ideal suffering found an explanation; the tremendous gap seemed filled; the door to all suicidal Nihilism was closed. The explanation—there is no doubt about it—brought in its train new suffering, deeper, more penetrating, more venomous, gnawing more brutally into life: it brought all suffering under the perspective of guilt; but in spite of all that—man was saved thereby, he had a meaning, and from henceforth was no more like a leaf in the wind, a shuttle-cock of chance, of nonsense, he could now "will" something—absolutely immaterial to what end, to what purpose, with what means he wished: the will itself was saved. It is absolutely impossible to disguise what in point of fact is made clear by every complete will that has taken its direction from the ascetic ideal: this hate of the human, and even more of the animal, and more still of the material, this horror of the senses, of reason itself, this fear of happiness and beauty, this desire to get right away from all illusion, change, growth, death, wishing and even desiring—all this means—let us have the courage to grasp it—a will for Nothingness, a will opposed to life, a repudiation of the most fundamental conditions of life, but it is and remains a will!—and to say at the end that which I said at the beginning—man will wish Nothingness rather than not wish at all.

PEOPLES AND COUNTRIES.

Translated by J. M. KENNEDY.

[The following twenty-seven fragments were intended by Nietzsche to form a supplement to Chapter VIII. of Beyond Good and Evil, dealing with Peoples and Countries.]

1.

The Europeans now imagine themselves as representing, in the main, the highest types of men on earth.

2.

A characteristic of Europeans: inconsistency between word and deed; the Oriental is true to himself in daily life. How the European has established colonies is explained by his nature, which resembles that of a beast of prey.

This inconsistency is explained by the fact that Christianity has abandoned the class from which it sprang.

This is the difference between us and the Hellenes: their morals grew up among the governing castes. Thucydides' morals are the same as those that exploded everywhere with Plato.

Attempts towards honesty at the Renaissance, for example: always for the benefit of the arts. Michael Angelo's conception of God as the "Tyrant of the World" was an honest one.

3.

I rate Michael Angelo higher than Raphael, because, through all the Christian clouds and prejudices of his time, he saw the ideal of a culture nobler than the Christo-Raphaelian: whilst Raphael truly and modestly glorified only the values handed down to him, and did not carry within himself any inquiring, yearning instincts. Michael Angelo, on the other hand, saw and felt the problem of the law-giver of new values: the problem of the conqueror made perfect, who first had to subdue the "hero within himself," the man exalted to his highest pedestal, master even of his pity, who mercilessly shatters and annihilates everything that does not bear his own stamp, shining in Olympian divinity. Michael Angelo was naturally only at certain moments so high and so far beyond his age and Christian Europe: for the most part he adopted a condescending attitude towards the eternal feminine in Christianity; it would seem, indeed, that in the end he broke down before her, and gave up the ideal of his most inspired hours. It was an ideal which only a man in the strongest and highest vigour of life could bear; but not a man advanced in years! Indeed, he would have had to demolish Christianity with his ideal! But he was not thinker and philosopher enough for that Perhaps Leonardo da Vinci alone of those artists had a really super-Christian outlook. He knows the East, the "land of dawn," within himself as well as without himself. There is something super-European and silent in him: a characteristic of every one who has seen too wide a circle of things good and bad.

4.

How much we have learnt and learnt anew in fifty years! The whole Romantic School with its belief in "the people" is refuted! No Homeric poetry as "popular" poetry! No deification of the great powers of Nature! No deduction from language-relationship to race-relationship! No "intellectual contemplations" of the supernatural! No truth enshrouded in religion!

The problem of truthfulness is quite a new one. I am astonished. From this standpoint we regard such natures as

Bismarck as culpable out of carelessness, such as Richard Wagner out of want of modesty; we would condemn Plato for his pia fraus, Kant for the derivation of his Categorical Imperative, his own belief certainly not having come to him from this source.

Finally, even doubt turns against itself: doubt in doubt. And the question as to the value of truthfulness and its extent lies there.

5.

What I observe with pleasure in the German is his Mephistophelian nature; but, to tell the truth, one must have a higher conception of Mephistopheles than Goethe had, who found it necessary to diminish his Mephistopheles in order to magnify his "inner Faust." The true German Mephistopheles is much more dangerous, bold, wicked, and cunning, and consequently more open-hearted: remember the nature of Frederick the Great, or of that much greater Frederick, the Hohenstaufen, Frederick II.

The real German Mephistopheles crosses the Alps, and believes that everything there belongs to him. Then he recovers himself, like Winckelmann, like Mozart. He looks upon Faust and Hamlet as caricatures, invented to be laughed at, and upon Luther also. Goethe had his good German moments, when he laughed inwardly at all these things. But then he fell back again into his cloudy moods.

6.

Perhaps the Germans have only grown up in a wrong climate! There is something in them that might be Hellenic!—something that is awakened when they are brought into touch with the South—Winckelmann, Goethe, Mozart. We should not forget, however, that we are still young. Luther is still our last event; our last book is still the Bible. The Germans have never yet "moralised." Also, the very food of the Germans was their doom: its consequence, Philistinism.

7.

The Germans are a dangerous people: they are experts at inventing intoxicants. Gothic, rococo (according to Semper), the historical sense and exoticism, Hegel, Richard Wagner—Leibniz, too (dangerous at the present day)—(they even idealised the serving soul as the virtue of scholars and soldiers, also as the simple mind). The Germans may well be the most composite people on earth.

"The people of the Middle," the inventors of porcelain, and of a kind of Chinese breed of Privy Councillor.

8.

The smallness and baseness of the German soul were not and are not consequences of the system of small states; for it is well known that the inhabitants of much smaller states were proud and independent: and it is not a large state per sethat makes souls freer and more manly. The man whose soul obeys the slavish command: "Thou shalt and must kneel!" in whose body there is an involuntary bowing and scraping to titles, orders, gracious glances from above—well, such a man in an "Empire" will only bow all the more deeply and lick the dust more fervently in the presence of the greater sovereign than in the presence of the lesser: this cannot be doubted. We can still see in the lower classes of Italians that aristocratic self-sufficiency; manly discipline and self- confidence still form a part of the long history of their country: these are virtues which once manifested themselves before their eyes. A poor Venetian gondolier makes a far better figure than a Privy Councillor from Berlin, and is even a better man in the end—any one can see this. Just ask the women.

9.

Most artists, even some of the greatest (including the historians) have up to the present belonged to the serving classes (whether they serve people of high position or princes or women or "the masses"), not to speak of their dependence upon the Church and upon moral law. Thus Rubens portrayed the nobility of his age; but only according to their vague conception of taste, not according to his own measure of beauty on the whole, therefore, against his own taste. Van Dyck was nobler in this respect: who in all those whom he painted added a certain amount of what he himself most highly valued: he did not descend from himself, but rather lifted up others to himself when he "rendered."

The slavish humility of the artist to his public (as Sebastian Bach has testified in undying and outrageous words in the dedication of his High Mass) is perhaps more difficult to perceive in music; but it is all the more deeply engrained. A hearing would be refused me if I endeavoured to impart my views on this subject. Chopin possesses distinction, like Van Dyck. The disposition of Beethoven is that of a proud peasant; of Haydn, that of a proud servant. Mendelssohn, too, possesses distinction—like Goethe, in the most natural way in the world.

10.

We could at any time have counted on the fingers of one hand those German learned men who possessed wit: the remainder have understanding, and a few of them, happily, that famous "childlike character" which divines.   It is our privilege: with this "divination"

German science has discovered some things which we can hardly conceive of, and which, after all, do not exist, perhaps. It is only the Jews among the Germans who do not "divine" like them.

11.

As Frenchmen reflect the politeness and esprit of French society, so do Germans reflect something of the deep, pensive earnestness of their mystics and musicians, and also of their silly childishness. The Italian exhibits a great deal of republican distinction and art, and can show himself to be noble and proud without vanity.

12.

A larger number of the higher and better-endowed men will, I hope, have in the end so much self-restraint as to be able to get rid of their bad taste for affectation and sentimental darkness, and to turn against Richard Wagner as much as against Schopenhauer. These two Germans are leading us to ruin; they flatter our dangerous qualities. A stronger future is prepared for us in Goethe, Beethoven, and Bismarck than in these racial aberrations. We have had no philosophers yet.

13.

The peasant is the commonest type of noblesse, for he is dependent upon himself most of all. Peasant blood is still the best blood in Germany —for example, Luther, Niebuhr, Bismarck.

Bismarck a Slav. Let any one look upon the face of Germans. Everything that had manly, exuberant blood in it went abroad. Over the smug populace remaining, the slave-souled people, there came an improvement from abroad, especially by a mixture of Slavonic blood.

The Brandenburg nobility and the Prussian nobility in general (and the peasant of certain North German districts), comprise at present the most manly natures in Germany.

That the manliest men shall rule: this is only the natural order of things. 14.

The future of German culture rests with the sons of the Prussian officers. 15.

There has always been a want of wit in Germany, and mediocre heads attain there to the highest honours, because even they are rare. What is most highly prized is diligence and perseverance and a certain cold- blooded, critical outlook, and, for the sake of such qualities, German scholarship and the German military system have become paramount in Europe.

16.

Parliaments may be very useful to a strong and versatile statesman: he has something there to rely upon (every such thing must, however, be able to resist!)—upon which he can throw a great deal of responsibility. On the whole, however, I could wish that the counting mania and the superstitious belief in majorities were not established in Germany, as with the Latin races, and that one could finally invent something new even in politics! It is senseless and dangerous to let the custom of universal suffrage—which is still but a short time under cultivation, and could easily be uprooted—take a deeper root: whilst, of course, its introduction was merely an expedient to steer clear of temporary difficulties.

17.

Can any one interest himself in this German Empire? Where is the new thought? Is it only a new combination of power? All the worse, if it does not know its own mind. Peace and laisser aller are not types of politics for which I have any respect. Ruling, and helping the highest thoughts to victory— the only things that can make me interested in Germany.

England's small-mindedness is the great danger now on earth. I observe more inclination towards greatness in the feelings of the Russian Nihilists than in those of the English Utilitarians. We require an intergrowth of the German and Slav races, and we require, too, the cleverest financiers, the Jews, for us to become masters of the world.

(a) The sense of reality.

(b) A giving-up of the English principle of the people's right of representation. We require the representation of the great interests.

(c) We require an unconditional union with Russia, together with a mutual plan of action which shall not permit any English schemata to obtain the mastery in Russia. No American future!

(d) A national system of politics is untenable, and embarrassment by Christian views is a very great evil. In Europe all sensible people are sceptics, whether they say so or not.

18.

I see over and beyond all these national wars, new "empires," and whatever else lies in the foreground. What I am concerned with—for I see it preparing itself slowly and hesitatingly—is the United Europe. It was the only real work, the one impulse in the souls, of all the broad- minded and deep-thinking men of this century—this preparation of a new synthesis, and the tentative effort to anticipate the future of "the European." Only in their weaker moments, or when they grew old, did they fall back again into the national narrowness of the "Fatherlanders"—then they were once more "patriots." I am thinking of men like Napoleon, Heinrich Heine, Goethe, Beethoven, Stendhal, Schopenhauer. Perhaps Richard Wagner likewise belongs to their number, concerning whom, as a successful type of German obscurity, nothing can be said without some such "perhaps."

But to the help of such minds as feel the need of a new unity there comes a great explanatory economic fact: the small States of Europe—I refer to all our present kingdoms and "empires"—will in a short time become economically untenable, owing to the mad, uncontrolled struggle for the possession of local and international trade. Money is even now compelling European nations to amalgamate into one

Power. In order, however, that Europe may enter into the battle for the mastery of the world with good prospects of victory (it is easy to perceive against whom this battle will be waged), she must probably "come to an understanding" with England. The English colonies are needed for this struggle, just as much as modern Germany, to play her new rôle of broker and middleman, requires the colonial possessions of Holland. For no one any longer believes that England alone is strong enough to continue to act her old part for fifty years more; the impossibility of shutting out homines novi from the government will ruin her, and her continual change of political parties is a fatal obstacle to the carrying out of any tasks which require to be spread out over a long period of time. A man must to-day be a soldier first and foremost that he may not afterwards lose his credit as a merchant. Enough; here, as in other matters, the coming century will be found following in the footsteps of Napoleon—the first man, and the man of greatest initiative and advanced views, of modern times. For the tasks of the next century, the methods of popular representation and parliaments are the most inappropriate imaginable.

19.

The condition of Europe in the next century will once again lead to the breeding of manly virtues, because men will live in continual danger. Universal military service is already the curious antidote which we possess for the effeminacy of democratic ideas, and it has grown up out of the struggle of the nations. (Nation—men who speak one language and read the same newspapers. These men now call themselves "nations," and would far too readily trace their descent from the same source and through the same history; which, however, even with the assistance of the most malignant lying in the past, they have not succeeded in doing.)

20.

What quagmires and mendacity must there be about if it is possible, in the modern European hotch-potch, to raise questions of "race"! (It being premised that the origin of such writers is not in Horneo and Borneo.)

21.

Maxim: To associate with no man who takes any part in the mendacious race swindle.

22.

With the freedom of travel now existing, groups of men of the same kindred can join together and establish communal habits and customs. The overcoming of "nations."

23.

To make Europe a centre of culture, national stupidities should not make us blind to the fact that in the higher regions there is already a continuous reciprocal dependence. France and German philosophy.

Richard Wagner and Paris (1830-50). Goethe and Greece. All things are impelled towards, a synthesis of the European past in the highest types of mind.

24.

Mankind has still much before it—how, generally speaking, could the ideal be taken from the past? Perhaps merely in relation to the present, which latter is possibly a lower region.

25.

This is our distrust, which recurs again and again; our care, which never lets us sleep; our question, which no one listens to or wishes to listen to; our Sphinx, near which there is more than one precipice: we believe that the men of present-day Europe are deceived in regard to the things which we love best, and a pitiless demon (no, not pitiless, only indifferent and puerile)—plays with our hearts and their enthusiasm, as it may perhaps have already played with everything that lived and loved; I believe that everything which we Europeans of to-day are in the habit of admiring as the values of all these respected things called "humanity," "mankind," "sympathy," "pity," may be of some value as the debilitation and moderating of certain powerful and dangerous primitive impulses.

Nevertheless, in the long run all these things are nothing else than the belittlement of the entire type "man," his mediocrisation, if in such a desperate situation I may make use of such a desperate expression. I think that the commedia umana for an epicurean spectator-god must consist in this: that the Europeans, by virtue of their growing morality, believe in all their innocence and vanity that they are rising higher and higher, whereas the truth is that they are sinking lower and lower— i.e. through the cultivation of all the virtues which are useful to a herd, and through the repression of the other and contrary virtues which give rise to a new, higher, stronger, masterful race of men—the first-named virtues merely develop the herd-animal in man and stabilitate the animal "man," for until now man has been "the animal as yet unstabilitated." Genius and Epoch.—Heroism is no form of selfishness, for one is shipwrecked by it The direction of power is often conditioned by the state of the period in which the great man happens to be born; and this fact brings about the superstition that he is the expression of his time. But this same power could be applied in several different ways; and between him and his time there is always this difference: that public opinion always worships the herd instinct,—i.e. the instinct of the weak,— while he, the strong man, rights for strong ideals.

27.

The fate now overhanging Europe is simply this: that it is exactly her strongest sons that come rarely and late to the spring-time of their existence; that, as a rule, when they are already in their early youth they perish, saddened, disgusted, darkened in mind, just because they have already, with the entire passion of their strength, drained to the dregs the cup of disillusionment, which in our days means the cup of knowledge, and they would not have been the strongest had they not also been the most disillusionised. For that is the test of their power—they must first of all rise out of the illness of their epoch to reach their own health. A late spring-time is their mark of distinction; also, let us add, late merriment, late folly, the late exuberance of joy! For this is the danger of to-day: everything that we loved when we were young has betrayed us. Our last love—the love which makes us acknowledge her, our love for Truth—let us take care that she, too, does not betray us!

THE BIRTH OF TRAGEDY

AN ATTEMPT AT SELF-CRITICISM

I.

Whatever may lie at the bottom of this doubtful book must be a question of the first rank and attractiveness, moreover a deeply personal question,—in proof thereof observe the time in which it originated, in spite of which it originated, the exciting period of the Franco-German war of 1870-71. While the thunder of the battle of Wörth rolled over Europe, the ruminator and riddle-lover, who had to be the parent of this book, sat somewhere in a nook of the Alps, lost in riddles and ruminations, consequently very much concerned and unconcerned at the same time, and wrote down his meditations on the Greeks,—the kernel of the curious and almost inaccessible book, to which this belated prologue (or epilogue) is to be devoted. A few weeks later: and he found himself under the walls of Metz, still wrestling with the notes of interrogation he had set down concerning the alleged "cheerfulness" of the Greeks and of Greek art; till at last, in that month of deep suspense, when peace was debated at Versailles, he too attained to peace with himself, and, slowly recovering from a disease brought home from the field, made up his mind definitely regarding the "Birth of Tragedy from the Spirit of Music."—From music? Music and Tragedy? Greeks and tragic music? Greeks and the Art-work of pessimism? A race of men, well-fashioned, beautiful, envied, life-inspiring, like no other race hitherto, the Greeks—indeed? The Greeks were in need of tragedy? Yea— of art? Wherefore—Greek art?...

We can thus guess where the great note of interrogation

concerning the value of existence had been set. Is pessimism necessarily the sign of decline, of decay, of failure, of exhausted and weakened instincts?—as was the case with the Indians, as is, to all appearance, the case with us "modern" men and Europeans? Is there a pessimism of strength? An intellectual predilection for what is hard, awful, evil, problematical in existence, owing to well-being, to exuberant health, to fullness of existence? Is there perhaps suffering in overfullness itself? A seductive fortitude with the keenest of glances, which yearns for the terrible, as for the enemy, the worthy enemy, with whom it may try its strength? from whom it is willing to learn what "fear" is? What means tragic myth to the Greeks of the best, strongest, bravest era? And the prodigious phenomenon of the Dionysian? And that which was born thereof, tragedy?— And again: that of which tragedy died, the Socratism of morality, the dialectics, contentedness and cheerfulness of the theoretical man—indeed? might not this very Socratism be a sign of decline, of weariness, of disease, of anarchically disintegrating instincts? And the "Hellenic cheerfulness" of the later Hellenism merely a glowing sunset? The Epicurean will counter to pessimism merely a precaution of the sufferer? And science itself, our science—ay, viewed as a symptom of life, what really signifies all science? Whither, worse still, whence—all science? Well? Is scientism perhaps only fear and evasion of pessimism? A subtle defence against—truth! Morally speaking, something like falsehood and cowardice? And, unmorally speaking, an artifice? O Socrates, Socrates, was this perhaps thy secret? Oh mysterious ironist, was this perhaps thine—irony?...

2.

What I then laid hands on, something terrible and dangerous, a problem with horns, not necessarily a bull itself, but at all events a new problem: I should say to-day it was the problem of science itself—science conceived for the first time as problematic, as questionable. But the book, in which my youthful ardour and suspicion then discharged themselves— what an impossible book must needs grow out of a task so disagreeable to youth. Constructed of nought but precocious, unripened self- experiences, all of which lay close to the threshold of the communicable, based on the groundwork of art—for the problem of science cannot be discerned on the groundwork of science,—a book perhaps for artists, with collateral analytical and retrospective aptitudes (that is, an exceptional kind of artists, for whom one must seek and does not even care to seek ...), full of psychological innovations and artists' secrets, with an artists' metaphysics in the background, a work of youth, full of youth's mettle and youth's melancholy, independent, defiantly self-sufficient even when it seems to bow to some authority and self-veneration; in short, a firstling-work, even in every bad sense of the term; in spite of its senile problem, affected with every fault of youth, above all with youth's prolixity and youth's "storm and stress": on the other hand, in view of the success it had (especially with the great artist to whom it addressed itself, as it were, in a duologue, Richard Wagner) a demonstrated book, I mean a book which, at any rate, sufficed "for the best of its time." On this account, if for no other reason, it should be treated with some consideration and reserve; yet I shall not altogether conceal how disagreeable it now appears to me, how after sixteen years it stands a total stranger before me,—before an eye which is more mature, and a hundred times more fastidious, but which has by no means grown colder nor lost any of its interest in that self-same task essayed for the first time by this daring book,—to view science through the optics of the artist, and art moreover through the optics of life....

3.

I say again, to-day it is an impossible book to me,—I call it badly written, heavy, painful, image-angling and image-entangling, maudlin, sugared at times even to femininism, uneven in tempo, void of the will to logical cleanliness, very convinced and therefore rising above the necessity of demonstration, distrustful even of the propriety of demonstration, as being a book for initiates, as "music" for those who are baptised with the name of Music, who are united from the beginning of things by common ties of rare experiences in art, as a countersign for blood-relations in artibus.—a haughty and fantastic book, which from the very first withdraws even more from the profanum vulgus of the "cultured" than from the "people," but which also, as its effect has shown and still shows, knows very well how to seek fellow-enthusiasts and lure them to new by- ways and dancing-grounds. Here, at any rate—thus much was acknowledged with curiosity as well as with aversion—a strange voice spoke, the disciple of a still "unknown God," who for the time being had hidden himself under the hood of the scholar, under the German's gravity and disinclination for dialectics, even under the bad manners of the Wagnerian; here was a spirit with strange and still nameless needs, a memory bristling with questions, experiences and obscurities, beside which stood the name Dionysos like one more note of interrogation; here spoke—people said to themselves with misgivings— something like a mystic and almost mænadic soul, which, undecided whether it should disclose or conceal itself, stammers with an effort and capriciously as in a strange tongue. It should have sung, this "new soul"—and not spoken!

What a pity, that I did not dare to say what I then had to say, as a poet: I could have done so perhaps! Or at least as a philologist:—for even at the present day well-nigh everything in this domain remains to be discovered and disinterred by the philologist! Above all the problem, that here there is a problem before us,—and that, so long as we have no answer to the question "what is Dionysian?" the Greeks are now as ever wholly unknown and inconceivable....

4.

Ay, what is Dionysian?—In this book may be found an answer,—a "knowing one" speaks here, the votary and disciple of his god. Perhaps I should now speak more guardedly and less eloquently of a psychological question so difficult as the origin of tragedy among the Greeks. A fundamental question is the relation of the Greek to pain, his degree of sensibility,—did this relation remain constant? or did it veer about?—the question, whether his ever-increasing longing for beauty, for festivals, gaieties, new cults, did really grow out of want, privation, melancholy, pain? For suppose even this to be true—and Pericles (or Thucydides) intimates as much in the great Funeral Speech:—whence then the opposite longing, which appeared first in the order of time, the longing for the ugly, the good, resolute desire of the Old Hellene for pessimism, for tragic myth, for the picture of all that is terrible, evil, enigmatical, destructive, fatal at the basis of existence,— whence then must tragedy have sprung? Perhaps from joy, from strength, from exuberant health, from over-fullness. And what then, physiologically speaking, is the meaning of that madness, out of which comic as well as tragic art has grown, the Dionysian madness? What? perhaps madness is not necessarily the symptom of degeneration, of decline, of belated culture? Perhaps there are—a question for alienists— neuroses of health? of folk- youth and youthfulness? What does that synthesis of god and goat in the Satyr point to? What self-experience what "stress," made the Greek think of the Dionysian reveller and primitive man as a satyr? And as regards the origin of the tragic chorus: perhaps there were endemic ecstasies in the eras when the Greek body bloomed and the Greek soul brimmed over with life? Visions and hallucinations, which took hold of entire communities, entire cult-assemblies? What if the Greeks in the very wealth of their youth had the will to be tragic and were pessimists? What if it was madness itself, to use a word of Plato's, which brought the greatest blessings upon Hellas? And what if, on the other hand and conversely, at the very time of their dissolution and weakness, the Greeks became always more optimistic, more superficial, more histrionic, also more ardent for logic and the logicising of the world,—consequently at the same time more "cheerful" and more "scientific"? Ay, despite all "modern ideas" and prejudices of the democratic taste, may not the triumph of optimism, the common sense that has gained the upper hand, the practical and theoretical utilitarianism, like democracy itself, with which it is synchronous—be symptomatic of declining vigour, of approaching age, of physiological weariness? And not at all—pessimism? Was Epicurus an optimist—because a sufferer?... We see it is a whole bundle of weighty questions which this book has taken upon itself,—let us not fail to add its weightiest question! Viewed through the optics of life, what is the meaning of—morality?...

5.

Already in the foreword to Richard Wagner, art——and not morality—is set down as the properly metaphysical activity of man; in the book itself the piquant proposition recurs time and again, that the existence of the world is justified only as an æsthetic phenomenon. Indeed, the entire book recognises only an artist-thought and artist-after-thought behind all occurrences,—a "God," if you will, but certainly only an altogether thoughtless and unmoral artist-God, who, in construction as in destruction, in good as in evil, desires to become conscious of his own equable joy and sovereign glory; who, in creating worlds, frees himself from the anguish of fullness and overfullness, from the suffering of the contradictions concentrated within him. The world, that is, the redemption of God attained at every moment, as the perpetually changing, perpetually new vision of the most suffering, most antithetical, most contradictory being, who contrives to redeem himself only in appearance: this entire artist-metaphysics, call it arbitrary, idle, fantastic, if you will,—the point is, that it already betrays a spirit, which is determined some day, at all hazards, to make a stand against the moral interpretation and significance of life. Here, perhaps for the first time, a pessimism "Beyond Good and Evil" announces itself, here that "perverseness of disposition" obtains expression and formulation, against which Schopenhauer never grew tired of hurling beforehand his angriest imprecations and thunderbolts,—a philosophy which dares to put, derogatorily put, morality itself in the world of phenomena, and not only among "phenomena" (in the sense of the idealistic terminus technicus), but among the "illusions," as appearance, semblance, error, interpretation, accommodation, art. Perhaps the depth of this antimoral tendency may be best estimated from the guarded and hostile silence with which Christianity is treated throughout this book,— Christianity, as being the most extravagant burlesque of the moral theme to which mankind has hitherto been obliged to listen. In fact, to the purely æsthetic world-interpretation and justification taught in this book, there is no greater antithesis than the Christian dogma, which is only and will be only moral, and which, with its absolute standards, for instance, its truthfulness of God, relegates—that is, disowns, convicts, condemns— art, all art, to the realm of falsehood. Behind such a mode of thought and valuation, which, if at all genuine, must be hostile to art, I always experienced what was hostile to life, the wrathful, vindictive counterwill to life itself: for all life rests on appearance, art, illusion, optics, necessity of perspective and error. From the very first Christianity was, essentially and thoroughly, the nausea and surfeit of Life for Life, which only disguised, concealed and decked itself out under the belief in "another" or "better" life. The hatred of the "world," the curse on the affections, the fear of beauty and sensuality, another world, invented for the purpose of slandering this world the more, at bottom a longing for.

Nothingness, for the end, for rest, for the "Sabbath of Sabbaths"—all this, as also the unconditional will of Christianity to recognise only moral values, has always appeared to me as the most dangerous and ominous of all possible forms of a "will to perish"; at the least, as the symptom of a most fatal disease, of profoundest weariness, despondency, exhaustion, impoverishment of life,—for before the tribunal of morality (especially Christian, that is, unconditional morality) life must constantly and inevitably be the loser, because life is something essentially unmoral,— indeed, oppressed with the weight of contempt and the everlasting No, life must finally be regarded as unworthy of desire, as in itself unworthy. Morality itself what?—may not morality be a "will to disown life," a secret instinct for annihilation, a principle of decay, of depreciation, of slander, a beginning of the end? And, consequently, the danger of dangers?... It was against morality, therefore, that my instinct, as an intercessory-instinct for life, turned in this questionable book, inventing for itself a fundamental counter—dogma and counter-valuation of life, purely artistic, purely anti-Christian. What should I call it? As a philologist and man of words I baptised it, not without some liberty—for who could be sure of the proper name of the Antichrist?— with the name of a Greek god: I called it Dionysian.

6.

You see which problem I ventured to touch upon in this early work?... How I now regret, that I had not then the courage (or immodesty?) to allow myself, in all respects, the use of an individual language for such individual contemplations and ventures in the field of thought— that I laboured to express, in Kantian and Schopenhauerian formulæ, strange and new valuations, which ran fundamentally counter to the spirit of Kant and Schopenhauer, as well as to their taste! What, forsooth, were Schopenhauer's views on tragedy? "What gives"—he says in Welt als Wille und Vorstellung, II. 495— "to all tragedy that singular swing towards elevation, is the awakening of the knowledge that the world, that life, cannot satisfy us thoroughly, and consequently is not worthy of our attachment In this consists the tragic spirit: it therefore leads to resignation." Oh, how differently Dionysos spoke to me! Oh how far from me then was just this entire resignationism!— But there is something far worse in this book, which I now regret even more than having obscured and spoiled Dionysian anticipations with Schopenhauerian formulæ: to wit, that, in general, I spoiled the grand Hellenic problem, as it had opened up before me, by the admixture of the most modern things! That I entertained hopes, where nothing was to be hoped for, where everything pointed all-too-clearly to an approaching end! That, on the basis of our latter-day German music, I began to fable about the "spirit of Teutonism," as if it were on the point of discovering and returning to itself,—ay, at the very time that the German spirit which not so very long before had had the will to the lordship over Europe, the strength to lead and govern Europe, testamentarily and conclusively resigned and, under the pompous pretence of empire-founding, effected its transition to mediocritisation, democracy, and "modern ideas." In very fact, I have since learned to regard this "spirit of Teutonism" as something to be despaired of and unsparingly treated, as also our present German music, which is Romanticism through and through and the most un-Grecian of all possible forms of art: and moreover a first-rate nerve-destroyer, doubly dangerous for a people given to drinking and revering the unclear as a virtue, namely, in its twofold capacity of an intoxicating and stupefying narcotic. Of course, apart from all precipitate hopes and faulty applications to matters specially modern, with which I then spoiled my first book, the great Dionysian note of interrogation, as set down therein, continues standing on and on, even with reference to music: how must we conceive of a music, which is no longer of Romantic origin, like the German; but of Dionysian?...

7.

—But, my dear Sir, if your book is not Romanticism, what in the world is? Can the deep hatred of the present, of "reality" and "modern ideas" be pushed farther than has been done in your artist-metaphysics?—which would rather believe in Nothing, or in the devil, than in the "Now"? Does not a radical bass of wrath and annihilative pleasure growl on beneath all your contrapuntal vocal art and aural seduction, a mad determination to oppose all that "now" is, a will which is not so very far removed from practical nihilism and which seems to say: "rather let nothing be true, than that you should be in the right, than that your truth should prevail!" Hear, yourself, my dear Sir Pessimist and art-deifier, with ever so unlocked ears, a single select passage of your own book, that not ineloquent dragon-slayer passage, which may sound insidiously rat- charming to young ears and hearts. What? is not that the true blue romanticist-confession of 1830 under the mask of the pessimism of 1850? After which, of course, the usual romanticist finale at once strikes up,—rupture, collapse, return and prostration before an old belief, before the old God What? is not your pessimist book itself a piece of anti-Hellenism and Romanticism, something "equally intoxicating and befogging," a narcotic at all events, ay, a piece of music, of German music? But listen:

Let us imagine a rising generation with this undauntedness of vision, with this heroic impulse towards the prodigious, let us imagine the bold step of these dragon-slayers, the proud daring with which they turn their backs on all the effeminate doctrines of optimism, in order "to live resolutely" in the Whole and in the Full: would it not be necessary for the tragic man of this culture, with his self-discipline to earnestness and terror, to desire a new art, the art of metaphysical comfort, tragedy as the Helena belonging to him, and that he should exclaim with Faust:

"Und sollt ich nicht, sehnsüchtigster Gewalt,

In's Leben ziehn die einzigste Gestalt?"1

"Would it not be necessary?" ... No, thrice no! ye young romanticists: it would not be necessary! But it is very probable, that things may end thus, that ye may end thus, namely "comforted," as it is written, in spite of all self-discipline to earnestness and terror; metaphysically comforted, in short, as Romanticists are wont to end, as Christians   No! ye should first of all learn the art of earthly comfort, ye should learn to laugh, my young friends, if ye are at all determined to remain pessimists: if so, you will perhaps, as laughing ones, eventually send all metaphysical comfortism to the devil—and metaphysics first of all! Or, to say it in the language of that Dionysian ogre, called Zarathustra:

"Lift up your hearts, my brethren, high, higher! And do not forget your legs! Lift up also your legs, ye good dancers—and better still if ye stand also on your heads!

"This crown of the laughter, this rose-garland crown—I myself have put on this crown; I myself have consecrated my laughter. No one else have I found to-day strong enough for this.

"Zarathustra the dancer, Zarathustra the light one, who beckoneth with his pinions, one ready for flight, beckoning unto all birds, ready and prepared, a blissfully light-spirited one:—

"Zarathustra the soothsayer, Zarathustra the sooth-laugher, no impatient one, no absolute one, one who loveth leaps and side-leaps: I myself have put on this crown!

"This crown of the laughter, this rose-garland crown—to you my brethren do I cast this crown! Laughing have I consecrated: ye higher men, learn, I pray you—to laugh!"

Thus spake Zarathustra, lxxiii. 17, 18, and 20. SILS-MARIA, OBERENGADIN, August 1886.

1 And shall not I, by mightiest desire,

In living shape that sole fair form acquire? SWANWICK, trans. of Faust.

FOREWORD TO RICHARD WAGNER

In order to keep at a distance all the possible scruples, excitements, and misunderstandings to which the thoughts gathered in this essay will give occasion, considering the peculiar character of our æsthetic publicity, and to be able also to write the introductory remarks with the same contemplative delight, the impress of which, as the petrifaction of good and elevating hours, it bears on every page, I form a conception of the moment when you, my highly honoured friend, will receive this essay; how you, say after an evening walk in the winter snow, will behold the unbound Prometheus on the title-page, read my name, and be forthwith convinced that, whatever this essay may contain, the author has something earnest and impressive to say, and, moreover, that in all his meditations he communed with you as with one present and could thus write only what befitted your presence. You will thus remember that it was at the same time as your magnificent dissertation on Beethoven originated, viz., amidst the horrors and sublimities of the war which had just then broken out, that I collected myself for these thoughts. But those persons would err, to whom this collection suggests no more perhaps than the antithesis of patriotic excitement and æsthetic revelry, of gallant earnestness and sportive delight. Upon a real perusal of this essay, such readers will, rather to their surprise, discover how earnest is the German problem we have to deal with, which we properly place, as a vortex and turning-point, in the very midst of German hopes. Perhaps, however, this same class of readers will be shocked at seeing an æsthetic problem taken so seriously, especially if they can recognise in art no more than a merry diversion, a readily dispensable court-jester to the "earnestness of existence": as if no one were aware of the real meaning of this confrontation with the "earnestness of existence." These earnest ones may be informed that I am convinced that art is the highest task and the properly metaphysical activity of this life, as it is understood by the man, to whom, as my sublime protagonist on this path, I would now dedicate this essay.

BASEL, end of the year 1871.

THE BIRTH OF TRAGEDY

1.

We shall have gained much for the science of æsthetics, when once we have perceived not only by logical inference, but by the immediate certainty of intuition, that the continuous development of art is bound up with the duplexity of the Apollonian and the Dionysian: in like manner as procreation is dependent on the duality of the sexes, involving perpetual conflicts with only periodically intervening reconciliations.

These names we borrow from the Greeks, who disclose to the intelligent observer the profound mysteries of their view of art, not indeed in concepts, but in the impressively clear figures of their world of deities. It is in connection with Apollo and Dionysus, the two art-deities of the Greeks, that we learn that there existed in the Grecian world a wide antithesis, in origin and aims, between the art of the shaper, the Apollonian, and the non-plastic art of music, that of Dionysus: both these so heterogeneous tendencies run parallel to each other, for the most part openly at variance, and continually inciting each other to new and more powerful births, to perpetuate in them the strife of this antithesis, which is but seemingly bridged over by their mutual term "Art"; till at last, by a metaphysical miracle of the Hellenic will, they appear paired with each other, and through this pairing eventually generate the equally Dionysian and Apollonian art-work of Attic tragedy.

In order to bring these two tendencies within closer range, let us conceive them first of all as the separate art-worlds of dreamland and drunkenness; between which physiological phenomena a contrast may be observed analogous to that existing between the Apollonian and the Dionysian. In dreams, according to the conception of Lucretius, the glorious divine figures first appeared to the souls of men, in dreams the great shaper beheld the charming corporeal structure of superhuman beings, and the Hellenic poet, if consulted on the mysteries of poetic inspiration, would likewise have suggested dreams and would have offered an explanation resembling that of Hans Sachs in the Meistersingers:—

Mein Freund, das grad' ist Dichters Werk, dass er sein Träumen deut' und merk'.

Glaubt mir, des Menschen wahrster Wahn wird ihm im Traume aufgethan: all' Dichtkunst und Poeterei ist nichts als Wahrtraum-Deuterei.2

The beauteous appearance of the dream-worlds, in the production of which every man is a perfect artist, is the presupposition of all plastic art, and in fact, as we shall see, of an important half of poetry also. We take delight in the immediate apprehension of form; all forms speak to us; there is nothing indifferent, nothing superfluous. But, together with the highest life of this dream-reality we also have, glimmering through it, the sensation of its appearance: such at least is my experience, as to the frequency, ay, normality of which I could adduce many proofs, as also the sayings of the poets. Indeed, the man of philosophic turn has a foreboding that underneath this reality in which we live and have our being, another and altogether different reality lies concealed, and that therefore it is also an appearance; and Schopenhauer actually designates the gift of occasionally regarding men and things as mere phantoms and dream-pictures as the criterion of philosophical ability. Accordingly, the man susceptible to art stands in the same relation to the reality of dreams as the philosopher to the reality of existence; he is a close and willing observer, for from these pictures he reads the meaning of life, and by these processes he trains himself for life. And it is perhaps not only the agreeable and friendly pictures that he realises in himself with such perfect understanding: the earnest, the troubled, the dreary, the gloomy, the sudden checks, the tricks of fortune, the uneasy presentiments, in short, the whole "Divine Comedy" of life, and the Inferno, also pass before him, not merely like pictures on the wall—for he too lives and suffers in these scenes,—and yet not without that fleeting sensation of appearance. And perhaps many a one will, like myself, recollect having sometimes called out cheeringly and not without success amid the dangers and terrors of dream-life: "It is a dream! I will dream on!" I have 2 My friend, just this is poet's task: His dreams to read and to unmask.

Trust me, illusion's truths thrice sealed In dream to man will be revealed.

All verse-craft and poetisation Is but soothdream interpretation.likewise been told of persons capable of continuing the causality of one and the same dream for three and even more successive nights: all of which facts clearly testify that our innermost being, the common substratum of all of us, experiences our dreams with deep joy and cheerful acquiescence.

This cheerful acquiescence in the dream-experience has likewise been embodied by the Greeks in their Apollo: for Apollo, as the god of all shaping energies, is also the soothsaying god. He, who (as the etymology of the name indicates) is the "shining one," the deity of light, also rules over the fair appearance of the inner world of fantasies. The higher truth, the perfection of these states in contrast to the only partially intelligible everyday world, ay, the deep consciousness of nature, healing and helping in sleep and dream, is at the same time the symbolical analogue of the faculty of soothsaying and, in general, of the arts, through which life is made possible and worth living. But also that delicate line, which the dream-picture must not overstep—lest it act pathologically (in which case appearance, being reality pure and simple, would impose upon us)— must not be wanting in the picture of Apollo: that measured limitation, that freedom from the wilder emotions, that philosophical calmness of the sculptor-god. His eye must be "sunlike," according to his origin; even when it is angry and looks displeased, the sacredness of his beauteous appearance is still there. And so we might apply to Apollo, in an eccentric sense, what Schopenhauer says of the man wrapt in the veil of

Mâyâ3: Welt als Wille und Vorstellung, I. p. 416: "Just as in a stormy sea, unbounded in every direction, rising and falling with howling mountainous waves, a sailor sits in a boat and trusts in his frail barque: so in the midst of a world of sorrows the individual sits quietly supported by and trusting in his principium individuationis." Indeed, we might say of Apollo, that in him the unshaken faith in this principium and the quiet sitting of the man wrapt therein have received their sublimest expression; and we might even designate Apollo as the glorious divine image of the principium individuationis, from out of the gestures and looks of which all the joy and wisdom of "appearance," together with its beauty, speak to us. 3 Cf. World and Will as Idea, 1. 455 ff., trans, by Haldane and Kemp.

In the same work Schopenhauer has described to us the stupendous awe which seizes upon man, when of a sudden he is at a loss to account for the cognitive forms of a phenomenon, in that the principle of reason, in some one of its manifestations, seems to admit of an exception. Add to this awe the blissful ecstasy which rises from the innermost depths of man, ay, of nature, at this same collapse of the principium individuationis, and we shall gain an insight into the being of the Dionysian, which is brought within closest ken perhaps by the analogy of drunkenness. It is either under the influence of the narcotic draught, of which the hymns of all primitive men and peoples tell us, or by the powerful approach of spring penetrating all nature with joy, that those Dionysian emotions awake, in the augmentation of which the subjective vanishes to complete self-forgetfulness. So also in the German Middle Ages singing and dancing crowds, ever increasing in number, were borne from place to place under this same Dionysian power. In these St. John's and St. Vitus's dancers we again perceive the Bacchic choruses of the Greeks, with their previous history in Asia Minor, as far back as Babylon and the orgiastic Sacæa. There are some, who, from lack of experience or obtuseness, will turn away from such phenomena as "folk-diseases" with a smile of contempt or pity prompted by the consciousness of their own health: of course, the poor wretches do not divine what a cadaverous-looking and ghastly aspect this very "health" of theirs presents when the glowing life of the Dionysian revellers rushes past them.

Under the charm of the Dionysian not only is the covenant between man and man again established, but also estranged, hostile or subjugated nature again celebrates her reconciliation with her lost son, man. Of her own accord earth proffers her gifts, and peacefully the beasts of prey approach from the desert and the rocks. The chariot of Dionysus is bedecked with flowers and garlands: panthers and tigers pass beneath his yoke. Change Beethoven's "jubilee-song" into a painting, and, if your imagination be equal to the occasion when the awestruck millions sink into the dust, you will then be able to approach the Dionysian. Now is the slave a free man, now all the stubborn, hostile barriers, which necessity, caprice, or "shameless fashion" has set up between man and man, are broken down. Now, at the evangel of cosmic harmony, each one feels himself not only united, reconciled, blended with his neighbour, but as one with him, as if the veil of Mâyâ has been torn and were now merely fluttering in tatters before the mysterious Primordial Unity. In song and in dance man exhibits himself as a member of a higher community, he has forgotten how to walk and speak, and is on the point of taking a dancing flight into the air. His gestures bespeak enchantment. Even as the animals now talk, and as the earth yields milk and honey, so also something super-natural sounds forth from him: he feels himself a god, he himself now walks about enchanted and elated even as the gods whom he saw walking about in his dreams. Man is no longer an artist, he has become a work of art: the artistic power of all nature here reveals itself in the tremors of drunkenness to the highest gratification of the Primordial Unity. The noblest clay, the costliest marble, namely man, is here kneaded and cut, and the chisel strokes of the Dionysian world- artist are accompanied with the cry of the Eleusinian mysteries: "Ihr stürzt nieder, Millionen? Ahnest du den Schöpfer, Welt?"4

2.

Thus far we have considered the Apollonian and his antithesis, the Dionysian, as artistic powers, which burst forth from nature herself, without the mediation of the human artist, and in which her art- impulses are satisfied in the most immediate and direct way: first, as the pictorial world of dreams, the perfection of which has no connection whatever with the intellectual height or artistic culture of the unit man, and again, as drunken reality, which likewise does not heed the unit man, but even seeks to destroy the individual and redeem him by a mystic feeling of Oneness. Anent these immediate art-states of nature every artist is either an "imitator," to wit, either an

Apollonian, an artist in dreams, or a Dionysian, an artist in ecstasies, or finally—as for instance in Greek tragedy—an artist in both dreams and ecstasies: so we may perhaps picture him, as in his Dionysian drunkenness and mystical self-abnegation, lonesome and apart from the revelling choruses, he sinks down, and how now, through Apollonian dream-inspiration, his 4 Te bow in the dust, oh millions? Thy maker, mortal, dost divine?

Cf. Schiller's "Hymn to Joy"; and Beethoven, Ninth Symphony.—TR. own state, i.e., his oneness with the primal source of the universe, reveals itself to him in a symbolical dream-picture.

After these general premisings and contrastings, let us now approach the Greeks in order to learn in what degree and to what height these art- impulses of nature were developed in them: whereby we shall be enabled to understand and appreciate more deeply the relation of the Greek artist to his archetypes, or, according to the Aristotelian expression, "the imitation of nature." In spite of all the dream-literature and the numerous dream-anecdotes of the Greeks, we can speak only conjecturally, though with a fair degree of certainty, of their dreams. Considering the incredibly precise and unerring plastic power of their eyes, as also their manifest and sincere delight in colours, we can hardly refrain (to the shame of every one born later) from assuming for their very dreams a logical causality of lines and contours, colours and groups, a sequence of scenes resembling their best reliefs, the perfection of which would certainly justify us, if a comparison were possible, in designating the dreaming Greeks as Homers and Homer as a dreaming Greek: in a deeper sense than when modern man, in respect to his dreams, ventures to compare himself with Shakespeare.

On the other hand, we should not have to speak conjecturally, if asked to disclose the immense gap which separated the Dionysian Greek from the Dionysian barbarian. From all quarters of the Ancient World—to say nothing of the modern—from Rome as far as Babylon, we can prove the existence of Dionysian festivals, the type of which bears, at best, the same relation to the Greek festivals as the bearded satyr, who borrowed his name and attributes from the goat, does to Dionysus himself. In nearly every instance the centre of these festivals lay in extravagant sexual licentiousness, the waves of which overwhelmed all family life and its venerable traditions; the very wildest beasts of nature were let loose here, including that detestable mixture of lust and cruelty which has always seemed to me the genuine "witches' draught." For some time, however, it would seem that the Greeks were perfectly secure and guarded against the feverish agitations of these festivals (—the knowledge of which entered Greece by all the channels of land and sea) by the figure of Apollo himself rising here in full pride, who could not have held out the Gorgon's head to a more dangerous power than this grotesquely uncouth Dionysian. It is in Doric art that this majestically- rejecting attitude of Apollo perpetuated itself. This opposition became more precarious and even impossible, when, from out of the deepest root of the Hellenic nature, similar impulses finally broke forth and made way for themselves: the Delphic god, by a seasonably effected reconciliation, was now contented with taking the destructive arms from the hands of his powerful antagonist. This reconciliation marks the most important moment in the history of the Greek cult: wherever we turn our eyes we may observe the revolutions resulting from this event. It was the reconciliation of two antagonists, with the sharp demarcation of the boundary-lines to be thenceforth observed by each, and with periodical transmission of testimonials;— in reality, the chasm was not bridged over. But if we observe how, under the pressure of this conclusion of peace, the

Dionysian power manifested itself, we shall now recognise in the Dionysian orgies of the Greeks, as compared with the Babylonian Sacæa and their retrogression of man to the tiger and the ape, the significance of festivals of world-redemption and days of transfiguration. Not till then does nature attain her artistic jubilee; not till then does the rupture of the principium individuationis become an artistic phenomenon. That horrible "witches' draught" of sensuality and cruelty was here powerless: only the curious blending and duality in the emotions of the Dionysian revellers reminds one of it—just as medicines remind one of deadly poisons,—that phenomenon, to wit, that pains beget joy, that jubilation wrings painful sounds out of the breast. From the highest joy sounds the cry of horror or the yearning wail over an irretrievable loss. In these Greek festivals a sentimental trait, as it were, breaks forth from nature, as if she must sigh over her dismemberment into individuals. The song and pantomime of such dually-minded revellers was something new and unheard-of in the Homeric-Grecian world; and the Dionysian music in particular excited awe and horror. If music, as it would seem, was previously known as an Apollonian art, it was, strictly speaking, only as the wave-beat of rhythm, the formative power of which was developed to the representation of Apollonian conditions. The music of Apollo was Doric architectonics in tones, but in merely suggested tones, such as those of the cithara. The very element which forms the essence of Dionysian music (and hence of music in general) is carefully excluded as un-Apollonian; namely, the thrilling power of the tone, the uniform stream of the melos, and the thoroughly incomparable world of harmony. In the Dionysian dithyramb man is incited to the highest exaltation of all his symbolic faculties; something never before experienced struggles for utterance—the annihilation of the veil of Mâyâ, Oneness as genius of the race, ay, of nature. The essence of nature is now to be expressed symbolically; a new world of symbols is required; for once the entire symbolism of the body, not only the symbolism of the lips, face, and speech, but the whole pantomime of dancing which sets all the members into rhythmical motion. Thereupon the other symbolic powers, those of music, in rhythmics, dynamics, and harmony, suddenly become impetuous. To comprehend this collective discharge of all the symbolic powers, a man must have already attained that height of self-abnegation, which wills to express itself symbolically through these powers: the Dithyrambic votary of Dionysus is therefore understood only by those like himself! With what astonishment must the Apollonian Greek have beheld him! With an astonishment, which was all the greater the more it was mingled with the shuddering suspicion that all this was in reality not so very foreign to him, yea, that, like unto a veil, his Apollonian consciousness only hid this Dionysian world from his view.

3.

In order to comprehend this, we must take down the artistic structure of the Apollonian culture, as it were, stone by stone, till we behold the foundations on which it rests. Here we observe first of all the glorious Olympian figures of the gods, standing on the gables of this structure, whose deeds, represented in far-shining reliefs, adorn its friezes. Though Apollo stands among them as an individual deity, side by side with others, and without claim to priority of rank, we must not suffer this fact to mislead us. The same impulse which embodied itself in Apollo has, in general, given birth to this whole Olympian world, and in this sense we may regard Apollo as the father thereof. What was the enormous need from which proceeded such an illustrious group of Olympian beings?

Whosoever, with another religion in his heart, approaches these Olympians and seeks among them for moral elevation, even for sanctity, for incorporeal spiritualisation, for sympathetic looks of love, will soon be obliged to turn his back on them, discouraged and disappointed. Here nothing suggests asceticism, spirituality, or duty: here only an exuberant, even triumphant life speaks to us, in which everything existing is deified, whether good or bad. And so the spectator will perhaps stand quite bewildered before this fantastic exuberance of life, and ask himself what magic potion these madly merry men could have used for enjoying life, so that, wherever they turned their eyes, Helena, the ideal image of their own existence "floating in sweet sensuality," smiled upon them. But to this spectator, already turning backwards, we must call out: "depart not hence, but hear rather what Greek folk-wisdom says of this same life, which with such inexplicable cheerfulness spreads out before thee." There is an ancient story that king Midas hunted in the forest a long time for the wise Silenus, the companion of Dionysus, without capturing him. When at last he fell into his hands, the king asked what was best of all and most desirable for man. Fixed and immovable, the demon remained silent; till at last, forced by the king, he broke out with shrill laughter into these words: "Oh, wretched race of a day, children of chance and misery, why do ye compel me to say to you what it were most expedient for you not to hear? What is best of all is for ever beyond your reach: not to be born, not to be, to be nothing. The second best for you, however, is soon to die."

How is the Olympian world of deities related to this folk-wisdom? Even as the rapturous vision of the tortured martyr to his sufferings.

Now the Olympian magic mountain opens, as it were, to our view and shows to us its roots. The Greek knew and felt the terrors and horrors of existence: to be able to live at all, he had to interpose the shining dream- birth of the Olympian world between himself and them. The excessive distrust of the titanic powers of nature, the Moira throning inexorably over all knowledge, the vulture of the great philanthropist Prometheus, the terrible fate of the wise Œdipus, the family curse of the Atridæ which drove Orestes to matricide; in short, that entire philosophy of the sylvan god, with its mythical exemplars, which wrought the ruin of the melancholy Etruscans—was again and again surmounted anew by the Greeks through the artistic middle world of the Olympians, or at least veiled and withdrawn from sight. To be able to live, the Greeks had, from direst necessity, to create these gods: which process we may perhaps picture to ourselves in this manner: that out of the original Titan thearchy of terror the Olympian thearchy of joy was evolved, by slow transitions, through the Apollonian impulse to beauty, even as roses break forth from thorny bushes. How else could this so sensitive people, so vehement in its desires, so singularly qualified for sufferings have endured existence, if it had not been exhibited to them in their gods, surrounded with a higher glory? The same impulse which calls art into being, as the complement and consummation of existence, seducing to a continuation of life, caused also the Olympian world to arise, in which the Hellenic "will" held up before itself a transfiguring mirror. Thus do the gods justify the life of man, in that they themselves live it—the only satisfactory Theodicy! Existence under the bright sunshine of such gods is regarded as that which is desirable in itself, and the real grief of the Homeric men has reference to parting from it, especially to early parting: so that we might now say of them, with a reversion of the Silenian wisdom, that "to die early is worst of all for them, the second worst is— some day to die at all." If once the lamentation is heard, it will ring out again, of the short-lived Achilles, of the leaf-like change and vicissitude of the human race, of the decay of the heroic age. It is not unworthy of the greatest hero to long for a continuation of life, ay, even as a day- labourer. So vehemently does the "will," at the Apollonian stage of development, long for this existence, so completely at one does the Homeric man feel himself with it, that the very lamentation becomes its song of praise.

Here we must observe that this harmony which is so eagerly contemplated by modern man, in fact, this oneness of man with nature, to express which Schiller introduced the technical term "naïve," is by no means such a simple, naturally resulting and, as it were, inevitable condition, which must be found at the gate of every culture leading to a paradise of man: this could be believed only by an age which sought to picture to itself Rousseau's Émile also as an artist, and imagined it had found in Homer such an artist Émile, reared at Nature's bosom.

Wherever we meet with the "naïve" in art, it behoves us to recognise the highest effect of the Apollonian culture, which in the first place has always to overthrow some Titanic empire and slay monsters, and which, through powerful dazzling representations and pleasurable illusions, must have triumphed over a terrible depth of world-contemplation and a most keen susceptibility to suffering. But how seldom is the naïve—that complete absorption, in the beauty of appearance—attained! And hence how inexpressibly sublime is Homer, who, as unit being, bears the same relation to this Apollonian folk-culture as the unit dream-artist does to the dream-faculty of the people and of Nature in general. The Homeric "naïveté" can be comprehended only as the complete triumph of the Apollonian illusion: it is the same kind of illusion as Nature so frequently employs to compass her ends. The true goal is veiled by a phantasm: we stretch out our hands for the latter, while Nature attains the former through our illusion. In the Greeks the "will" desired to contemplate itself in the transfiguration of the genius and the world of art; in order to glorify themselves, its creatures had to feel themselves worthy of glory; they had to behold themselves again in a higher sphere, without this consummate world of contemplation acting as an imperative or reproach. Such is the sphere of beauty, in which, as in a mirror, they saw their images, the Olympians. With this mirroring of beauty the Hellenic will combated its talent—correlative to the artistic—for suffering and for the wisdom of suffering: and, as a monument of its victory, Homer, the naïve artist, stands before us.

4.

Concerning this naïve artist the analogy of dreams will enlighten us to some extent. When we realise to ourselves the dreamer, as, in the midst of the illusion of the dream-world and without disturbing it, he calls out to himself: "it is a dream, I will dream on"; when we must thence infer a deep inner joy in dream-contemplation; when, on the other hand, to be at all able to dream with this inner joy in contemplation, we must have completely forgotten the day and its terrible obtrusiveness, we may, under the direction of the dream-reading Apollo, interpret all these phenomena to ourselves somewhat as follows. Though it is certain that of the two halves of life, the waking and the dreaming, the former appeals to us as by far the more preferred, important, excellent and worthy of being lived, indeed, as that which alone is lived: yet, with reference to that mysterious ground of our being of which we are the phenomenon, I should, paradoxical as it may seem, be inclined to maintain the very opposite estimate of the value of dream life. For the more clearly I perceive in nature those all-powerful art impulses, and in them a fervent longing for appearance, for redemption through appearance, the more I feel myself driven to the metaphysical assumption that the Verily-Existent and Primordial Unity, as the Eternally Suffering and Self-Contradictory, requires the rapturous vision, the joyful appearance, for its continuous salvation: which appearance we, who are completely wrapt in it and composed of it, must regard as the Verily Non-existent,—i.e., as a perpetual unfolding in time, space and causality,—in other words, as empiric reality. If we therefore waive the consideration of our own "reality" for the present, if we conceive our empiric existence, and that of the world generally, as a representation of the Primordial Unity generated every moment, we shall then have to regard the dream as an appearance of appearance, hence as a still higher gratification of the primordial desire for appearance. It is for this same reason that the innermost heart of Nature experiences that indescribable joy in the naïve artist and in the naïve work of art, which is likewise only "an appearance of appearance." In a symbolic painting, Raphael, himself one of these immortal "naïve" ones, has represented to us this depotentiating of appearance to appearance, the primordial process of the naïve artist and at the same time of Apollonian culture. In his Transfiguration, the lower half, with the possessed boy, the despairing bearers, the helpless, terrified disciples, shows to us the reflection of eternal primordial pain, the sole basis of the world: the "appearance" here is the counter-appearance of eternal Contradiction, the father of things. Out of this appearance then arises, like an ambrosial vapour, a vision like new world of appearances, of which those wrapt in the first appearance see nothing—a radiant floating in purest bliss and painless Contemplation beaming from wide- open eyes. Here there is presented to our view, in the highest symbolism of art, that Apollonian world of beauty and its substratum, the terrible wisdom of Silenus, and we comprehend, by intuition, their necessary interdependence. Apollo, however, again appears to us as the apotheosis of the principium individuationis, in which alone the perpetually attained end of the Primordial Unity, its redemption through appearance, is consummated: he shows us, with sublime attitudes, how the entire world of torment is necessary, that thereby the individual may be impelled to realise the redeeming vision, and then, sunk in contemplation thereof, quietly sit in his fluctuating barque, in the midst of the sea.

This apotheosis of individuation, if it be at all conceived as imperative and laying down precepts, knows but one law— the individual, i.e., the observance of the boundaries of the individual, measure in the Hellenic sense. Apollo, as ethical deity, demands due proportion of his disciples, and, that this may be observed, he demands self-knowledge. And thus, parallel to the æsthetic necessity for beauty, there run the demands "know thyself" and "not too much," while presumption and undueness are regarded as the truly hostile demons of the non-Apollonian sphere, hence as characteristics of the pre-Apollonian age, that of the Titans, and of the extra-Apollonian world, that of the barbarians. Because of his Titan-like love for man, Prometheus had to be torn to pieces by vultures; because of his excessive wisdom, which solved the riddle of the Sphinx, Œdipus had to plunge into a bewildering vortex of monstrous crimes: thus did the Delphic god interpret the Grecian past.

So also the effects wrought by the Dionysian appeared "titanic" and "barbaric" to the Apollonian Greek: while at the same time he could not conceal from himself that he too was inwardly related to these overthrown Titans and heroes. Indeed, he had to recognise still more than this: his entire existence, with all its beauty and moderation, rested on a hidden substratum of suffering and of knowledge, which was again disclosed to him by the Dionysian. And lo! Apollo could not live without Dionysus! The "titanic" and the "barbaric" were in the end not less necessary than the Apollonian. And now let us imagine to ourselves how the ecstatic tone of the Dionysian festival sounded in ever more luring and bewitching strains into this artificially confined world built on appearance and moderation, how in these strains all the undueness of nature, in joy, sorrow, and knowledge, even to the transpiercing shriek, became audible: let us ask ourselves what meaning could be attached to the psalmodising artist of Apollo, with the phantom harp-sound, as compared with this demonic folk-song! The muses of the arts of "appearance" paled before an art which, in its intoxication, spoke the truth, the wisdom of Silenus cried "woe! woe!" against the cheerful Olympians. The individual, with all his boundaries and due proportions, went under in the self-oblivion of the Dionysian states and forgot the Apollonian precepts. The Undueness revealed itself as truth, contradiction, the bliss born of pain, declared itself but of the heart of nature. And thus, wherever the Dionysian prevailed, the Apollonian was routed and annihilated. But it is quite as certain that, where the first assault was successfully withstood, the authority and majesty of the Delphic god exhibited itself as more rigid and menacing than ever. For I can only explain to myself the Doric state and Doric art as a permanent war-camp of the Apollonian: only by incessant opposition to the titanic-barbaric nature of the Dionysian was it possible for an art so defiantly- prim, so encompassed with bulwarks, a training so warlike and rigorous, a constitution so cruel and relentless, to last for any length of time.

Up to this point we have enlarged upon the observation made at the beginning of this essay: how the Dionysian and the Apollonian, in ever new births succeeding and mutually augmenting one another, controlled the Hellenic genius: how from out the age of "bronze," with its Titan struggles and rigorous folk-philosophy, the Homeric world develops under the fostering sway of the Apollonian impulse to beauty, how this "naïve" splendour is again overwhelmed by the inbursting flood of the Dionysian, and how against this new power the

Apollonian rises to the austere majesty of Doric art and the Doric view of things. If, then, in this way, in the strife of these two hostile principles, the older Hellenic history falls into four great periods of art, we are now driven to inquire after the ulterior purpose of these unfoldings and processes, unless perchance we should regard the last-attained period, the period of Doric art, as the end and aim of these artistic impulses: and here the sublime and highly celebrated art-work of Attic tragedy and dramatic dithyramb presents itself to our view as the common goal of both these impulses, whose mysterious union, after many and long precursory struggles, found its glorious consummation in such a child,—which is at once Antigone and Cassandra.

5.

We now approach the real purpose of our investigation, which aims at acquiring a knowledge of the Dionyso-Apollonian genius and his art- work, or at least an anticipatory understanding of the mystery of the aforesaid union. Here we shall ask first of all where that new germ which subsequently developed into tragedy and dramatic dithyramb first makes itself perceptible in the Hellenic world. The ancients themselves supply the answer in symbolic form, when they place Homer and Archilochus as the forefathers and torch-bearers of Greek poetry side by side on gems, sculptures, etc., in the sure conviction that only these two thoroughly original compeers, from whom a stream of fire flows over the whole of Greek posterity, should be taken into consideration. Homer, the aged dreamer sunk in himself, the type of the Apollonian naïve artist, beholds now with astonishment the impassioned genius of the warlike votary of the muses, Archilochus, violently tossed to and fro on the billows of existence: and modern æsthetics could only add by way of interpretation, that here the "objective" artist is confronted by the first "subjective" artist. But this interpretation is of little service to us, because we know the subjective artist only as the poor artist, and in every type and elevation of art we demand specially and first of all the conquest of the Subjective, the redemption from the "ego" and the cessation of every individual will and desire; indeed, we find it impossible to believe in any truly artistic production, however insignificant, without objectivity, without pure, interestless contemplation. Hence our æsthetics must first solve the problem as to how the "lyrist" is possible as an artist: he who according to the experience of all ages continually says "I" and sings off to us the entire chromatic scale of his passions and desires. This very Archilochus appals us, alongside of Homer, by his cries of hatred and scorn, by the drunken outbursts of his desire. Is not just he then, who has been called the first subjective artist, the non-artist proper? But whence then the reverence which was shown to him— the poet—in very remarkable utterances by the Delphic oracle itself, the focus of "objective" art?

Schiller has enlightened us concerning his poetic procedure by a psychological observation, inexplicable to himself, yet not apparently open to any objection. He acknowledges that as the preparatory state to the act of poetising he had not perhaps before him or within him a series of pictures with co-ordinate causality of thoughts, but rather a musical mood ("The perception with me is at first without a clear and definite object; this forms itself later. A certain musical mood of mind precedes, and only after this does the poetical idea follow with me.") Add to this the most important phenomenon of all ancient lyric poetry, the union, regarded everywhere as natural, of the lyrist with the musician, their very identity, indeed,— compared with which our modern lyric poetry is like the statue of a god without a head,—and we may now, on the basis of our metaphysics of æsthetics set forth above, interpret the lyrist to ourselves as follows. As Dionysian artist he is in the first place become altogether one with the Primordial Unity, its pain and contradiction, and he produces the copy of this Primordial Unity as music, granting that music has been correctly termed a repetition and a recast of the world; but now, under the Apollonian dream-inspiration, this music again becomes visible to him as in a symbolic dream- picture. The formless and intangible reflection of the primordial pain in music, with its redemption in appearance, then generates a second mirroring as a concrete symbol or example. The artist has already surrendered his subjectivity in the Dionysian process: the picture which now shows to him his oneness with the heart of the world, is a dream- scene, which embodies the primordial contradiction and primordial pain, together with the primordial joy, of appearance. The "I" of the lyrist sounds therefore from the abyss of being: its "subjectivity," in the sense of the modern æsthetes, is a fiction. When Archilochus, the first lyrist of the Greeks, makes known both his mad love and his contempt to the daughters of Lycambes, it is not his passion which dances before us in orgiastic frenzy: we see Dionysus and the Mænads, we see the drunken reveller Archilochus sunk down to sleep—as Euripides depicts it in the Bacchæ, the sleep on the high Alpine pasture, in the noonday sun:—and now Apollo approaches and touches him with the laurel. The Dionyso- musical enchantment of the sleeper now emits, as it were, picture sparks, lyrical poems, which in their highest development are called tragedies and dramatic dithyrambs.

The plastic artist, as also the epic poet, who is related to him, is sunk in the pure contemplation of pictures. The Dionysian musician is, without any picture, himself just primordial pain and the primordial re-echoing thereof. The lyric genius is conscious of a world of pictures and symbols—growing out of the state of mystical self-abnegation and oneness,—which has a colouring causality and velocity quite different from that of the world of the plastic artist and epic poet. While the latter lives in these pictures, and only in them, with joyful satisfaction, and never grows tired of contemplating them with love, even in their minutest characters, while even the picture of the angry Achilles is to him but a picture, the angry expression of which he enjoys with the dream-joy in appearance— so that, by this mirror of appearance, he is guarded against being unified and blending with his figures;—the pictures of the lyrist on the other hand are nothing but his very self and, as it were, only different projections of himself, on account of which he as the moving centre of this world is entitled to say "I": only of course this self is not the same as that of the waking, empirically real man, but the only verily existent and eternal self resting at the basis of things, by means of the images whereof the lyric genius sees through even to this basis of things. Now let us suppose that he beholds himself also among these images as non-genius, i.e., his subject, the whole throng of subjective passions and impulses of the will directed to a definite object which appears real to him; if now it seems as if the lyric genius and the allied non-genius were one, and as if the former spoke that little word "I" of his own accord, this appearance will no longer be able to lead us astray, as it certainly led those astray who designated the lyrist as the subjective poet. In truth, Archilochus, the passionately inflamed, loving and hating man, is but a vision of the genius, who by this time is no longer Archilochus, but a genius of the world, who expresses his primordial pain symbolically in the figure of the man Archilochus: while the subjectively willing and desiring man, Archilochus, can never at any time be a poet. It is by no means necessary, however, that the lyrist should see nothing but the phenomenon of the man Archilochus before him as a reflection of eternal being; and tragedy shows how far the visionary world of the lyrist may depart from this phenomenon, to which, of course, it is most intimately related.

Schopenhauer, who did not shut his eyes to the difficulty presented by the lyrist in the philosophical contemplation of art, thought he had found a way out of it, on which, however, I cannot accompany him; while he alone, in his profound metaphysics of music, held in his hands the means whereby this difficulty could be definitely removed: as I believe I have removed it here in his spirit and to his honour. In contrast to our view, he describes the peculiar nature of song as follows5 (Welt als Wille und Vorstellung, I. 295):—"It is the subject of the will, i.e., his own volition, which fills the consciousness of the singer; often as an unbound and satisfied desire (joy), but still more often as a restricted desire (grief), always as an emotion, a passion, or an agitated frame of mind. Besides this, however, and along with it, by the sight of surrounding nature, the singer becomes conscious of himself as the subject of pure will-less knowing, the unbroken, blissful peace of which now appears, in contrast to the stress of desire, which is always restricted and always needy. The 5 World as Will and Idea, I. 323, 4th ed. of Haldane and Kemp's translation. Quoted with a few changes. feeling of this contrast, this alternation, is really what the song as a whole expresses and what principally constitutes the lyrical state of mind. In it pure knowing comes to us as it were to deliver us from desire and the stress thereof: we follow, but only for an instant; for desire, the remembrance of our personal ends, tears us anew from peaceful contemplation; yet ever again the next beautiful surrounding in which the pure will-less knowledge presents itself to us, allures us away from desire. Therefore, in song and in the lyrical mood, desire (the personal interest of the ends) and the pure perception of the surrounding which presents itself, are wonderfully mingled with each other; connections between them are sought for and imagined; the subjective disposition, the affection of the will, imparts its own hue to the contemplated surrounding, and conversely, the surroundings communicate the reflex of their colour to the will. The true song is the expression of the whole of this mingled and divided state of mind."

Who could fail to see in this description that lyric poetry is here characterised as an imperfectly attained art, which seldom and only as it were in leaps arrives at its goal, indeed, as a semi-art, the essence of which is said to consist in this, that desire and pure contemplation, i.e., the unæsthetic and the æsthetic condition, are wonderfully mingled with each other? We maintain rather, that this entire antithesis, according to which, as according to some standard of value, Schopenhauer, too, still classifies the arts, the antithesis between the subjective and the objective, is quite out of place in æsthetics, inasmuch as the subject i.e., the desiring individual who furthers his own egoistic ends, can be conceived only as the adversary, not as the origin of art. In so far as the subject is the artist, however, he has already been released from his individual will, and has become as it were the medium, through which the one verily existent Subject celebrates his redemption in appearance. For this one thing must above all be clear to us, to our humiliation and exaltation, that the entire comedy of art is not at all performed, say, for our betterment and culture, and that we are just as little the true authors of this art-world: rather we may assume with regard to ourselves, that its true author uses us as pictures and artistic projections, and that we have our highest dignity in our significance as works of art—for only as an æsthetic phenomenon is existence and the world eternally justified:—while of course our consciousness of this our specific significance hardly differs from the kind of consciousness which the soldiers painted on canvas have of the battle represented thereon.

Hence all our knowledge of art is at bottom quite illusory,

because, as knowing persons we are not one and identical with the Being who, as the sole author and spectator of this comedy of art, prepares a perpetual entertainment for himself. Only in so far as the genius in the act of artistic production coalesces with this primordial artist of the world, does he get a glimpse of the eternal essence of art, for in this state he is, in a marvellous manner, like the weird picture of the fairy-tale which can at will turn its eyes and behold itself; he is now at once subject and object, at once poet, actor, and spectator.

6.

With reference to Archilochus, it has been established by critical research that he introduced the folk-song into literature, and, on account thereof, deserved, according to the general estimate of the Greeks, his unique position alongside of Homer. But what is this popular folk-song in contrast to the wholly Apollonian epos? What else but the perpetuum vestigium of a union of the Apollonian and the Dionysian? Its enormous diffusion among all peoples, still further enhanced by ever new births, testifies to the power of this artistic double impulse of nature: which leaves its vestiges in the popular song in like manner as the orgiastic movements of a people perpetuate themselves in its music. Indeed, one might also furnish historical proofs, that every period which is highly productive in popular songs has been most violently stirred by Dionysian currents, which we must always regard as the substratum and prerequisite of the popular song.

First of all, however, we regard the popular song as the musical mirror of the world, as the Original melody, which now seeks for itself a parallel dream-phenomenon and expresses it in poetry. Melody is therefore primary and universal, and as such may admit of several objectivations, in several texts. Likewise, in the naïve estimation of the people, it is regarded as by far the more important and necessary. Melody generates the poem out of itself by an ever-recurring process. The strophic form of the popular song points to the same phenomenon, which I always beheld with astonishment, till at last I found this explanation. Any one who in accordance with this theory examines a collection of popular songs, such as "Des Knaben Wunderhorn," will find innumerable instances of the perpetually productive melody scattering picture sparks all around: which in their variegation, their abrupt change, their mad precipitance, manifest a power quite unknown to the epic appearance and its steady flow. From the point of view of the epos, this unequal and irregular pictorial world of lyric poetry must be simply condemned: and the solemn epic rhapsodists of the Apollonian festivals in the age of Terpander have certainly done so.

Accordingly, we observe that in the poetising of the popular song, language is strained to its utmost to imitate music; and hence a new world of poetry begins with Archilochus, which is fundamentally opposed to the Homeric. And in saying this we have pointed out the only possible relation between poetry and music, between word and tone: the word, the picture, the concept here seeks an expression analogous to music and now experiences in itself the power of music. In this sense we may discriminate between two main currents in the history of the language of the Greek people, according as their language imitated either the world of phenomena and of pictures, or the world of music. One has only to reflect seriously on the linguistic difference with regard to colour, syntactical structure, and vocabulary in Homer and Pindar, in order to comprehend the significance of this contrast; indeed, it becomes palpably clear to us that in the period between Homer and Pindar the orgiastic flute tones of Olympus must have sounded forth, which, in an age as late as Aristotle's, when music was infinitely more developed, transported people to drunken enthusiasm, and which, when their influence was first felt, undoubtedly incited all the poetic means of expression of contemporaneous man to imitation. I here call attention to a familiar phenomenon of our own times, against which our æsthetics raises many objections. We again and again have occasion to observe how a symphony of Beethoven compels the individual hearers to use figurative speech, though the appearance presented by a collocation of the different pictorial world generated by a piece of music may be never so fantastically diversified and even contradictory. To practise its small wit on such compositions, and to overlook a phenomenon which is certainly worth explaining, is quite in keeping with this æsthetics.

Indeed, even if the tone-poet has spoken in pictures concerning a composition, when for instance he designates a certain symphony as the "pastoral" symphony, or a passage therein as "the scene by the brook," or another as the "merry gathering of rustics," these are likewise only symbolical representations born out of music—and not perhaps the imitated objects of music—representations which can give us no information whatever concerning the Dionysian content of music, and which in fact have no distinctive value of their own alongside of other pictorical expressions. This process of a discharge of music in pictures we have now to transfer to some youthful, linguistically productive people, to get a notion as to how the strophic popular song originates, and how the entire faculty of speech is stimulated by this new principle of imitation of music.

If, therefore, we may regard lyric poetry as the effulguration of music in pictures and concepts, we can now ask: "how does music appear in the mirror of symbolism and conception?" It appears as will, taking the word in the Schopenhauerian sense, i.e., as the antithesis of the æsthetic, purely contemplative, and passive frame of mind. Here, however, we must discriminate as sharply as possible between the concept of essentiality and the concept of phenominality; for music, according to its essence, cannot be will, because as such it would have to be wholly banished from the domain of art—for the will is the unæsthetic-in- itself;—yet it appears as will. For in order to express the phenomenon of music in pictures, the lyrist requires all the stirrings of passion, from the whispering of infant desire to the roaring of madness. Under the impulse to speak of music in Apollonian symbols, he conceives of all nature, and himself therein, only as the eternally willing, desiring, longing existence. But in so far as he interprets music by means of pictures, he himself rests in the quiet calm of Apollonian contemplation, however much all around him which he beholds through the medium of music is in a state of confused and violent motion. Indeed, when he beholds himself through this same medium, his own image appears to him in a state of unsatisfied feeling: his own willing, longing, moaning and rejoicing are to him symbols by which he interprets music. Such is the phenomenon of the lyrist: as Apollonian genius he interprets music through the image of the will, while he himself, completely released from the avidity of the will, is the pure, undimmed eye of day.

Our whole disquisition insists on this, that lyric poetry is dependent on the spirit of music just as music itself in its absolute sovereignty does not require the picture and the concept, but only endures them as accompaniments. The poems of the lyrist can express nothing which has not already been contained in the vast universality and absoluteness of the music which compelled him to use figurative speech. By no means is it possible for language adequately to render the cosmic symbolism of music, for the very reason that music stands in symbolic relation to the primordial contradiction and primordial pain in the heart of the Primordial Unity, and therefore symbolises a sphere which is above all appearance and before all phenomena. Rather should we say that all phenomena, compared with it, are but symbols: hence language, as the organ and symbol of phenomena, cannot at all disclose the innermost essence, of music; language can only be in superficial contact with music when it attempts to imitate music; while the profoundest significance of the latter cannot be brought one step nearer to us by all the eloquence of lyric poetry.

7.

We shall now have to avail ourselves of all the principles of art hitherto considered, in order to find our way through the labyrinth, as we must designate the origin of Greek tragedy. I shall not be charged with absurdity in saying that the problem of this origin has as yet not even been seriously stated, not to say solved, however often the fluttering tatters of ancient tradition have been sewed together in sundry combinations and torn asunder again. This tradition tells us in the most unequivocal terms, that tragedy sprang from the tragic chorus, and was originally only chorus and nothing but chorus: and hence we feel it our duty to look into the heart of this tragic chorus as being the real proto- drama, without in the least contenting ourselves with current art- phraseology—according to which the chorus is the ideal spectator, or represents the people in contrast to the regal side of the scene. The latter explanatory notion, which sounds sublime to many a politician—that the immutable moral law was embodied by the democratic Athenians in the popular chorus, which always carries its point over the passionate excesses and extravagances of kings—may be ever so forcibly suggested by an observation of Aristotle: still it has no bearing on the original formation of tragedy, inasmuch as the entire antithesis of king and people, and, in general, the whole politico-social sphere, is excluded from the purely religious beginnings of tragedy; but, considering the well-known classical form of the chorus in Æschylus and Sophocles, we should even deem it blasphemy to speak here of the anticipation of a "constitutional representation of the people," from which blasphemy others have not shrunk, however. The ancient governments knew of no constitutional representation of the people in praxi, and it is to be hoped that they did not even so much as "anticipate" it in tragedy.

Much more celebrated than this political explanation of the chorus is the notion of A. W. Schlegel, who advises us to regard the chorus, in a manner, as the essence and extract of the crowd of spectators,—as the "ideal spectator." This view when compared with the historical tradition that tragedy was originally only chorus, reveals itself in its true character, as a crude, unscientific, yet brilliant assertion, which, however, has acquired its brilliancy only through its concentrated form of expression, through the truly Germanic bias in favour of whatever is called "ideal," and through our momentary astonishment. For we are indeed astonished the moment we compare our well-known theatrical public with this chorus, and ask ourselves if it could ever be possible to idealise something analogous to the Greek chorus out of such a public.

We tacitly deny this, and now wonder as much at the boldness of Schlegel's assertion as at the totally different nature of the Greek public. For hitherto we always believed that the true spectator, be he who he may, had always to remain conscious of having before him a work of art, and not an empiric reality: whereas the tragic chorus of the Greeks is compelled to recognise real beings in the figures of the stage. The chorus of the Oceanides really believes that it sees before it the Titan Prometheus, and considers itself as real as the god of the scene. And are we to own that he is the highest and purest type of spectator, who, like the Oceanides, regards

Prometheus as real and present in body? And is it characteristic of the ideal spectator that he should run on the stage and free the god from his torments? We had believed in an æsthetic public, and considered the individual spectator the better qualified the more he was capable of viewing a work of art as art, that is, æsthetically; but now the Schlegelian expression has intimated to us, that the perfect ideal spectator does not at all suffer the world of the scenes to act æsthetically on him, but corporeo-empirically. Oh, these Greeks! we have sighed; they will upset our æsthetics! But once accustomed to it, we have reiterated the saying of Schlegel, as often as the subject of the chorus has been broached.

But the tradition which is so explicit here speaks against Schlegel: the chorus as such, without the stage,—the primitive form of tragedy,—and the chorus of ideal spectators do not harmonise. What kind of art would that be which was extracted from the concept of the spectator, and whereof we are to regard the "spectator as such" as the true form? The spectator without the play is something absurd. We fear that the birth of tragedy can be explained neither by the high esteem for the moral intelligence of the multitude nor by the concept of the spectator without the play; and we regard the problem as too deep to be even so much as touched by such superficial modes of contemplation.

An infinitely more valuable insight into the signification of the chorus had already been displayed by Schiller in the celebrated Preface to

his Bride of Messina, where he regarded the chorus as a living wall which tragedy draws round herself to guard her from contact with the world of reality, and to preserve her ideal domain and poetical freedom.

It is with this, his chief weapon, that Schiller combats the ordinary conception of the natural, the illusion ordinarily required in dramatic poetry. He contends that while indeed the day on the stage is merely artificial, the architecture only symbolical, and the metrical dialogue purely ideal in character, nevertheless an erroneous view still prevails in the main: that it is not enough to tolerate merely as a poetical

license that which is in reality the essence of all poetry. The introduction of the chorus is, he says, the decisive step by which war is declared openly and honestly against all naturalism in art.—It is, methinks, for disparaging this mode of contemplation that our would-be superior age has coined the disdainful catchword "pseudo-idealism." I fear, however, that we on the other hand with our present worship of the natural and the real have landed at the nadir of all idealism, namely in the region of cabinets of wax-figures. An art indeed exists also here, as in certain novels much in vogue at present: but let no one pester us with the claim that by this art the Schiller-Goethian "Pseudo-idealism" has been vanquished.

It is indeed an "ideal" domain, as Schiller rightly perceived, upon—which the Greek satyric chorus, the chorus of primitive tragedy, was wont to walk, a domain raised far above the actual path of mortals. The Greek framed for this chorus the suspended scaffolding of a fictitious natural state and placed thereon fictitious natural beings. It is on this foundation that tragedy grew up, and so it could of course dispense from the very first with a painful portrayal of reality. Yet it is, not an arbitrary world placed by fancy betwixt heaven and earth; rather is it a world possessing the same reality and trustworthiness that Olympus with its dwellers possessed for the believing Hellene. The satyr, as being the Dionysian chorist, lives in a religiously acknowledged reality under the sanction of the myth and cult. That tragedy begins with him, that the Dionysian wisdom of tragedy speaks through him, is just as surprising a phenomenon to us as, in general, the derivation of tragedy from the chorus.

Perhaps we shall get a starting-point for our inquiry, if I put forward the proposition that the satyr, the fictitious natural being, is to the man of culture what Dionysian music is to civilisation. Concerning this latter, Richard Wagner says that it is neutralised by music even as lamplight by daylight. In like manner, I believe, the Greek man of culture felt himself neutralised in the presence of the satyric chorus: and this is the most immediate effect of the Dionysian tragedy, that the state and society, and, in general, the gaps between man and man give way to an overwhelming feeling of oneness, which leads back to the heart of nature. The metaphysical comfort,—with which, as I have here intimated, every true tragedy dismisses us—that, in spite of the perpetual change of phenomena, life at bottom is indestructibly powerful and pleasurable, this comfort appears with corporeal lucidity as the satyric chorus, as the chorus of natural beings, who live ineradicable as it were behind all civilisation, and who, in spite of the ceaseless change of generations and the history of nations, remain for ever the same.

With this chorus the deep-minded Hellene, who is so singularly qualified for the most delicate and severe suffering, consoles himself:—he who has glanced with piercing eye into the very heart of the terrible destructive processes of so-called universal history, as also into the cruelty of nature, and is in danger of longing for a Buddhistic negation of the will. Art saves him, and through art life saves him—for herself.

For we must know that in the rapture of the Dionysian state, with its annihilation of the ordinary bounds and limits of existence, there is a lethargic element, wherein all personal experiences of the past are submerged. It is by this gulf of oblivion that the everyday world and the world of Dionysian reality are separated from each other. But as soon as this everyday reality rises again in consciousness, it is felt as such, and nauseates us; an ascetic will-paralysing mood is the fruit of these states. In this sense the Dionysian man may be said to resemble Hamlet: both have for once seen into the true nature of things, —they have perceived, but they are loath to act; for their action cannot change the eternal nature of things; they regard it as shameful or ridiculous that one should require of them to set aright the time which is out of joint.

Knowledge kills action, action requires the veil of illusion—it is this lesson which Hamlet teaches, and not the cheap wisdom of John-a- Dreams who from too much reflection, as it were from a surplus of possibilities, does not arrive at action at all. Not reflection, no!—true knowledge, insight into appalling truth, preponderates over all motives inciting to action, in Hamlet as well as in the Dionysian man. No comfort avails any longer; his longing goes beyond a world after death, beyond the gods themselves; existence with its glittering reflection in the gods, or in an immortal other world is abjured. In the consciousness of the truth he has perceived, man now sees everywhere only the awfulness or the absurdity of existence, he now understands the symbolism in the fate of Ophelia, he now discerns the wisdom of the sylvan god Silenus: and loathing seizes him.

Here, in this extremest danger of the will, art approaches, as a saving and healing enchantress; she alone is able to transform these nauseating reflections on the awfulness or absurdity of existence into representations wherewith it is possible to live: these are the representations of the sublime as the artistic subjugation of the awful, and the comic as the artistic delivery from the nausea of the absurd. The satyric chorus of dithyramb is the saving deed of Greek art; the paroxysms described above spent their force in the intermediary world of these Dionysian followers.

8.

The satyr, like the idyllic shepherd of our more recent

time, is the offspring of a longing after the Primitive and the Natural; but mark with what firmness and fearlessness the Greek embraced the man of the woods, and again, how coyly and mawkishly the modern man dallied with the flattering picture of a tender, flute-playing, soft-natured shepherd! Nature, on which as yet no knowledge has been at work, which maintains unbroken barriers to culture—this is what the Greek saw in his satyr, which still was not on this account supposed to coincide with the ape. On the contrary: it was the archetype of man, the embodiment of his highest and strongest emotions, as the enthusiastic reveller enraptured By the proximity of his god, as the fellow-suffering companion in whom the suffering of the god repeats itself, as the herald of wisdom speaking from the very depths of nature, as the emblem of the sexual omnipotence of nature, which the Greek was wont to contemplate with reverential awe. The satyr was something sublime and godlike: he could not but appear so, especially to the sad and wearied eye of the Dionysian man.

He would have been offended by our spurious tricked-up shepherd, while his eye dwelt with sublime satisfaction on the naked and unstuntedly magnificent characters of nature: here the illusion of culture was brushed away from the archetype of man; here the true man, the bearded satyr, revealed himself, who shouts joyfully to his god.

Before him the cultured man shrank to a lying caricature. Schiller is right also with reference to these beginnings of tragic art: the chorus is a living bulwark against the onsets of reality, because it—the satyric chorus— portrays existence more truthfully, more realistically, more perfectly than the cultured man who ordinarily considers himself as the only reality. The sphere of poetry does not lie outside the world, like some fantastic impossibility of a poet's imagination: it seeks to be the very opposite, the unvarnished expression of truth, and must for this very reason cast aside the false finery of that supposed reality of the cultured man. The contrast between this intrinsic truth of nature and the falsehood of culture, which poses as the only reality, is similar to that existing between the eternal kernel of things, the thing in itself, and the collective world of phenomena. And even as tragedy, with its metaphysical comfort, points to the eternal life of this kernel of existence, notwithstanding the perpetual dissolution of phenomena, so the symbolism of the satyric chorus already expresses figuratively this primordial relation between the thing in itself and phenomenon. The idyllic shepherd of the modern man is but a copy of the sum of the illusions of culture which he calls nature; the Dionysian Greek desires truth and nature in their most potent form;—he sees himself metamorphosed into the satyr.

The revelling crowd of the votaries of Dionysus rejoices, swayed by such moods and perceptions, the power of which transforms them before their own eyes, so that they imagine they behold themselves as reconstituted genii of nature, as satyrs. The later constitution of the tragic chorus is the artistic imitation of this natural phenomenon, which of course required a separation of the Dionysian spectators from the enchanted Dionysians. However, we must never lose sight of the fact that the public of the Attic tragedy rediscovered itself in the chorus of the orchestra, that there was in reality no antithesis of public and chorus: for all was but one great sublime chorus of dancing and singing satyrs, or of such as allowed themselves to be represented by the satyrs. The Schlegelian observation must here reveal itself to us in a deeper sense.

The chorus is the "ideal spectator"[6] in so far as it is the only beholder,[7] the beholder of the visionary world of the scene. A public of spectators, as known to us, was unknown to the Greeks. In their theatres the terraced structure of the spectators' space rising in concentric arcs enabled every one, in the strictest sense, to overlook the entire world of culture around him, and in surfeited contemplation to imagine himself a chorist. According to this view, then, we may call the chorus in its primitive stage in proto-tragedy, a self-mirroring of the Dionysian man: a phenomenon which may be best exemplified by the process of the actor, who, if he be truly gifted, sees hovering before his eyes with almost tangible perceptibility the character he is to represent. The satyric chorus is first of all a vision of the Dionysian throng, just as the world of the stage is, in turn, a vision of the satyric chorus: the power of this vision is great enough to render the eye dull and insensible to the impression of "reality," to the presence of the cultured men occupying the tiers of seats on every side. The form of the Greek theatre reminds one of a lonesome mountain-valley: the architecture of the scene appears like a luminous cloud-picture which the Bacchants swarming on the mountains behold from the heights, as the splendid encirclement in the midst of which the image of Dionysus is revealed to them.

Owing to our learned conception of the elementary artistic processes, this artistic proto-phenomenon, which is here introduced to explain the tragic chorus, is almost shocking: while nothing can be more certain than that the poet is a poet only in that he beholds himself surrounded by forms which live and act before him, into the innermost being of which his glance penetrates. By reason of a strange defeat in our capacities, we modern men are apt to represent to ourselves the æsthetic proto- phenomenon as too complex and abstract. For the true poet the metaphor is not a rhetorical figure, but a vicarious image which actually hovers before him in place of a concept. The character is not for him an aggregate composed of a studied collection of particular traits, but an irrepressibly live person appearing before his eyes, and differing only from the corresponding vision of the painter by its ever continued life and action. Why is it that Homer sketches much more vividly8 than all the other poets? Because he contemplates9 much more. We talk so abstractly about poetry, because we are all wont to be bad poets. At bottom the æsthetic phenomenon is simple: let a man but have the faculty of perpetually seeing a lively play and of constantly living surrounded by hosts of spirits, then he is a poet: let him but feel the impulse to transform himself and to talk from out the bodies and souls of others, then he is a dramatist.

The Dionysian excitement is able to impart to a whole mass of men this artistic faculty of seeing themselves surrounded by such a host of spirits, with whom they know themselves to be inwardly one. This function of the tragic chorus is the dramatic proto-phenomenon: to see one's self transformed before one's self, and then to act as if one had really entered into another body, into another character. This function stands at the beginning of the development of the drama. Here we have something different from the rhapsodist, who does not blend with his pictures, but only sees them, like the painter, with contemplative eye outside of him; here we actually have a surrender of the individual by his entering into another nature. Moreover this phenomenon appears in the form of an epidemic: a whole throng feels itself metamorphosed in this wise. Hence it is that the dithyramb is essentially different from every other variety of the choric song. The virgins, who with laurel twigs in their hands solemnly proceed to the temple of Apollo and sing a processional hymn, remain what they are and retain their civic names: the dithyrambic chorus is a chorus of transformed beings, whose civic past and social rank are totally forgotten: they have become the timeless servants of their god that live aloof from all the spheres of society. Every other variety of the choric lyric of the Hellenes is but an enormous enhancement of the Apollonian unit-singer: while in the dithyramb we have before us a community of unconscious actors, who mutually regard themselves as transformed among one another.

This enchantment is the prerequisite of all dramatic art. In this enchantment the Dionysian reveller sees himself as a satyr, and as satyr he in turn beholds the god, that is, in his transformation he sees a new vision outside him as the Apollonian consummation of his state. With this new vision the drama is complete.

According to this view, we must understand Greek tragedy as the Dionysian chorus, which always disburdens itself anew in an Apollonian world of pictures. The choric parts, therefore, with which tragedy is interlaced, are in a manner the mother-womb of the entire so-called dialogue, that is, of the whole stage-world, of the drama proper. In several successive outbursts does this primordial basis of tragedy beam forth the vision of the drama, which is a dream-phenomenon throughout, and, as such, epic in character: on the other hand, however, as objectivation of a Dionysian state, it does not represent the Apollonian redemption in appearance, but, conversely, the dissolution of the individual and his unification with primordial existence. Accordingly, the drama is the Apollonian embodiment of Dionysian perceptions and influences, and is thereby separated from the epic as by an immense gap.

The chorus of Greek tragedy, the symbol of the mass of the people moved by Dionysian excitement, is thus fully explained by our conception of it as here set forth. Whereas, being accustomed to the position of a chorus on the modern stage, especially an operatic chorus, we could never comprehend why the tragic chorus of the Greeks should be older, more primitive, indeed, more important than the "action" proper,—as has been so plainly declared by the voice of tradition; whereas, furthermore, we could not reconcile with this traditional paramount importance and primitiveness the fact of the chorus' being composed only of humble, ministering beings; indeed, at first only of goatlike satyrs; whereas, finally, the orchestra before the scene was always a riddle to us; we have learned to comprehend at length that the scene, together with the action, was fundamentally and originally conceived only as a vision, that the only reality is just the chorus, which of itself generates the vision and speaks thereof with the entire symbolism of dancing, tone, and word. This chorus beholds in the vision its lord and master Dionysus, and is thus for ever the serving chorus: it sees how he, the god, suffers and glorifies himself, and therefore does not itself act. But though its attitude towards the god is throughout the attitude of ministration, this is nevertheless the highest expression, the Dionysian expression of Nature, and therefore, like Nature herself, the chorus utters oracles and wise sayings when transported with enthusiasm: as fellow-sufferer it is also the sage proclaiming truth from out the heart of Nature. Thus, then, originates the fantastic figure, which seems so shocking, of the wise and enthusiastic satyr, who is at the same time "the dumb man" in contrast to the god: the image of Nature and her strongest impulses, yea, the symbol of Nature, and at the same time the herald of her art and wisdom: musician, poet, dancer, and visionary in one person.

Agreeably to this view, and agreeably to tradition, Dionysus, the proper stage-hero and focus of vision, is not at first actually present in the oldest period of tragedy, but is only imagined as present: i.e., tragedy is originally only "chorus" and not "drama." Later on the attempt is made to exhibit the god as real and to display the visionary figure together with its glorifying encirclement before the eyes of all; it is here that the "drama" in the narrow sense of the term begins. To the dithyrambic chorus is now assigned the task of exciting the minds of the hearers to such a pitch of Dionysian frenzy, that, when the tragic hero appears on the stage, they do not behold in him, say, the unshapely masked man, but a visionary figure, born as it were of their own ecstasy. Let us picture Admetes thinking in profound meditation of his lately departed wife Alcestis, and quite consuming himself in spiritual contemplation thereof—when suddenly the veiled figure of a woman resembling her in form and gait is led towards him: let us picture his sudden trembling anxiety, his agitated comparisons, his instinctive conviction—and we shall have an analogon to the sensation with which the spectator, excited to Dionysian frenzy, saw the god approaching on the stage, a god with whose sufferings he had already become identified. He involuntarily transferred the entire picture of the god, fluttering magically before his soul, to this masked figure and resolved its reality as it were into a phantasmal unreality. This is the Apollonian dream-state, in which the world of day is veiled, and a new world, clearer, more intelligible, more striking than the former, and nevertheless more shadowy, is ever born anew in perpetual change before our eyes. We accordingly recognise in tragedy a thorough-going stylistic contrast: the language, colour, flexibility and dynamics of the dialogue fall apart in the Dionysian lyrics of the chorus on the one hand, and in the Apollonian dream-world of the scene on the other, into entirely separate spheres of expression. The Apollonian appearances, in which Dionysus objectifies himself, are no longer "ein ewiges Meer, ein wechselnd Weben, ein glühend Leben,"10 as is the music of the chorus, they are no longer the forces merely felt, but not condensed into a picture, by which the inspired votary of Dionysus divines the proximity of his god: the clearness and firmness of epic form now speak to him from the scene, Dionysus now no longer speaks through forces, but as an epic hero, almost in the language of Homer.

9.

Whatever rises to the surface in the dialogue of the Apollonian part of Greek tragedy, appears simple, transparent, beautiful. In this sense the dialogue is a copy of the Hellene, whose nature reveals itself in the dance, because in the dance the greatest energy is merely potential, but betrays itself nevertheless in flexible and vivacious movements. The language of the Sophoclean heroes, for instance, surprises us by its Apollonian precision and clearness, so that we at once imagine we see into the innermost recesses of their being, and marvel not a little that the way to these recesses is so short. But if for the moment we disregard the character of the hero which rises to the surface and grows visible—and which at bottom is nothing but the light-picture cast on a dark wall, that is, appearance through and through,—if rather we enter into the myth which projects itself in these bright mirrorings, we shall of a sudden experience a phenomenon which bears a reverse relation to one familiar in optics. When, after a vigorous effort to gaze into the sun, we turn away blinded, we have dark-coloured spots before our eyes as restoratives, so to speak; while, on the contrary, those light-picture phenomena of the An eternal sea, A weaving, flowing, Life, all glowing. Faust, trans. of Bayard Taylor.—TR.

Sophoclean hero,—in short, the Apollonian of the mask,—are the necessary productions of a glance into the secret and terrible things of nature, as it were shining spots to heal the eye which dire night has seared. Only in this sense can we hope to be able to grasp the true meaning of the serious and significant notion of "Greek cheerfulness"; while of course we encounter the misunderstood notion of this cheerfulness, as resulting from a state of unendangered comfort, on all the ways and paths of the present time.

The most sorrowful figure of the Greek stage, the hapless

Œdipus, was understood by Sophocles as the noble man, who in spite of his wisdom was destined to error and misery, but nevertheless through his extraordinary sufferings ultimately exerted a magical, wholesome influence on all around him, which continues effective even after his death. The noble man does not sin; this is what the thoughtful poet wishes to tell us: all laws, all natural order, yea, the moral world itself, may be destroyed through his action, but through this very action a higher magic circle of influences is brought into play, which establish a new world on the ruins of the old that has been overthrown. This is what the poet, in so far as he is at the same time a religious thinker, wishes to tell us: as poet, he shows us first of all a wonderfully complicated legal mystery, which the judge slowly unravels, link by link, to his own destruction. The truly Hellenic delight at this dialectical loosening is so great, that a touch of surpassing cheerfulness is thereby communicated to the entire play, which everywhere blunts the edge of the horrible presuppositions of the procedure. In the "Œdipus at Colonus" we find the same cheerfulness, elevated, however, to an infinite transfiguration: in contrast to the aged king, subjected to an excess of misery, and exposed solely as a sufferer to all that befalls him, we have here a supermundane cheerfulness, which descends from a divine sphere and intimates to us that in his purely passive attitude the hero attains his highest activity, the influence of which extends far beyond his life, while his earlier conscious musing and striving led him only to passivity. Thus, then, the legal knot of the fable of Œdipus, which to mortal eyes appears indissolubly entangled, is slowly unravelled—and the profoundest human joy comes upon us in the presence of this divine counterpart of dialectics. If this explanation does justice to the poet, it may still be asked whether the substance of the myth is thereby exhausted; and here it turns out that the entire conception of the poet is nothing but the light-picture which healing nature holds up to us after a glance into the abyss. Œdipus, the murderer of his father, the husband of his mother, Œdipus, the interpreter of the riddle of the Sphinx! What does the mysterious triad of these deeds of destiny tell us? There is a primitive popular belief, especially in Persia, that a wise Magian can be born only of incest: which we have forthwith to interpret to ourselves with reference to the riddle- solving and mother-marrying Œdipus, to the effect that when the boundary of the present and future, the rigid law of individuation and, in general, the intrinsic spell of nature, are broken by prophetic and magical powers, an extraordinary counter-naturalness—as, in this case, incest—must have preceded as a cause; for how else could one force nature to surrender her secrets but by victoriously opposing her, i.e., by means of the Unnatural? It is this intuition which I see imprinted in the awful triad of the destiny of Œdipus: the very man who solves the riddle of nature—that double-constituted Sphinx—must also, as the murderer of his father and husband of his mother, break the holiest laws of nature. Indeed, it seems as if the myth sought to whisper into our ears that wisdom, especially Dionysian wisdom, is an unnatural abomination, and that whoever, through his knowledge, plunges nature into an abyss of annihilation, must also experience the dissolution of nature in himself. "The sharpness of wisdom turns round upon the sage: wisdom is a crime against nature": such terrible expressions does the myth call out to us: but the Hellenic poet touches like a sunbeam the sublime and formidable Memnonian statue of the myth, so that it suddenly begins to sound—in Sophoclean melodies.

With the glory of passivity I now contrast the glory of activity which illuminates the Prometheus of Æschylus. That which Æschylus the thinker had to tell us here, but which as a poet he only allows us to surmise by his symbolic picture, the youthful Goethe succeeded in disclosing to us in the daring words of his Prometheus:—

"Hier sitz' ich, forme Menschen Nach meinem Bilde,

Ein Geschlecht, das mir gleich sei, Zu leiden, zu weinen,

Zu geniessen und zu freuen sich,

Und dein nicht zu achten, Wie ich!"11

Man, elevating himself to the rank of the Titans, acquires his culture by his own efforts, and compels the gods to unite with him, because in his self-sufficient wisdom he has their existence and their limits in his hand. What is most wonderful, however, in this Promethean form, which according to its fundamental conception is the specific hymn of impiety, is the profound Æschylean yearning for justice: the untold sorrow of the bold "single-handed being" on the one hand, and the divine need, ay, the foreboding of a twilight of the gods, on the other, the power of these two worlds of suffering constraining to reconciliation, to metaphysical oneness—all this suggests most forcibly the central and main position of the Æschylean view of things, which sees Moira as eternal justice enthroned above gods and men. In view of the astonishing boldness with which Æschylus places the Olympian world on his scales of justice, it must be remembered that the deep-minded Greek had an immovably firm substratum of metaphysical thought in his mysteries, and that all his sceptical paroxysms could be discharged upon the Olympians. With reference to these deities, the Greek artist, in particular, had an obscure feeling as to mutual dependency: and it is just in the Prometheus of Æschylus that this feeling is symbolised. The Titanic artist found in himself the daring belief that he could create men and at least destroy Olympian deities: namely, by his superior wisdom, for which, to be sure, he had to atone by eternal suffering. The splendid "can-ing" of the great genius, bought too cheaply even at the price of eternal suffering, the stern pride of the artist: this is the essence and soul of Æschylean poetry, while Sophocles in his Œdipus preludingly strikes up the victory-song of the saint. But even this interpretation which Æschylus has given to the myth does not fathom its astounding depth of terror; the fact is rather that the artist's delight in unfolding, the cheerfulness of artistic creating bidding defiance to all calamity, is but a shining stellar and nebular 11 "Here sit I, forming mankind In my image,

A race resembling me,—

To sorrow and to weep,

To taste, to hold, to enjoy,

And not have need of thee, As I!"

(Translation in Hæckel's History of the Evolution of Man.) image reflected in a black sea of sadness. The tale of Prometheus is an original possession of the entire Aryan family of races, and documentary evidence of their capacity for the profoundly tragic; indeed, it is not improbable that this myth has the same characteristic significance for the Aryan race that the myth of the fall of man has for the Semitic, and that there is a relationship between the two myths like that of brother and sister. The presupposition of the Promethean myth is the transcendent value which a naïve humanity attach to fire as the true palladium of every ascending culture: that man, however, should dispose at will of this fire, and should not receive it only as a gift from heaven, as the igniting lightning or the warming solar flame, appeared to the contemplative primordial men as crime and robbery of the divine nature. And thus the first philosophical problem at once causes a painful, irreconcilable antagonism between man and God, and puts as it were a mass of rock at the gate of every culture. The best and highest that men can acquire they obtain by a crime, and must now in their turn take upon themselves its consequences, namely the whole flood of sufferings and sorrows with which the offended celestials must visit the nobly aspiring race of man: a bitter reflection, which, by the dignity it confers on crime, contrasts strangely with the Semitic myth of the fall of man, in which curiosity, beguilement, seducibility, wantonness,—in short, a whole series of pre-eminently feminine passions,—were regarded as the origin of evil. What distinguishes the Aryan representation is the sublime view of active sin as the properly Promethean virtue, which suggests at the same time the ethical basis of pessimistic tragedy as the justification of human evil— of human guilt as well as of the suffering incurred thereby. The misery in the essence of things—which the contemplative Aryan is not disposed to explain away—the antagonism in the heart of the world, manifests itself to him as a medley of different worlds, for instance, a Divine and a human world, each of which is in the right individually, but as a separate existence alongside of another has to suffer for its individuation. With the heroic effort made by the individual for universality, in his attempt to pass beyond the bounds of individuation and become the one universal being, he experiences in himself the primordial contradiction concealed in the essence of things, i.e., he trespasses and suffers. Accordingly crime12 is understood by the Aryans to be a man, sin13 by the Semites a woman; as also, the original crime is committed by man, the original sin by woman. Besides, the witches' chorus says:

"Wir nehmen das nicht so genau:

Mit tausend Schritten macht's die Frau; Doch wie sie auch sich eilen kann

Mit einem Sprunge macht's der Mann."14

He who understands this innermost core of the tale of Prometheus— namely the necessity of crime imposed on the titanically striving individual—will at once be conscious of the un-Apollonian nature of this pessimistic representation: for

Apollo seeks to pacify individual beings precisely by drawing boundary lines between them, and by again and again calling attention thereto, with his requirements of self-knowledge and due proportion, as the holiest laws of the universe. In order, however, to prevent the form from congealing to Egyptian rigidity and coldness in consequence of this Apollonian tendency, in order to prevent the extinction of the motion of the entire lake in the effort to prescribe to the individual wave its path and compass, the high tide of the Dionysian tendency destroyed from time to time all the little circles in which the one-sided Apollonian "will" sought to confine the Hellenic world. The suddenly swelling tide of the Dionysian then takes the separate little wave-mountains of individuals on its back, just as the brother of Prometheus, the Titan Atlas, does with the earth. This Titanic impulse, to become as it were the Atlas of all individuals, and to carry them on broad shoulders higher and higher, farther and farther, is what the Promethean and the Dionysian have in common. In this respect the Æschylean Prometheus is a Dionysian mask, while, in the afore-mentioned profound yearning for justice, Æschylus betrays to the intelligent observer his paternal descent from Apollo, the god of individuation and of the boundaries of justice. And so the double-being of the Æschylean Prometheus, his conjoint Dionysian and Apollonian nature, might be Die Sünde.

We do not measure with such care: Woman in thousand steps is there, But howsoe'er she hasten may.

Man in one leap has cleared the way.

Faust, trans. of Bayard Taylor.—TR. thus expressed in an abstract formula: "Whatever exists is alike just and unjust, and equally justified in both."

Das ist deine Welt! Das heisst eine Welt!15

10.

It is an indisputable tradition that Greek tragedy in its earliest form had for its theme only the sufferings of Dionysus, and that for some time the only stage-hero therein was simply Dionysus himself. With the same confidence, however, we can maintain that not until Euripides did Dionysus cease to be the tragic hero, and that in fact all the celebrated figures of the Greek stage—Prometheus, Œdipus, etc.—are but masks of this original hero, Dionysus. The presence of a god behind all these masks is the one essential cause of the typical "ideality," so oft exciting wonder, of these celebrated figures. Some one, I know not whom, has maintained that all individuals are comic as individuals and are consequently un-tragic: from whence it might be inferred that the Greeks in general could not endure individuals on the tragic stage. And they really seem to have had these sentiments: as, in general, it is to be observed that the Platonic discrimination and valuation of the "idea" in contrast to the "eidolon," the image, is deeply rooted in the Hellenic being. Availing ourselves of Plato's terminology, however, we should have to speak of the tragic figures of the Hellenic stage somewhat as follows. The one truly real Dionysus appears in a multiplicity of forms, in the mask of a fighting hero and entangled, as it were, in the net of an individual will. As the visibly appearing god now talks and acts, he resembles an erring, striving, suffering individual: and that, in general, he appears with such epic precision and clearness, is due to the dream-reading Apollo, who reads to the chorus its Dionysian state through this symbolic appearance. In reality, however, this hero is the suffering Dionysus of the mysteries, a god experiencing in himself the sufferings of individuation, of whom wonderful myths tell that as a boy he was dismembered by the Titans and has been worshipped in this state as Zagreus:16 whereby is intimated that this dismemberment, the properly Dionysian suffering, is like a transformation into air, water, earth, and fire, that we must therefore regard the state of individuation as the source and primal cause of all suffering, as something objectionable in itself. From the smile of this Dionysus sprang the Olympian gods, from his tears sprang man. In his existence as a dismembered god, Dionysus has the dual nature of a cruel barbarised demon, and a mild pacific ruler. But the hope of the epopts looked for a new birth of Dionysus, which we have now to conceive of in anticipation as the end of individuation: it was for this coming third Dionysus that the stormy jubilation-hymns of the epopts resounded. And it is only this hope that sheds a ray of joy upon the features of a world torn asunder and shattered into individuals: as is symbolised in the myth by Demeter sunk in eternal sadness, who rejoices again only when told that she may once more give birth to Dionysus In the views of things here given we already have all the elements of a profound and pessimistic contemplation of the world, and along with these we have the mystery doctrine of tragedy: the fundamental knowledge of the oneness of all existing things, the consideration of individuation as the primal cause of evil, and art as the joyous hope that the spell of individuation may be broken, as the augury of a restored oneness.

It has already been intimated that the Homeric epos is the poem of Olympian culture, wherewith this culture has sung its own song of triumph over the terrors of the war of the Titans. Under the predominating influence of tragic poetry, these Homeric myths are now reproduced anew, and show by this metempsychosis that meantime the Olympian culture also has been vanquished by a still deeper view of things. The haughty Titan Prometheus has announced to his Olympian tormentor that the extremest danger will one day menace his rule, unless he ally with him betimes. In Æschylus we perceive the terrified Zeus, apprehensive of his end, in alliance with the Titan. Thus, the former age of the Titans is subsequently brought from Tartarus once more to the light of day. The philosophy of wild and naked nature beholds with the undissembled mien of truth the myths of the Homeric world as they dance past: they turn pale, they tremble before the lightning glance of See article by Mr. Arthur Symons in The Academy, 30th August 1902. this goddess—till the powerful fist17 of the Dionysian artist forces them into the service of the new deity. Dionysian truth takes over the entire domain of myth as symbolism of its knowledge, which it makes known partly in the public cult of tragedy and partly in the secret celebration of the dramatic mysteries, always, however, in the old mythical garb. What was the power, which freed Prometheus from his vultures and transformed the myth into a vehicle of Dionysian wisdom? It is the Heracleian power of music: which, having reached its highest manifestness in tragedy, can invest myths with a new and most profound significance, which we have already had occasion to characterise as the most powerful faculty of music. For it is the fate of every myth to insinuate itself into the narrow limits of some alleged historical reality, and to be treated by some later generation as a solitary fact with historical claims: and the Greeks were already fairly on the way to restamp the whole of their mythical juvenile dream sagaciously and arbitrarily into a historico-pragmatical juvenile history. For this is the manner in which religions are wont to die out: when of course under the stern, intelligent eyes of an orthodox dogmatism, the mythical presuppositions of a religion are systematised as a completed sum of historical events, and when one begins apprehensively to defend the credibility of the myth, while at the same time opposing all continuation of their natural vitality and luxuriance; when, accordingly, the feeling for myth dies out, and its place is taken by the claim of religion to historical foundations. This dying myth was now seized by the new-born genius of Dionysian music, in whose hands it bloomed once more, with such colours as it had never yet displayed, with a fragrance that awakened a longing anticipation of a metaphysical world. After this final effulgence it collapses, its leaves wither, and soon the scoffing Lucians of antiquity catch at the discoloured and faded flowers which the winds carry off in every direction. Through tragedy the myth attains its profoundest significance, its most expressive form; it rises once more like a wounded hero, and the whole surplus of vitality, together with the philosophical calmness of the Dying, burns in its eyes with a last powerful gleam.

What meantest thou, oh impious Euripides, in seeking once more to enthral this dying one? It died under thy ruthless hands: and then thou madest use of counterfeit, masked myth, which like the ape of Heracles Die mächtige Faust.—Cf. Faust, Chorus of Spirits.—TR could only trick itself out in the old finery. And as myth died in thy hands, so also died the genius of music; though thou couldst covetously plunder all the gardens of music—thou didst only realise a counterfeit, masked music. And because thou hast forsaken Dionysus. Apollo hath also forsaken thee; rout up all the passions from their haunts and conjure them into thy sphere, sharpen and polish a sophistical dialectics for the speeches of thy heroes—thy very heroes have only counterfeit, masked passions, and speak only counterfeit, masked music.

11.

Greek tragedy had a fate different from that of all her older sister arts: she died by suicide, in consequence of an irreconcilable conflict; accordingly she died tragically, while they all passed away very calmly and beautifully in ripe old age. For if it be in accordance with a happy state of things to depart this life without a struggle, leaving behind a fair posterity, the closing period of these older arts exhibits such a happy state of things: slowly they sink out of sight, and before their dying eyes already stand their fairer progeny, who impatiently lift up their heads with courageous mien. The death of Greek tragedy, on the other hand, left an immense void, deeply felt everywhere. Even as certain Greek sailors in the time of Tiberius once heard upon a lonesome island the thrilling cry, "great Pan is dead": so now as it were sorrowful wailing sounded through the Hellenic world: "Tragedy is dead! Poetry itself has perished with her! Begone, begone, ye stunted, emaciated epigones!

Begone to Hades, that ye may for once eat your fill of the crumbs of your former masters!"

But when after all a new Art blossomed forth which revered tragedy as her ancestress and mistress, it was observed with horror that she did indeed bear the features of her mother, but those very features the latter had exhibited in her long death-struggle. It was Euripides who fought this death-struggle of tragedy; the later art is known as the New Attic Comedy. In it the degenerate form of tragedy lived on as a monument of the most painful and violent death of tragedy proper.

This connection between the two serves to explain the passionate attachment to Euripides evinced by the poets of the New Comedy, and hence we are no longer surprised at the wish of Philemon, who would have got himself hanged at once, with the sole design of being able to visit Euripides in the lower regions: if only he could be assured generally that the deceased still had his wits. But if we desire, as briefly as possible, and without professing to say aught exhaustive on the subject, to characterise what Euripides has in common with Menander and Philemon, and what appealed to them so strongly as worthy of imitation: it will suffice to say that the spectator was brought upon the stage by Euripides. He who has perceived the material of which the Promethean tragic writers prior to Euripides formed their heroes, and how remote from their purpose it was to bring the true mask of reality on the stage, will also know what to make of the wholly divergent tendency of Euripides. Through him the commonplace individual forced his way from the spectators' benches to the stage itself; the mirror in which formerly only great and bold traits found expression now showed the painful exactness that conscientiously reproduces even the abortive lines of nature. Odysseus, the typical Hellene of the Old Art, sank, in the hands of the new poets, to the figure of the Græculus, who, as the good- naturedly cunning domestic slave, stands henceforth in the centre of dramatic interest. What Euripides takes credit for in the Aristophanean "Frogs," namely, that by his household remedies he freed tragic art from its pompous corpulency, is apparent above all in his tragic heroes. The spectator now virtually saw and heard his double on the Euripidean stage, and rejoiced that he could talk so well. But this joy was not all: one even learned of Euripides how to speak: he prides himself upon this in his contest with Æschylus: how the people have learned from him how to observe, debate, and draw conclusions according to the rules of art and with the cleverest sophistications. In general it may be said that through this revolution of the popular language he made the New Comedy possible. For it was henceforth no longer a secret, how—and with what saws—the commonplace could represent and express itself on the stage. Civic mediocrity, on which Euripides built all his political hopes, was now suffered to speak, while heretofore the demigod in tragedy and the drunken satyr, or demiman, in comedy, had determined the character of the language. And so the Aristophanean Euripides prides himself on having portrayed the common, familiar, everyday life and dealings of the people, concerning which all are qualified to pass judgment. If now the entire populace philosophises, manages land and goods with unheard-of circumspection, and conducts law-suits, he takes all the credit to himself, and glories in the splendid results of the wisdom with which he inoculated the rabble.

It was to a populace prepared and enlightened in this manner that the New Comedy could now address itself, of which Euripides had become as it were the chorus-master; only that in this case the chorus of spectators had to be trained.

As soon as this chorus was trained to sing in the Euripidean key, there arose that chesslike variety of the drama, the New Comedy, with its perpetual triumphs of cunning and artfulness. But Euripides—the chorus-master—was praised incessantly: indeed, people would have killed themselves in order to learn yet more from him, had they not known that tragic poets were quite as dead as tragedy. But with it the Hellene had surrendered the belief in his immortality; not only the belief in an ideal past, but also the belief in an ideal future. The saying taken from the well-known epitaph, "as an old man, frivolous and capricious," applies also to aged Hellenism. The passing moment, wit, levity, and caprice, are its highest deities; the fifth class, that of the slaves, now attains to power, at least in sentiment: and if we can still speak at all of "Greek cheerfulness," it is the cheerfulness of the slave who has nothing of consequence to answer for, nothing great to strive for, and cannot value anything of the past or future higher than the present. It was this semblance of "Greek cheerfulness" which so revolted the deep-minded and formidable natures of the first four centuries of Christianity: this womanish flight from earnestness and terror, this cowardly contentedness with easy pleasure, was not only contemptible to them, but seemed to be a specifically anti-Christian sentiment. And we must ascribe it to its influence that the conception of Greek antiquity, which lived on for centuries, preserved with almost enduring persistency that peculiar hectic colour of cheerfulness—as if there had never been a Sixth Century with its birth of tragedy, its Mysteries, its Pythagoras and Heraclitus, indeed as if the art-works of that great period did not at all exist, which in fact—each by itself—can in no wise be explained as having sprung from the soil of such a decrepit and slavish love of existence and cheerfulness, and point to an altogether different conception of things as their source.

The assertion made a moment ago, that Euripides introduced the spectator on the stage to qualify him the better to pass judgment on the drama, will make it appear as if the old tragic art was always in a false relation to the spectator: and one would be tempted to extol the radical tendency of Euripides to bring about an adequate relation between art- work and public as an advance on Sophocles. But, as things are, "public" is merely a word, and not at all a homogeneous and constant quantity.

Why should the artist be under obligations to accommodate himself to a power whose strength is merely in numbers? And if by virtue of his endowments and aspirations he feels himself superior to every one of these spectators, how could he feel greater respect for the collective expression of all these subordinate capacities than for the relatively highest-endowed individual spectator? In truth, if ever a Greek artist treated his public throughout a long life with presumptuousness and self-sufficiency, it was Euripides, who, even when the masses threw themselves at his feet, with sublime defiance made an open assault on his own tendency, the very tendency with which he had triumphed over the masses. If this genius had had the slightest reverence for the pandemonium of the public, he would have broken down long before the middle of his career beneath the weighty blows of his own failures. These considerations here make it obvious that our formula— namely, that Euripides brought the spectator upon the stage, in order to make him truly competent to pass judgment—was but a provisional one, and that we must seek for a deeper understanding of his tendency. Conversely, it is undoubtedly well known that Æschylus and Sophocles, during all their lives, indeed, far beyond their lives, enjoyed the full favour of the people, and that therefore in the case of these predecessors of Euripides the idea of a false relation between art-work and public was altogether excluded. What was it that thus forcibly diverted this highly gifted artist, so incessantly impelled to production, from the path over which shone the sun of the greatest names in poetry and the cloudless heaven of popular favour? What strange consideration for the spectator led him to defy, the spectator? How could he, owing to too much respect for the public —dis- respect the public?

Euripides—and this is the solution of the riddle just propounded—felt himself, as a poet, undoubtedly superior to the masses, but not to two of his spectators: he brought the masses upon the stage; these two spectators he revered as the only competent judges and masters of his art: in compliance with their directions and admonitions, he transferred the entire world of sentiments, passions, and experiences, hitherto present at every festival representation as the invisible chorus on the spectators' benches, into the souls of his stage-heroes; he yielded to their demands when he also sought for these new characters the new word and the new tone; in their voices alone he heard the conclusive verdict on his work, as also the cheering promise of triumph when he found himself condemned as usual by the justice of the public.

Of these two, spectators the one is—Euripides himself, Euripides as thinker, not as poet. It might be said of him, that his unusually large fund of critical ability, as in the case of Lessing, if it did not create, at least constantly fructified a productively artistic collateral impulse. With this faculty, with all the clearness and dexterity of his critical thought, Euripides had sat in the theatre and striven to recognise in the masterpieces of his great predecessors, as in faded paintings, feature and feature, line and line. And here had happened to him what one initiated in the deeper arcana of Æschylean tragedy must needs have expected: he observed something incommensurable in every feature and in every line, a certain deceptive distinctness and at the same time an enigmatic profundity, yea an infinitude, of background. Even the clearest figure had always a comet's tail attached to it, which seemed to suggest the uncertain and the inexplicable. The same twilight shrouded the structure of the drama, especially the significance of the chorus. And how doubtful seemed the solution of the ethical problems to his mind! How questionable the treatment of the myths! How unequal the distribution of happiness and misfortune! Even in the language of the Old Tragedy there was much that was objectionable to him, or at least enigmatical; he found especially too much pomp for simple affairs, too many tropes and immense things for the plainness of the characters. Thus he sat restlessly pondering in the theatre, and as a spectator he acknowledged to himself that he did not understand his great predecessors. If, however, he thought the understanding the root proper of all enjoyment and productivity, he had to inquire and look about to see whether any one else thought as he did, and also acknowledged this incommensurability. But most people, and among them the best individuals, had only a distrustful smile for him, while none could explain why the great masters were still in the right in face of his scruples and objections. And in this painful condition he found that other spectator, who did not comprehend, and therefore did not esteem, tragedy. In alliance with him he could venture, from amid his lonesomeness, to begin the prodigious struggle against the art of Æschylus and Sophocles—not with polemic writings, but as a dramatic poet, who opposed his own conception of tragedy to the traditional one.

12.

Before we name this other spectator, let us pause here a moment in order to recall our own impression, as previously described, of the discordant and incommensurable elements in the nature of Æschylean tragedy. Let us think of our own astonishment at the chorus and the tragic hero of that type of tragedy, neither of which we could reconcile with our practices any more than with tradition—till we rediscovered this duplexity itself as the origin and essence of Greek tragedy, as the expression of two interwoven artistic impulses, the Apollonian and the Dionysian.

To separate this primitive and all-powerful Dionysian element from tragedy, and to build up a new and purified form of tragedy on the basis of a non-Dionysian art, morality, and conception of things—such is the tendency of Euripides which now reveals itself to us in a clear light.

In a myth composed in the eve of his life, Euripides himself most urgently propounded to his contemporaries the question as to the value and signification of this tendency. Is the Dionysian entitled to exist at all? Should it not be forcibly rooted out of the Hellenic soil? Certainly, the poet tells us, if only it were possible: but the god Dionysus is too powerful; his most intelligent adversary—like Pentheus in the "Bacchæ"—is unwittingly enchanted by him, and in this enchantment meets his fate. The judgment of the two old sages, Cadmus and Tiresias, seems to be also the judgment of the aged poet: that the reflection of the wisest individuals does not overthrow old popular traditions, nor the perpetually propagating worship of Dionysus, that in fact it behoves us to display at least a diplomatically cautious concern in the presence of such strange forces: where however it is always possible that the god may take offence at such lukewarm participation, and finally change the diplomat—in this case Cadmus—into a dragon. This is what a poet tells us, who opposed Dionysus with heroic valour throughout a long life—in order finally to wind up his career with a glorification of his adversary, and with suicide, like one staggering from giddiness, who, in order to escape the horrible vertigo he can no longer endure, casts himself from a tower. This tragedy—the Bacchæ—is a protest against the practicability of his own tendency; alas, and it has already been put into practice! The surprising thing had happened: when the poet recanted, his tendency had already conquered. Dionysus had already been scared from the tragic stage, and in fact by a demonic power which spoke through Euripides. Even Euripides was, in a certain sense, only a mask: the deity that spoke through him was neither Dionysus nor Apollo, but an altogether new-born demon, called Socrates. This is the new antithesis: the Dionysian and the Socratic, and the art-work of Greek tragedy was wrecked on it. What if even Euripides now seeks to comfort us by his recantation? It is of no avail: the most magnificent temple lies in ruins.

What avails the lamentation of the destroyer, and his confession that it was the most beautiful of all temples? And even that Euripides has been changed into a dragon as a punishment by the art-critics of all ages—who could be content with this wretched compensation?

Let us now approach this Socratic tendency with which Euripides combated and vanquished Æschylean tragedy.

We must now ask ourselves, what could be the ulterior aim of the Euripidean design, which, in the highest ideality of its execution, would found drama exclusively on the non-Dionysian? What other form of drama could there be, if it was not to be born of the womb of music, in the mysterious twilight of the Dionysian? Only the dramatised epos: in which Apollonian domain of art the tragic effect is of course unattainable. It does not depend on the subject-matter of the events here represented; indeed, I venture to assert that it would have been impossible for Goethe in his projected "Nausikaa" to have rendered tragically effective the suicide of the idyllic being with which he intended to complete the fifth act; so extraordinary is the power of the epic-Apollonian representation, that it charms, before our eyes, the most terrible things by the joy in appearance and in redemption through appearance. The poet of the dramatised epos cannot completely blend with his pictures any more than the epic rhapsodist. He is still just the calm, unmoved embodiment of Contemplation whose wide eyes see the picture before them. The actor in this dramatised epos still remains intrinsically rhapsodist: the consecration of inner dreaming is on all his actions, so that he is never wholly an actor.

How, then, is the Euripidean play related to this ideal of the Apollonian drama? Just as the younger rhapsodist is related to the solemn rhapsodist of the old time. The former describes his own character in the Platonic "Ion" as follows: "When I am saying anything sad, my eyes fill with tears; when, however, what I am saying is awful and terrible, then my hair stands on end through fear, and my heart leaps." Here we no longer observe anything of the epic absorption in appearance, or of the unemotional coolness of the true actor, who precisely in his highest activity is wholly appearance and joy in appearance. Euripides is the actor with leaping heart, with hair standing on end; as Socratic thinker he designs the plan, as passionate actor he executes it. Neither in the designing nor in the execution is he an artist pure and simple. And so the Euripidean drama is a thing both cool and fiery, equally capable of freezing and burning; it is impossible for it to attain the Apollonian, effect of the epos, while, on the other hand, it has severed itself as much as possible from Dionysian elements, and now, in order to act at all, it requires new stimulants, which can no longer lie within the sphere of the two unique art-impulses, the Apollonian and the Dionysian. The stimulants are cool, paradoxical thoughts, in place of Apollonian intuitions—and fiery passions—in place Dionysean ecstasies; and in fact, thoughts and passions very realistically copied, and not at all steeped in the ether of art.

Accordingly, if we have perceived this much, that Euripides

did not succeed in establishing the drama exclusively on the Apollonian, but that rather his non-Dionysian inclinations deviated into a naturalistic and inartistic tendency, we shall now be able to approach nearer to the character æsthetic Socratism. supreme law of which reads about as follows: "to be beautiful everything must be intelligible," as the parallel to the Socratic proposition, "only the knowing is one virtuous." With this canon in his hands Euripides measured all the separate elements of the drama, and rectified them according to his principle: the language, the characters, the dramaturgic structure, and the choric music. The poetic deficiency and retrogression, which we are so often wont to impute to Euripides in comparison with Sophoclean tragedy, is for the most part the product of this penetrating critical process, this daring intelligibility.

The Euripidian prologue may serve us as an example of the productivity of this, rationalistic method. Nothing could be more opposed to the technique of our stage than the prologue in the drama of Euripides. For a single person to appear at the outset of the play telling us who he is, what precedes the action, what has happened thus far, yea, what will happen in the course of the play, would be designated by a modern playwright as a wanton and unpardonable abandonment of the effect of suspense.

Everything that is about to happen is known beforehand; who then cares to wait for it actually to happen?—considering, moreover, that here there is not by any means the exciting relation of a predicting dream to a reality taking place later on. Euripides speculated quite differently. The effect of tragedy never depended on epic suspense, on the fascinating uncertainty as to what is to happen now and afterwards: but rather on the great rhetoro-lyric scenes in which the passion and dialectics of the chief hero swelled to a broad and mighty stream. Everything was arranged for pathos, not for action: and whatever was not arranged for pathos was regarded as objectionable. But what interferes most with the hearer's pleasurable satisfaction in such scenes is a missing link, a gap in the texture of the previous history. So long as the spectator has to divine the meaning of this or that person, or the presuppositions of this or that conflict of inclinations and intentions, his complete absorption in the doings and sufferings of the chief persons is impossible, as is likewise breathless fellow-feeling and fellow-fearing. The Æschyleo-Sophoclean tragedy employed the most ingenious devices in the first scenes to place in the hands of the spectator as if by chance all the threads requisite for understanding the whole: a trait in which that noble artistry is approved, which as it were masks the inevitably formal, and causes it to appear as something accidental. But nevertheless Euripides thought he observed that during these first scenes the spectator was in a strange state of anxiety to make out the problem of the previous history, so that the poetic beauties and pathos of the exposition were lost to him.

Accordingly he placed the prologue even before the exposition, and put it in the mouth of a person who could be trusted: some deity had often as it were to guarantee the particulars of the tragedy to the public and remove every doubt as to the reality of the myth: as in the case of Descartes, who could only prove the reality of the empiric world by an appeal to the truthfulness of God and His inability to utter falsehood. Euripides makes use of the same divine truthfulness once more at the close of his drama, in order to ensure to the public the future of his heroes; this is the task of the notorious deus ex machina. Between the preliminary and the additional epic spectacle there is the dramatico-lyric present, the "drama" proper.

Thus Euripides as a poet echoes above all his own conscious knowledge; and it is precisely on this account that he occupies such a notable position in the history of Greek art. With reference to his critico- productive activity, he must often have felt that he ought to actualise in the drama the words at the beginning of the essay of Anaxagoras: "In the beginning all things were mixed together; then came the understanding and created order." And if Anaxagoras with his seemed like the first sober person among nothing but drunken philosophers, Euripides may also have conceived his relation to the other tragic poets under a similar figure. As long as the sole ruler and disposer of the universe, the was still excluded from artistic activity, things were all mixed together in a chaotic, primitive mess;—it is thus Euripides was obliged to think, it is thus he was obliged to condemn the "drunken" poets as the first "sober" one among them. What Sophocles said of Æschylus, that he did what was right, though unconsciously, was surely not in the mind of Euripides: who would have admitted only thus much, that because he wrought unconsciously, did what was wrong. So also the divine Plato speaks for the most part only ironically of the creative faculty of the poet, in so far as it is not conscious insight, and places it on a par with the gift of the soothsayer and dream-interpreter; insinuating that the poet is incapable of composing until he has become unconscious and reason has deserted him. Like Plato, Euripides undertook to show to the world the reverse of the "unintelligent" poet; his æsthetic principle that "to be beautiful everything must be known" is, as I have said, the parallel to the Socratic "to be good everything must be known." Accordingly we may regard Euripides as the poet of æsthetic Socratism. Socrates, however, was that second spectator who did not comprehend and therefore did not esteem the Old Tragedy; in alliance with him Euripides ventured to be the herald of a new artistic activity. If, then, the Old Tragedy was here destroyed, it follows that æsthetic Socratism was the murderous principle; but in so far as the struggle is directed against the Dionysian element in the old art, we recognise in Socrates the opponent of Dionysus, the new Orpheus who rebels against Dionysus; and although destined to be torn to pieces by the Mænads of the Athenian court, yet puts to flight the overpowerful god himself, who, when he fled from Lycurgus, the king of Edoni, sought refuge in the depths of the ocean—namely, in the mystical flood of a secret cult which gradually overspread the earth.

13.

That Socrates stood in close relationship to Euripides in the tendency of his teaching, did not escape the notice of contemporaneous antiquity; the most eloquent expression of this felicitous insight being the tale current in Athens, that Socrates was accustomed to help Euripides in poetising.

Both names were mentioned in one breath by the adherents of the "good old time," whenever they came to enumerating the popular agitators of the day: to whose influence they attributed the fact that the old Marathonian stalwart capacity of body and soul was more and more being sacrificed to a dubious enlightenment, involving progressive degeneration of the physical and mental powers. It is in this tone, half indignantly and half contemptuously, that Aristophanic comedy is wont to speak of both of them—to the consternation of modern men, who would indeed be willing enough to give up Euripides, but cannot suppress their amazement that Socrates should appear in Aristophanes as the first and head sophist, as the mirror and epitome of all sophistical tendencies; in connection with which it offers the single consolation of putting Aristophanes himself in the pillory, as a rakish, lying Alcibiades of poetry. Without here defending the profound instincts of Aristophanes against such attacks, I shall now indicate, by means of the sentiments of the time, the close connection between Socrates and Euripides. With this purpose in view, it is especially to be remembered that Socrates, as an opponent of tragic art, did not ordinarily patronise tragedy, but only appeared among the spectators when a new play of Euripides was performed. The most noted thing, however, is the close juxtaposition of the two names in the Delphic oracle, which designated Socrates as the wisest of men, but at the same time decided that the second prize in the contest of wisdom was due to Euripides.

Sophocles was designated as the third in this scale of rank; he who could pride himself that, in comparison with Æschylus, he did what was right, and did it, moreover, because he knew what was right. It is evidently just the degree of clearness of this knowledge, which distinguishes these three men in common as the three "knowing ones" of their age.

The most decisive word, however, for this new and unprecedented esteem of knowledge and insight was spoken by Socrates when he found that he was the only one who acknowledged to himself that he knew nothing while in his critical pilgrimage through Athens, and calling on the greatest statesmen, orators, poets, and artists, he discovered everywhere the conceit of knowledge. He perceived, to his astonishment, that all these celebrities were without a proper and accurate insight, even with regard to their own callings, and practised them only by instinct. "Only by instinct": with this phrase we touch upon the heart and core of the Socratic tendency. Socratism condemns therewith existing art as well as existing ethics; wherever Socratism turns its searching eyes it beholds the lack of insight and the power of illusion; and from this lack infers the inner perversity and objectionableness of existing conditions. From this point onwards, Socrates believed that he was called upon to, correct existence; and, with an air of disregard and superiority, as the precursor of an altogether different culture, art, and morality, he enters single- handed into a world, of which, if we reverently touched the hem, we should count it our greatest happiness.

Here is the extraordinary hesitancy which always seizes upon us with regard to Socrates, and again and again invites us to ascertain the sense and purpose of this most questionable phenomenon of antiquity. Who is it that ventures single-handed to disown the Greek character, which, as Homer, Pindar, and Æschylus, as Phidias, as Pericles, as Pythia and Dionysus, as the deepest abyss and the highest height, is sure of our wondering admiration? What demoniac power is it which would presume to spill this magic draught in the dust? What demigod is it to whom the chorus of spirits of the noblest of mankind must call out: "Weh! Weh! Du hast sie zerstört, die schöne Welt, mit mächtiger Faust; sie stürzt, sie zerfällt!"18

18 Woe! Woe!

Thou hast it destroyed, The beautiful world; With powerful fist;

In ruin 'tis hurled!

Faust, trans. of Bayard Taylor.—TR.

A key to the character of Socrates is presented to us by the surprising phenomenon designated as the "daimonion" of Socrates. In special circumstances, when his gigantic intellect began to stagger, he got a secure support in the utterances of a divine voice which then spake to him. This voice, whenever it comes, always dissuades. In this totally abnormal nature instinctive wisdom only appears in order to hinder the progress of conscious perception here and there. While in all productive men it is instinct which is the creatively affirmative force, consciousness only comporting itself critically and dissuasively; with Socrates it is instinct which becomes critic; it is consciousness which becomes creator—a perfect monstrosity per defectum! And we do indeed observe here a monstrous defectus of all mystical aptitude, so that Socrates might be designated as the specific non-mystic, in whom the logical nature is developed, through a superfoetation, to the same excess as instinctive wisdom is developed in the mystic. On the other hand, however, the logical instinct which appeared in Socrates was absolutely prohibited from turning against itself; in its unchecked flow it manifests a native power such as we meet with, to our shocking surprise, only among the very greatest instinctive forces. He who has experienced even a breath of the divine naïveté and security of the Socratic course of life in the Platonic writings, will also feel that the enormous driving-wheel of logical Socratism is in motion, as it were, behind Socrates, and that it must be viewed through Socrates as through a shadow. And that he himself had a boding of this relation is apparent from the dignified earnestness with which he everywhere, and even before his judges, insisted on his divine calling. To refute him here was really as impossible as to approve of his instinct-disintegrating influence. In view of this indissoluble conflict, when he had at last been brought before the forum of the Greek state, there was only one punishment demanded, namely exile; he might have been sped across the borders as something thoroughly enigmatical, irrubricable and inexplicable, and so posterity would have been quite unjustified in charging the Athenians with a deed of ignominy. But that the sentence of death, and not mere exile, was pronounced upon him, seems to have been brought about by Socrates himself, with perfect knowledge of the circumstances, and without the natural fear of death: he met his death with the calmness with which, according to the description of Plato, he leaves the symposium at break of day, as the last of the revellers, to begin a new day; while the sleepy companions remain behind on the benches and the floor, to dream of Socrates, the true eroticist. The dying Socrates became the new ideal of the noble Greek youths,—an ideal they had never yet beheld,—and above all, the typical Hellenic youth, Plato, prostrated himself before this scene with all the fervent devotion of his visionary soul.

14.

Let us now imagine the one great Cyclopean eye of Socrates fixed on tragedy, that eye in which the fine frenzy of artistic enthusiasm had never glowed—let us think how it was denied to this eye to gaze with pleasure into the Dionysian abysses—what could it not but see in the "sublime and greatly lauded" tragic art, as Plato called it? Something very absurd, with causes that seemed to be without effects, and effects apparently without causes; the whole, moreover, so motley and diversified that it could not but be repugnant to a thoughtful mind, a dangerous incentive, however, to sensitive and irritable souls. We know what was the sole kind of poetry which he comprehended: the Æsopian fable: and he did this no doubt with that smiling complaisance with which the good honest Gellert sings the praise of poetry in the fable of the bee and the hen:—

"Du siehst an mir, wozu sie nützt, Dem, der nicht viel Verstand besitzt,

Die Wahrheit durch ein Bild zu sagen."19

But then it seemed to Socrates that tragic art did not even "tell the truth": not to mention the fact that it addresses itself to him who "hath but little wit"; consequently not to the philosopher: a twofold reason why it should be avoided. Like Plato, he reckoned it among the seductive arts which only represent the agreeable, not the useful, and hence he required of his disciples abstinence and strict separation from such unphilosophical allurements; with such success that the youthful tragic poet Plato first of all burned his poems to be able to become a scholar of Socrates. But where unconquerable native capacities bore up against the Socratic maxims, their power, together with the momentum of his In me thou seest its benefit,— To him who hath but little wit, Through parables to tell the truth. mighty character, still sufficed to force poetry itself into new and hitherto unknown channels.

An instance of this is the aforesaid Plato: he, who in the condemnation of tragedy and of art in general certainly did not fall short of the naïve cynicism of his master, was nevertheless constrained by sheer artistic necessity to create a form of art which is inwardly related even to the then existing forms of art which he repudiated. Plato's main objection to the old art— that it is the imitation of a phantom,20 and hence belongs to a sphere still lower than the empiric world—could not at all apply to the new art: and so we find Plato endeavouring to go beyond reality and attempting to represent the idea which underlies this pseudo-reality. But Plato, the thinker, thereby arrived by a roundabout road just at the point where he had always been at home as poet, and from which Sophocles and all the old artists had solemnly protested against that objection. If tragedy absorbed into itself all the earlier varieties of art, the same could again be said in an unusual sense of Platonic dialogue, which, engendered by a mixture of all the then existing forms and styles, hovers midway between narrative, lyric and drama, between prose and poetry, and has also thereby broken loose from the older strict law of unity of linguistic form; a movement which was carried still farther by the cynic writers, who in the most promiscuous style, oscillating to and fro betwixt prose and metrical forms, realised also the literary picture of the "raving Socrates" whom they were wont to represent in life. Platonic dialogue was as it were the boat in which the shipwrecked ancient poetry saved herself together with all her children: crowded into a narrow space and timidly obsequious to the one steersman, Socrates, they now launched into a new world, which never tired of looking at the fantastic spectacle of this procession. In very truth, Plato has given to all posterity the prototype of a new form of art, the prototype of the novel which must be designated as the infinitely evolved

Æsopian fable, in which poetry holds the same rank with reference to dialectic philosophy as this same philosophy held for many centuries with reference to theology: namely, the rank of ancilla. This was the new position of poetry into which Plato forced it under the pressure of the demon-inspired Socrates.

Here philosophic thought overgrows art and compels it to cling close to the trunk of dialectics. The Apollonian tendency has chrysalised in the logical schematism; just as something analogous in the case of Euripides (and moreover a translation of the Dionysian into the naturalistic emotion) was forced upon our attention. Socrates, the dialectical hero in Platonic drama, reminds us of the kindred nature of the Euripidean hero, who has to defend his actions by arguments and counter-arguments, and thereby so often runs the risk of forfeiting our tragic pity; for who could mistake the optimistic element in the essence of dialectics, which celebrates a jubilee in every conclusion, and can breathe only in cool clearness and consciousness: the optimistic element, which, having once forced its way into tragedy, must gradually overgrow its Dionysian regions, and necessarily impel it to self-destruction—even to the death-leap into the bourgeois drama. Let us but realise the consequences of the Socratic maxims: "Virtue is knowledge; man only sins from ignorance; he who is virtuous is happy": these three fundamental forms of optimism involve the death of tragedy. For the virtuous hero must now be a dialectician; there must now be a necessary, visible connection between virtue and knowledge, between belief and morality; the transcendental justice of the plot in Æschylus is now degraded to the superficial and audacious principle of poetic justice with its usual deus ex machina.

How does the chorus, and, in general, the entire Dionyso-musical substratum of tragedy, now appear in the light of this new Socrato-optimistic stage-world? As something accidental, as a readily dispensable reminiscence of the origin of tragedy; while we have in fact seen that the chorus can be understood only as the cause of tragedy, and of the tragic generally. This perplexity with respect to the chorus first manifests itself in Sophocles—an important sign that the Dionysian basis of tragedy already begins to disintegrate with him. He no longer ventures to entrust to the chorus the main share of the effect, but limits its sphere to such an extent that it now appears almost co-ordinate with the actors, just as if it were elevated from the orchestra into the scene: whereby of course its character is completely destroyed, notwithstanding that Aristotle countenances this very theory of the chorus. This alteration of the position of the chorus, which Sophocles at any rate recommended by his practice, and, according to tradition, even by a treatise, is the first step towards the annihilation of the chorus, the phases of which follow one another with alarming rapidity in Euripides, Agathon, and the New Comedy. Optimistic dialectics drives, music out of tragedy with the scourge of its syllogisms: that is, it destroys the essence of tragedy, which can be explained only as a manifestation and illustration of Dionysian states, as the visible symbolisation of music, as the dream-world of Dionysian ecstasy.

If, therefore, we are to assume an anti-Dionysian tendency operating even before Socrates, which received in him only an unprecedentedly grand expression, we must not shrink from the question as to what a phenomenon like that of Socrates indicates: whom in view of the Platonic dialogues we are certainly not entitled to regard as a purely disintegrating, negative power. And though there can be no doubt whatever that the most immediate effect of the Socratic impulse tended to the dissolution of Dionysian tragedy, yet a profound experience of Socrates' own life compels us to ask whether there is necessarily only an antipodal relation between Socratism and art, and whether the birth of an "artistic Socrates" is in general something contradictory in itself.

For that despotic logician had now and then the feeling of a gap, or void, a sentiment of semi-reproach, as of a possibly neglected duty with respect to art. There often came to him, as he tells his friends in prison, one and the same dream-apparition, which kept constantly repeating to him: "Socrates, practise music." Up to his very last days he solaces himself with the opinion that his philosophising is the highest form of poetry, and finds it hard to believe that a deity will remind him of the "common, popular music." Finally, when in prison, he consents to practise also this despised music, in order thoroughly to unburden his conscience. And in this frame of mind he composes a poem on Apollo and turns a few Æsopian fables into verse. It was something similar to the demonian warning voice which urged him to these practices; it was because of his Apollonian insight that, like a barbaric king, he did not understand the noble image of a god and was in danger of sinning against a deity—through ignorance. The prompting voice of the

Socratic dream-vision is the only sign of doubtfulness as to the limits of logical nature. "Perhaps "—thus he had to ask himself—"what is not intelligible to me is not therefore unreasonable? Perhaps there is a realm of wisdom from which the logician is banished? Perhaps art is even a necessary correlative of and supplement to science?"

15.

In the sense of these last portentous questions it must now be indicated how the influence of Socrates (extending to the present moment, indeed, to all futurity) has spread over posterity like an ever-increasing shadow in the evening sun, and how this influence again and again necessitates a regeneration of art,—yea, of art already with metaphysical, broadest and profoundest sense,—and its own eternity guarantees also the eternity of art.

Before this could be perceived, before the intrinsic dependence of every art on the Greeks, the Greeks from Homer to Socrates, was conclusively demonstrated, it had to happen to us with regard to these Greeks as it happened to the Athenians with regard to Socrates. Nearly every age and stage of culture has at some time or other sought with deep displeasure to free itself from the Greeks, because in their presence everything self- achieved, sincerely admired and apparently quite original, seemed all of a sudden to lose life and colour and shrink to an abortive copy, even to caricature. And so hearty indignation breaks forth time after time against this presumptuous little nation, which dared to designate as "barbaric" for all time everything not native: who are they, one asks one's self, who, though they possessed only an ephemeral historical splendour, ridiculously restricted institutions, a dubious excellence in their customs, and were even branded with ugly vices, yet lay claim to the dignity and singular position among the peoples to which genius is entitled among the masses. What a pity one has not been so fortunate as to find the cup of hemlock with which such an affair could be disposed of without ado: for all the poison which envy, calumny, and rankling resentment engendered within themselves have not sufficed to destroy that self- sufficient grandeur! And so one feels ashamed and afraid in the presence of the Greeks: unless one prize truth above all things, and dare also to acknowledge to one's self this truth, that the Greeks, as charioteers, hold in their hands the reins of our own and of every culture, but that almost always chariot and horses are of too poor material and incommensurate with the glory of their guides, who then will deem it sport to run such a team into an abyss: which they themselves clear with the leap of Achilles.

In order to assign also to Socrates the dignity of such a

leading position, it will suffice to recognise in him the type of an unheard-of form of existence, the type of the theoretical man, with regard to whose meaning and purpose it will be our next task to attain an insight. Like the artist, the theorist also finds an infinite satisfaction in what is and, like the former, he is shielded by this satisfaction from the practical ethics of pessimism with its lynx eyes which shine only in the dark. For if the artist in every unveiling of truth always cleaves with raptured eyes only to that which still remains veiled after the unveiling, the theoretical man, on the other hand, enjoys and contents himself with the cast-off veil, and finds the consummation of his pleasure in the process of a continuously successful unveiling through his own unaided efforts. There would have been no science if it had only been concerned about that one naked goddess and nothing else. For then its disciples would have been obliged to feel like those who purposed to dig a hole straight through the earth: each one of whom perceives that with the utmost lifelong exertion he is able to excavate only a very little of the enormous depth, which is again filled up before his eyes by the labours of his successor, so that a third man seems to do well when on his own account he selects a new spot for his attempts at tunnelling. If now some one proves conclusively that the antipodal goal cannot be attained in this direct way, who will still care to toil on in the old depths, unless he has learned to content himself in the meantime with finding precious stones or discovering natural laws? For that reason Lessing, the most honest theoretical man, ventured to say that he cared more for the search after truth than for truth itself: in saying which he revealed the fundamental secret of science, to the astonishment, and indeed, to the vexation of scientific men. Well, to be sure, there stands alongside of this detached perception, as an excess of honesty, if not of presumption, a profound illusion which first came to the world in the person of Socrates, the imperturbable belief that, by means of the clue of causality, thinking reaches to the deepest abysses of being, and that thinking is able not only to perceive being but even to correct it. This sublime metaphysical illusion is added as an instinct to science and again and again leads the latter to its limits, where it must change into art; which is really the end, to be attained by this mechanism.

If we now look at Socrates in the light of this thought, he appears to us as the first who could not only live, but— what is far more—also die under the guidance of this instinct of science: and hence the picture of the dying, Socrates, as the man delivered from the fear of death by knowledge and argument, is the escutcheon, above the entrance to science which reminds every one of its mission, namely, to make existence appear to be comprehensible, and therefore to be justified: for which purpose, if arguments do not suffice, myth also must be used, which I just now designated even as the necessary consequence, yea, as the end of science.

He who once makes intelligible to himself how, after the death of Socrates, the mystagogue of science, one philosophical school succeeds another, like wave upon wave,—how an entirely unfore-shadowed universal development of the thirst for knowledge in the widest compass of the cultured world (and as the specific task for every one highly gifted) led science on to the high sea from which since then it has never again been able to be completely ousted; how through the universality of this movement a common net of thought was first stretched over the entire globe, with prospects, moreover, of conformity to law in an entire solar system;—he who realises all this, together with the amazingly high pyramid of our present-day knowledge, cannot fail to see in Socrates the turning-point and vortex of so-called universal history. For if one were to imagine the whole incalculable sum of energy which has been used up by that universal tendency,—employed, not in the service of knowledge, but for the practical, i.e., egoistical ends of individuals and peoples,—then probably the instinctive love of life would be so much weakened in universal wars of destruction and incessant migrations of peoples, that, owing to the practice of suicide, the individual would perhaps feel the last remnant of a sense of duty, when, like the native of the Fiji Islands, as son he strangles his parents and, as friend, his friend: a practical pessimism which might even give rise to a horrible ethics of general slaughter out of pity—which, for the rest, exists and has existed wherever art in one form or another, especially as science and religion, has not appeared as a remedy and preventive of that pestilential breath.

In view of this practical pessimism, Socrates is the archetype of the theoretical optimist, who in the above-indicated belief in the fathomableness of the nature of things, attributes to knowledge and perception the power of a universal medicine, and sees in error and evil. To penetrate into the depths of the nature of things, and to separate true perception from error and illusion, appeared to the Socratic man the noblest and even the only truly human calling: just as from the time of Socrates onwards the mechanism of concepts, judgments, and inferences was prized above all other capacities as the highest activity and the most admirable gift of nature. Even the sublimest moral acts, the stirrings of pity, of self-sacrifice, of heroism, and that tranquillity of soul, so difficult of attainment, which the Apollonian Greek called Sophrosyne, were derived by Socrates, and his like-minded successors up to the present day, from the dialectics of knowledge, and were accordingly designated as teachable. He who has experienced in himself the joy of a Socratic perception, and felt how it seeks to embrace, in constantly widening circles, the entire world of phenomena, will thenceforth find no stimulus which could urge him to existence more forcible than the desire to complete that conquest and to knit the net impenetrably close. To a person thus minded the Platonic Socrates then appears as the teacher of an entirely new form of "Greek cheerfulness" and felicity of existence, which seeks to discharge itself in actions, and will find its discharge for the most part in maieutic and pedagogic influences on noble youths, with a view to the ultimate production of genius.

But now science, spurred on by its powerful illusion, hastens irresistibly to its limits, on which its optimism, hidden in the essence of logic, is wrecked. For the periphery of the circle of science has an infinite number of points, and while there is still no telling how this circle can ever be completely measured, yet the noble and gifted man, even before the middle of his career, inevitably comes into contact with those extreme points of the periphery where he stares at the inexplicable. When he here sees to his dismay how logic coils round itself at these limits and finally bites its own tail—then the new form of perception discloses itself, namely tragic perception, which, in order even to be endured, requires art as a safeguard and remedy.

If, with eyes strengthened and refreshed at the sight of the Greeks, we look upon the highest spheres of the world that surrounds us, we behold the avidity of the insatiate optimistic knowledge, of which Socrates is the typical representative, transformed into tragic resignation and the need of art: while, to be sure, this same avidity, in its lower stages, has to exhibit itself as antagonistic to art, and must especially have an inward detestation of Dionyso-tragic art, as was exemplified in the opposition of Socratism to Æschylean tragedy.

Here then with agitated spirit we knock at the gates of the present and the future: will that "transforming" lead to ever new configurations of genius, and especially of the music-practising Socrates? Will the net of art which is spread over existence, whether under the name of religion or of science, be knit always more closely and delicately, or is it destined to be torn to shreds under the restlessly barbaric activity and whirl which is called "the present day"?—Anxious, yet not disconsolate, we stand aloof for a little while, as the spectators who are permitted to be witnesses of these tremendous struggles and transitions. Alas! It is the charm of these struggles that he who beholds them must also fight them!

16.

By this elaborate historical example we have endeavoured to make it clear that tragedy perishes as surely by evanescence of the spirit of music as it can be born only out of this spirit. In order to qualify the singularity of this assertion, and, on the other hand, to disclose the source of this insight of ours, we must now confront with clear vision the analogous phenomena of the present time; we must enter into the midst of these struggles, which, as I said just now, are being carried on in the highest spheres of our present world between the insatiate optimistic perception and the tragic need of art. In so doing I shall leave out of consideration all other antagonistic tendencies which at all times oppose art, especially tragedy, and which at present again extend their sway triumphantly, to such an extent that of the theatrical arts only the farce and the ballet, for example, put forth their blossoms, which perhaps not every one cares to smell, in tolerably rich luxuriance. I will speak only of the Most Illustrious Opposition to the tragic conception of things—and by this I mean essentially optimistic science, with its ancestor Socrates at the head of it. Presently also the forces will be designated which seem to me to guarantee a re-birth of tragedy—and who knows what other blessed hopes for the German genius!

Before we plunge into the midst of these struggles, let us array ourselves in the armour of our hitherto acquired knowledge. In contrast to all those who are intent on deriving the arts from one exclusive principle, as the necessary vital source of every work of art, I keep my eyes fixed on the two artistic deities of the Greeks, Apollo and Dionysus, and recognise in them the living and conspicuous representatives of two worlds of art which differ in their intrinsic essence and in their highest aims. Apollo stands before me as the transfiguring genius of the principium individuationis through which alone the redemption in appearance is to be truly attained, while by the mystical cheer of Dionysus the spell of individuation is broken, and the way lies open to the Mothers of Being, to the innermost heart of things. This extraordinary antithesis, which opens up yawningly between plastic art as the Apollonian and music as the Dionysian art, has become manifest to only one of the great thinkers, to such an extent that, even without this key to the symbolism of the Hellenic divinities, he allowed to music a different character and origin in advance of all the other arts, because, unlike them, it is not a copy of the phenomenon, but a direct copy of the will itself, and therefore represents the metaphysical of everything physical in the world, the thing-in-itself of every phenomenon. (Schopenhauer, Welt als Wille und Vorstellung, I. 310.) To this most important perception of æsthetics (with which, taken in a serious sense, æsthetics properly commences), Richard Wagner, by way of confirmation of its eternal truth, affixed his seal, when he asserted in his Beethoven that music must be judged according to æsthetic principles quite different from those which apply to the plastic arts, and not, in general, according to the category of beauty: although an erroneous æsthetics, inspired by a misled and degenerate art, has by virtue of the concept of beauty prevailing in the plastic domain accustomed itself to demand of music an effect analogous to that of the works of plastic art, namely the suscitating delight in beautiful forms.

Upon perceiving this extraordinary antithesis, I felt a strong inducement to approach the essence of Greek tragedy, and, by means of it, the profoundest revelation of Hellenic genius: for I at last thought myself to be in possession of a charm to enable me—far beyond the phraseology of our usual æsthetics—to represent vividly to my mind the primitive problem of tragedy: whereby such an astounding insight into the Hellenic character was afforded me that it necessarily seemed as if our proudly comporting classico-Hellenic science had thus far contrived to subsist almost exclusively on phantasmagoria and externalities.

Perhaps we may lead up to this primitive problem with the question: what æsthetic effect results when the intrinsically separate art- powers, the Apollonian and the Dionysian, enter into concurrent actions? Or, in briefer form: how is music related to image and concept?—Schopenhauer, whom Richard Wagner, with especial reference to this point, accredits with an unsurpassable clearness and perspicuity of exposition, expresses himself most copiously on the subject in the following passage which I shall cite here at full length21 (Welt als Wille und Vorstellung, I. p. 309): "According to all this, we may regard the phenomenal world, or nature, and music as two different expressions of the same thing,22 WHich is therefore itself the only medium of the analogy between these two expressions, so that a knowledge of this medium is required in order to understand that analogy. Music, therefore, if regarded as an expression of the world, is in the highest degree a universal language, which is related indeed to the universality of concepts, much as these are related to the particular things. Its universality, however, is by no means the empty universality of abstraction, but of quite a different kind, and is united with thorough and distinct definiteness. In this respect it resembles geometrical figures and numbers, which are the universal forms of all possible objiects of experience and applicable to them all a priori, and yet are not abstract but perceptible and thoroughly determinate. All possible efforts, excitements and manifestations of will, all that goes on in the heart of man and that reason includes in the wide, negative concept of feeling, may be expressed by the infinite number of possible melodies, but always in the universality of mere form, without the material, always according to the thing-in-itself, not the phenomenon,—of which they reproduce the very soul and essence as it were, without the body. This deep relation which music bears to the true nature of all things also explains the fact that suitable music played to any scene, action, event, or surrounding seems to disclose to us its most secret meaning, and appears as the most accurate and distinct commentary upon it; as also the fact that whoever gives himself up entirely to the impression of a That is "the will" as understood by Schopenhauer.—TR. symphony seems to see all the possible events of life and the world take place in himself: nevertheless upon reflection he can find no likeness between the music and the things that passed before his mind. For, as we have said, music is distinguished from all the other arts by the fact that it is not a copy of the phenomenon, or, more accurately, the adequate objectivity of the will, but the direct copy of the will itself, and therefore represents the metaphysical of everything physical in the world, and the thing-in-itself of every phenomenon. We might, therefore, just as well call the world embodied music as embodied will: and this is the reason why music makes every picture, and indeed every scene of real life and of the world, at once appear with higher significance; all the more so, to be sure, in proportion as its melody is analogous to the inner spirit of the given phenomenon. It rests upon this that we are able to set a poem to music as a song, or a perceptible representation as a pantomime, or both as an opera. Such particular pictures of human life, set to the universal language of music, are never bound to it or correspond to it with stringent necessity, but stand to it only in the relation of an example chosen at will to a general concept. In the determinateness of the real they represent that which music expresses in the universality of mere form. For melodies are to a certain extent, like general concepts, an abstraction from the actual. This actual world, then, the world of particular things, affords the object of perception, the special and the individual, the particular case, both to the universality of concepts and to the universality of the melodies. But these two universalities are in a certain respect opposed to each other; for the concepts contain only the forms, which are first of all abstracted from perception,—the separated outward shell of things, as it were,—and hence they are, in the strictest sense of the term, abstracta; music, on the other hand, gives the inmost kernel which precedes all forms, or the heart of things. This relation may be very well expressed in the language of the schoolmen, by saying: the concepts are the universalia post rem, but music gives the universalia ante rem, and the real world the universalia in re.—But that in general a relation is possible between a composition and a perceptible representation rests, as we have said, upon the fact that both are simply different expressions of the same inner being of the world. When now, in the particular case, such a relation is actually given, that is to say, when the composer has been able to express in the universal language of music the emotions of will which constitute the heart of an event, then the melody of the song, the music of the opera, is expressive. But the analogy discovered by the composer between the two must have proceeded from the direct knowledge of the nature of the world unknown to his reason, and must not be an imitation produced with conscious intention by means of conceptions; otherwise the music does not express the inner nature of the will itself, but merely gives an inadequate imitation of its phenomenon: all specially imitative music does this."

We have therefore, according to the doctrine of

Schopenhauer, an immediate understanding of music as the language of the will, and feel our imagination stimulated to give form to this invisible and yet so actively stirred spirit-world which speaks to us, and prompted to embody it in an analogous example. On the other hand, image and concept, under the influence of a truly conformable music, acquire a higher significance. Dionysian art therefore is wont to exercise—two kinds of influences, on the Apollonian art-faculty: music firstly incites to the symbolic intuition of Dionysian universality, and, secondly, it causes the symbolic image to stand forth in its fullest significance. From these facts, intelligible in themselves and not inaccessible to profounder observation, I infer the capacity of music to give birth to myth, that is to say, the most significant exemplar, and precisely tragic myth: the myth which speaks of Dionysian knowledge in symbols. In the phenomenon of the lyrist, I have set forth that in him music strives to express itself with regard to its nature in Apollonian images. If now we reflect that music in its highest potency must seek to attain also to its highest symbolisation, we must deem it possible that it also knows how to find the symbolic expression of its inherent Dionysian wisdom; and where shall we have to seek for this expression if not in tragedy and, in general, in the conception of the tragic?

From the nature of art, as it is ordinarily conceived according to the single category of appearance and beauty, the tragic cannot be honestly deduced at all; it is only through the spirit of music that we understand the joy in the annihilation of the individual. For in the particular examples of such annihilation only is the eternal phenomenon of Dionysian art made clear to us, which gives expression to the will in its omnipotence, as it were, behind the principium individuationis, the eternal life beyond all phenomena, and in spite of all annihilation. The metaphysical delight in the tragic is a translation of the instinctively unconscious Dionysian wisdom into the language of the scene: the hero, the highest manifestation of the will, is disavowed for our pleasure, because he is only phenomenon, and because the eternal life of the will is not affected by his annihilation. "We believe in eternal life," tragedy exclaims; while music is the proximate idea of this life. Plastic art has an altogether different object: here Apollo vanquishes the suffering of the individual by the radiant glorification of the eternity of the phenomenon; here beauty triumphs over the suffering inherent in life; pain is in a manner surreptitiously obliterated from the features of nature. In Dionysian art and its tragic symbolism the same nature speaks to us with its true undissembled voice: "Be as I am! Amidst the ceaseless change of phenomena the eternally creative primordial mother, eternally impelling to existence, self-satisfying eternally with this change of phenomena!" Dionysian art, too, seeks to convince us of the eternal joy of existence: only we are to seek this joy not in phenomena, but behind phenomena. We are to perceive how all that comes into being must be ready for a sorrowful end; we are compelled to look into the terrors of individual existence— yet we are not to become torpid: a metaphysical comfort tears us momentarily from the bustle of the transforming figures. We are really for brief moments Primordial Being itself, and feel its indomitable desire for being and joy in existence; the struggle, the pain, the destruction of phenomena, now appear to us as something necessary, considering the surplus of innumerable forms of existence which throng and push one another into life, considering the exuberant fertility of the universal will. We are pierced by the maddening sting of these pains at the very moment when we have become, as it were, one with the immeasurable primordial joy in existence, and when we anticipate, in Dionysian ecstasy, the indestructibility and eternity of this joy. In spite of fear and pity, we are the happy living beings, not as individuals, but as the one living being, with whose procreative joy we are blended.

The history of the rise of Greek tragedy now tells us with luminous precision that the tragic art of the Greeks was really born of the spirit of music: with which conception we believe we have done justice for the first time to the original and most astonishing significance of the chorus. At the same time, however, we must admit that the import of tragic myth as set forth above never became transparent with sufficient lucidity to the Greek poets, let alone the Greek philosophers; their heroes speak, as it were, more superficially than they act; the myth does not at all find its adequate objectification in the spoken word. The structure of the scenes and the conspicuous images reveal a deeper wisdom than the poet himself can put into words and concepts: the same being also observed in Shakespeare, whose Hamlet, for instance, in an analogous manner talks more superficially than he acts, so that the previously mentioned lesson of Hamlet is to be gathered not from his words, but from a more profound contemplation and survey of the whole. With respect to Greek tragedy, which of course presents itself to us only as word-drama, I have even intimated that the incongruence between myth and expression might easily tempt us to regard it as shallower and less significant than it really is, and accordingly to postulate for it a more superficial effect than it must have had according to the testimony of the ancients: for how easily one forgets that what the word-poet did not succeed in doing, namely realising the highest spiritualisation and ideality of myth, he might succeed in doing every moment as creative musician! We require, to be sure, almost by philological method to reconstruct for ourselves the ascendency of musical influence in order to receive something of the incomparable comfort which must be characteristic of true tragedy. Even this musical ascendency, however, would only have been felt by us as such had we been Greeks: while in the entire development of Greek music—as compared with the infinitely richer music known and familiar to us—we imagine we hear only the youthful song of the musical genius intoned with a feeling of diffidence. The Greeks are, as the Egyptian priests say, eternal children, and in tragic art also they are only children who do not know what a sublime play-thing has originated under their hands and—is being demolished.

That striving of the spirit of music for symbolic and mythical manifestation, which increases from the beginnings of lyric poetry to Attic tragedy, breaks off all of a sudden immediately after attaining luxuriant development, and disappears, as it were, from the surface of Hellenic art: while the Dionysian view of things born of this striving lives on in Mysteries and, in its strangest metamorphoses and debasements, does not cease to attract earnest natures. Will it not one day rise again as art out of its mystic depth?

Here the question occupies us, whether the power by the counteracting influence of which tragedy perished, has for all time strength enough to prevent the artistic reawaking of tragedy and of the tragic view of things. If ancient tragedy was driven from its course by the dialectical desire for knowledge and the optimism of science, it might be inferred that there is an eternal conflict between the theoretic and the tragic view of things, and only after the spirit of science has been led to its boundaries, and its claim to universal validity has been destroyed by the evidence of these boundaries, can we hope for a re-birth of tragedy: for which form of culture we should have to use the symbol of the music-practising Socrates in the sense spoken of above. In this contrast, I understand by the spirit of science the belief which first came to light in the person of Socrates,—the belief in the fathomableness of nature and in knowledge as a panacea. He who recalls the immediate consequences of this restlessly onward- pressing spirit of science will realise at once that myth was annihilated by it, and that, in consequence of this annihilation, poetry was driven as a homeless being from her natural ideal soil. If we have rightly assigned to music the capacity to reproduce myth from itself, we may in turn expect to find the spirit of science on the path where it inimically opposes this mythopoeic power of music. This takes place in the development of the New Attic Dithyramb, the music of which no longer expressed the inner essence, the will itself, but only rendered the phenomenon insufficiently, in an imitation by means of concepts; from which intrinsically degenerate music the truly musical natures turned away with the same repugnance that they felt for the art-destroying tendency of Socrates. The unerring instinct of Aristophanes surely did the proper thing when it comprised Socrates himself, the tragedy of Euripides, and the music of the new Dithyrambic poets in the same feeling of hatred, and perceived in all three phenomena the symptoms of a degenerate culture. By this New Dithyramb, music has in an outrageous manner been made the imitative portrait of phenomena, for instance, of a battle or a storm at sea, and has thus, of course, been entirely deprived of its mythopoeic power. For if it endeavours to excite our delight only by compelling us to seek external analogies between a vital or natural process and certain rhythmical figures and characteristic sounds of music; if our understanding is expected to satisfy itself with the perception of these analogies, we are reduced to a frame of mind in which the reception of the mythical is impossible; for the myth as a unique exemplar of generality and truth towering into the infinite, desires to be conspicuously perceived. The truly Dionysean music presents itself to us as such a general mirror of the universal will: the conspicuous event which is refracted in this mirror expands at once for our consciousness to the copy of an eternal truth. Conversely, such a conspicious event is at once divested of every mythical character by the tone-painting of the New Dithyramb; music has here become a wretched copy of the phenomenon, and therefore infinitely poorer than the phenomenon itself: through which poverty it still further reduces even the phenomenon for our consciousness, so that now, for instance, a musically imitated battle of this sort exhausts itself in marches, signal- sounds, etc., and our imagination is arrested precisely by these superficialities. Tone-painting is therefore in every respect the counterpart of true music with its mythopoeic power: through it the phenomenon, poor in itself, is made still poorer, while through an isolated Dionysian music the phenomenon is evolved and expanded into a picture of the world. It was an immense triumph of the non-Dionysian spirit, when, in the development of the New Dithyramb, it had estranged music from itself and reduced it to be the slave of phenomena. Euripides, who, albeit in a higher sense, must be designated as a thoroughly unmusical nature, is for this very reason a passionate adherent of the New Dithyrambic Music, and with the liberality of a freebooter employs all its effective turns and mannerisms.

In another direction also we see at work the power of this un-Dionysian, myth-opposing spirit, when we turn our eyes to the prevalence of character representation and psychological refinement from Sophocles onwards. The character must no longer be expanded into an eternal type, but, on the contrary, must operate individually through artistic by-traits and shadings, through the nicest precision of all lines, in such a manner that the spectator is in general no longer conscious of the myth, but of the mighty nature-myth and the imitative power of the artist. Here also we observe the victory of the phenomenon over the Universal, and the delight in the particular quasi-anatomical preparation; we actually breathe the air of a theoretical world, in which scientific knowledge is valued more highly than the artistic reflection of a universal law. The movement along the line of the representation of character proceeds rapidly: while Sophocles still delineates complete characters and employs myth for their refined development, Euripides already delineates only prominent individual traits of character, which can express themselves in violent bursts of passion; in the New Attic Comedy, however, there are only masks with one expression: frivolous old men, duped panders, and cunning slaves in untiring repetition.

Where now is the mythopoeic spirit of music? What is still left now of music is either excitatory music or souvenir music, that is, either a stimulant for dull and used-up nerves, or tone-painting. As regards the former, it hardly matters about the text set to it: the heroes and choruses of Euripides are already dissolute enough when once they begin to sing; to what pass must things have come with his brazen successors?

The new un-Dionysian spirit, however, manifests itself most clearly in the dénouements of the new dramas. In the Old Tragedy one could feel at the close the metaphysical comfort, without which the delight in tragedy cannot be explained at all; the conciliating tones from another world sound purest, perhaps, in the Œdipus at Colonus. Now that the genius of music has fled from tragedy, tragedy is, strictly speaking, dead: for from whence could one now draw the metaphysical comfort? One sought, therefore, for an earthly unravelment of the tragic dissonance; the hero, after he had been sufficiently tortured by fate, reaped a well-deserved reward through a superb marriage or divine tokens of favour. The hero had turned gladiator, on whom, after being liberally battered about and covered with wounds, freedom was occasionally bestowed. The deus ex machina took the place of metaphysical comfort. I will not say that the tragic view of things was everywhere completely destroyed by the intruding spirit of the un-Dionysian: we only know that it was compelled to flee from art into the under-world as it were, in the degenerate form of a secret cult. Over the widest extent of the Hellenic character, however, there raged the consuming blast of this spirit, which manifests itself in the form of "Greek cheerfulness," which we have already spoken of as a senile, unproductive love of existence; this cheerfulness is the counterpart of the splendid "naïveté" of the earlier Greeks, which, according to the characteristic indicated above, must be conceived as the blossom of the Apollonian culture growing out of a dark abyss, as the victory which the Hellenic will, through its mirroring of beauty, obtains over suffering and the wisdom of suffering. The noblest manifestation of that other form of "Greek cheerfulness," the Alexandrine, is the cheerfulness of the theoretical man: it exhibits the same symptomatic characteristics as I have just inferred concerning the spirit of the un- Dionysian:—it combats Dionysian wisdom and art, it seeks to dissolve myth, it substitutes for metaphysical comfort an earthly consonance, in fact, a deus ex machina of its own, namely the god of machines and crucibles, that is, the powers of the genii of nature recognised and employed in the service of higher egoism; it believes in amending the world by knowledge, in guiding life by science, and that it can really confine the individual within a narrow sphere of solvable problems, where he cheerfully says to life: "I desire thee: it is worth while to know thee."

18.

It is an eternal phenomenon: the avidious will can always, by means of an illusion spread over things, detain its creatures in life and compel them to live on. One is chained by the Socratic love of knowledge and the vain hope of being able thereby to heal the eternal wound of existence; another is ensnared by art's seductive veil of beauty fluttering before his eyes; still another by the metaphysical comfort that eternal life flows on indestructibly beneath the whirl of phenomena: to say nothing of the more ordinary and almost more powerful illusions which the will has always at hand. These three specimens of illusion are on the whole designed only for the more nobly endowed natures, who in general feel profoundly the weight and burden of existence, and must be deluded into forgetfulness of their displeasure by exquisite stimulants. All that we call culture is made up of these stimulants; and, according to the proportion of the ingredients, we have either a specially Socratic or artistic or tragic culture: or, if historical exemplifications are wanted, there is either an Alexandrine or a Hellenic or a Buddhistic culture.

Our whole modern world is entangled in the meshes of Alexandrine culture, and recognises as its ideal the theorist equipped with the most potent means of knowledge, and labouring in the service of science, of whom the archetype and progenitor is Socrates. All our educational methods have originally this ideal in view: every other form of existence must struggle onwards wearisomely beside it, as something tolerated, but not intended. In an almost alarming manner the cultured man was here found for a long time only in the form of the scholar: even our poetical arts have been forced to evolve from learned imitations, and in the main effect of the rhyme we still recognise the origin of our poetic form from artistic experiments with a non-native and thoroughly learned language. How unintelligible must Faust, the modern cultured man, who is in himself intelligible, have appeared to a true Greek,—Faust, storming discontentedly through all the faculties, devoted to magic and the devil from a desire for knowledge, whom we have only to place alongside of Socrates for the purpose of comparison, in order to see that modern man begins to divine the boundaries of this Socratic love of perception and longs for a coast in the wide waste of the ocean of knowledge. When Goethe on one occasion said to Eckermann with reference to Napoleon: "Yes, my good friend, there is also a productiveness of deeds," he reminded us in a charmingly naïve manner that the non-theorist is something incredible and astounding to modern man; so that the wisdom of Goethe is needed once more in order to discover that such a surprising form of existence is comprehensible, nay even pardonable.

Now, we must not hide from ourselves what is concealed in the heart of this Socratic culture: Optimism, deeming itself absolute! Well, we must not be alarmed if the fruits of this optimism ripen,—if society, leavened to the very lowest strata by this kind of culture, gradually begins to tremble through wanton agitations and desires, if the belief in the earthly happiness of all, if the belief in the possibility of such a general intellectual culture is gradually transformed into the threatening demand for such an Alexandrine earthly happiness, into the conjuring of a Euripidean deus ex machina. Let us mark this well: the Alexandrine culture requires a slave class, to be able to exist permanently: but, in its optimistic view of life, it denies the necessity of such a class, and consequently, when the effect of its beautifully seductive and tranquillising utterances about the "dignity of man" and the "dignity of labour" is spent, it gradually drifts towards a dreadful destination. There is nothing more terrible than a barbaric slave class, who have learned to regard their existence as an injustice, and now prepare to take vengeance, not only for themselves, but for all generations. In the face of such threatening storms, who dares to appeal with confident spirit to our pale and exhausted religions, which even in their foundations have degenerated into scholastic religions?—so that myth, the necessary prerequisite of every religion, is already paralysed everywhere, and even in this domain the optimistic spirit—which we have just designated as the annihilating germ of society—has attained the mastery.

While the evil slumbering in the heart of theoretical

culture gradually begins to disquiet modern man, and makes him anxiously ransack the stores of his experience for means to avert the danger, though not believing very much in these means; while he, therefore, begins to divine the consequences his position involves: great, universally gifted natures have contrived, with an incredible amount of thought, to make use of the apparatus of science itself, in order to point out the limits and the relativity of knowledge generally, and thus definitely to deny the claim of science to universal validity and universal ends: with which demonstration the illusory notion was for the first time recognised as such, which pretends, with the aid of causality, to be able to fathom the innermost essence of things. The extraordinary courage and wisdom of Kant and Schopenhauer have succeeded in gaining the most, difficult, victory, the victory over the optimism hidden in the essence of logic, which optimism in turn is the basis of our culture. While this optimism, resting on apparently unobjectionable æterna veritates, believed in the intelligibility and solvability of all the riddles of the world, and treated space, time, and causality as totally unconditioned laws of the most universal validity, Kant, on the other hand, showed that these served in reality only to elevate the mere phenomenon, the work of Mâyâ, to the sole and highest reality, putting it in place of the innermost and true essence of things, thus making the actual knowledge of this essence impossible, that is, according to the expression of Schopenhauer, to lull the dreamer still more soundly asleep (Welt als Wille und Vorstellung, I. 498). With this knowledge a culture is inaugurated which I venture to designate as a tragic culture; the most important characteristic of which is that wisdom takes the place of science as the highest end,— wisdom, which, uninfluenced by the seductive distractions of the sciences, turns with unmoved eye to the comprehensive view of the world, and seeks to apprehend therein the eternal suffering as its own with sympathetic feelings of love. Let us imagine a rising generation with this undauntedness of vision, with this heroic desire for the prodigious, let us imagine the bold step of these dragon-slayers, the proud and daring spirit with which they turn their backs on all the effeminate doctrines of optimism in order "to live resolutely" in the Whole and in the Full: would it not be necessary for the tragic man of this culture, with his self- discipline to earnestness and terror, to desire a new art, the art of metaphysical comfort,—namely, tragedy, as the Hellena belonging to him, and that he should exclaim with Faust:

Und sollt' ich nicht, sehnsüchtigster Gewalt, In's Leben ziehn die einzigste Gestalt?23

But now that the Socratic culture has been shaken from two directions, and is only able to hold the sceptre of its infallibility with trembling hands,—once by the fear of its own conclusions which it at length begins to surmise, and again, because it is no longer convinced with its former naïve trust of the eternal validity of its foundation, —it is a sad spectacle to behold how the dance of its thought always rushes longingly on new forms, to embrace them, and then, shuddering, lets them go of a sudden, as Mephistopheles does the seductive Lamiæ. It is certainly the symptom of the "breach" which all are wont to speak of as the primordial suffering of modern culture that the theoretical man, alarmed and dissatisfied at his own conclusions, no longer dares to entrust himself to the terrible ice-stream of existence: he runs timidly up and down the bank. He no longer wants to have anything entire, with all the natural cruelty of things, so thoroughly has he been spoiled by his optimistic contemplation. Besides, he feels that a culture built up on the principles of science must perish when it begins to grow illogical, that is, to avoid its own conclusions. Our art reveals this universal trouble: in vain does one seek help by imitating all the great productive periods and natures, in vain does one accumulate the entire "world-literature" around modern man for his comfort, in vain does one place one's self in the midst of the art-styles and artists of all ages, so that one may give names to them as Adam did to the beasts: one still continues the eternal hungerer, the "critic" without joy and energy, the Alexandrine man, who is in the main a librarian and corrector of proofs, and who, pitiable wretch goes blind from the dust of books and printers' errors.

19.

We cannot designate the intrinsic substance of Socratic culture more distinctly than by calling it the culture of the opera: for it is in this department that culture has expressed itself with special naïveté concerning its aims and perceptions, which is sufficiently surprising when we compare the genesis of the opera and the facts of operatic development with the eternal truths of the Apollonian and Dionysian. I call to mind first of all the origin of the stilo rappresentativo and the recitative. Is it credible that this thoroughly externalised operatic music, incapable of devotion, could be received and cherished with enthusiastic favour, as a re-birth, as it were, of all true music, by the very age in which the ineffably sublime and sacred music of Palestrina had originated? And who, on the other hand, would think of making only the diversion-craving luxuriousness of those Florentine circles and the vanity of their dramatic singers responsible for the love of the opera which spread with such rapidity? That in the same age, even among the same people, this passion for a half-musical mode of speech should awaken alongside of the vaulted structure of Palestrine harmonies which the entire Christian Middle Age had been building up, I can explain to myself only by a co- operating extra-artistic tendency in the essence of the recitative.

The listener, who insists on distinctly hearing the words

under the music, has his wishes met by the singer in that he speaks rather than sings, and intensifies the pathetic expression of the words in this half- song: by this intensification of the pathos he facilitates the understanding of the words and surmounts the remaining half of the music. The specific danger which now threatens him is that in some unguarded moment he may give undue importance to music, which would forthwith result in the destruction of the pathos of the speech and the distinctness of the words: while, on the other hand, he always feels himself impelled to musical delivery and to virtuose exhibition of vocal talent. Here the "poet" comes to his aid, who knows how to provide him with abundant opportunities for lyrical interjections, repetitions of words and sentences, etc.,—at which places the singer, now in the purely musical element, can rest himself without minding the words. This alternation of emotionally impressive, yet only half-sung speech and wholly sung interjections, which is characteristic of the stilo rappresentativo, this rapidly changing endeavour to operate now on the conceptional and representative faculty of the hearer, now on his musical sense, is something so thoroughly unnatural and withal so intrinsically contradictory both to the Apollonian and Dionysian artistic impulses, that one has to infer an origin of the recitative foreign to all artistic instincts. The recitative must be defined, according to this description, as the combination of epic and lyric delivery, not indeed as an intrinsically stable combination which could not be attained in the case of such totally disparate elements, but an entirely superficial mosaic conglutination, such as is totally unprecedented in the domain of nature and experience. But this was not the opinion of the inventors of the recitative: they themselves, and their age with them, believed rather that the mystery of antique music had been solved by this stilo rappresentativo, in which, as they thought, the only explanation of the enormous influence of an Orpheus, an

Amphion, and even of Greek tragedy was to be found. The new style was regarded by them as the re- awakening of the most effective music, the Old Greek music: indeed, with the universal and popular conception of the Homeric world as the primitive world, they could abandon themselves to the dream of having descended once more into the paradisiac beginnings of mankind, wherein music also must needs have had the unsurpassed purity, power, and innocence of which the poets could give such touching accounts in their pastoral plays. Here we see into the internal process of development of this thoroughly modern variety of art, the opera: a powerful need here acquires an art, but it is a need of an unæsthetic kind: the yearning for the idyll, the belief in the prehistoric existence of the artistic, good man. The recitative was regarded as the rediscovered language of this primitive man; the opera as the recovered land of this idyllically or heroically good creature, who in every action follows at the same time a natural artistic impulse, who sings a little along with all he has to say, in order to sing immediately with full voice on the slightest emotional excitement. It is now a matter of indifference to us that the humanists of those days combated the old ecclesiastical representation of man as naturally corrupt and lost, with this new-created picture of the paradisiac artist: so that opera may be understood as the oppositional dogma of the good man, whereby however a solace was at the same time found for the pessimism to which precisely the seriously-disposed men of that time were most strongly incited, owing to the frightful uncertainty of all conditions of life. It is enough to have perceived that the intrinsic charm, and therefore the genesis, of this new form of art lies in the gratification of an altogether unæsthetic need, in the optimistic glorification of man as such, in the conception of the primitive man as the man naturally good and artistic: a principle of the opera which has gradually changed into a threatening and terrible demand, which, in face of the socialistic movements of the present time, we can no longer ignore. The "good primitive man" wants his rights: what paradisiac prospects!

I here place by way of parallel still another equally obvious confirmation of my view that opera is built up on the same principles as our Alexandrine culture. Opera is the birth of the theoretical man, of the critical layman, not of the artist: one of the most surprising facts in the whole history of art. It was the demand of thoroughly unmusical hearers that the words must above all be understood, so that according to them a re-birth of music is only to be expected when some mode of singing has been discovered in which the text-word lords over the counterpoint as the master over the servant. For the words, it is argued, are as much nobler than the accompanying harmonic system as the soul is nobler than the body. It was in accordance with the laically unmusical crudeness of these views that the combination of music, picture and expression was effected in the beginnings of the opera: in the spirit of this æsthetics the first experiments were also made in the leading laic circles of Florence by the poets and singers patronised there. The man incapable of art creates for himself a species of art precisely because he is the inartistic man as such. Because he does not divine the Dionysian depth of music, he changes his musical taste into appreciation of the understandable word-and-tone-rhetoric of the passions in the stilo rappresentativo, and into the voluptuousness of the arts of song; because he is unable to behold a vision, he forces the machinist and the decorative artist into his service; because he cannot apprehend the true nature of the artist, he conjures up the "artistic primitive man" to suit his taste, that is, the man who sings and recites verses under the influence of passion. He dreams himself into a time when passion suffices to generate songs and poems: as if emotion had ever been able to create anything artistic. The postulate of the opera is a false belief concerning the artistic process, in fact, the idyllic belief that every sentient man is an artist. In the sense of this belief, opera is the expression of the taste of the laity in art, who dictate their laws with the cheerful optimism of the theorist.

Should we desire to unite in one the two conceptions just set forth as influential in the origin of opera, it would only remain for us to speak of an idyllic tendency of the opera: in which connection we may avail ourselves exclusively of the phraseology and illustration of Schiller.24 "Nature and the ideal," he says, "are either objects of grief, when the former is represented as lost, the latter unattained; or both are objects of joy, in that they are represented as real. The first case furnishes the elegy in its narrower signification, the second the idyll in its widest sense." Here we must at once call attention to the common characteristic of these two conceptions in operatic genesis, namely, that in them the ideal is not regarded as unattained or nature as lost Agreeably to this sentiment, there was a primitive age of man when he lay close to the heart of nature, and, owing to this naturalness, had attained the ideal of mankind in a paradisiac goodness and artist- organisation: from which perfect primitive man all of us were supposed to be descended; whose faithful copy we were in fact still said to be: only we had to cast off some few things in order to recognise ourselves once more as this primitive man, on the strength of a voluntary renunciation of superfluous learnedness, of super-abundant culture. It was to such a concord of nature and the ideal, to an idyllic reality, that the cultured man of the Renaissance suffered himself to be led back by his operatic imitation of Greek tragedy; he made use of this tragedy, as Dante made use of Vergil, in order to be led up to the gates of paradise: while from this point he went on without assistance and passed over from an imitation of the highest form of Greek art to a "restoration of all things," to an imitation of man's original art-world. What delightfully naïve hopefulness of these daring endeavours, in the very heart of theoretical culture!—solely to be explained by the comforting belief, that "man-in- himself" is the eternally virtuous hero of the opera, the eternally fluting or singing shepherd, who must always in the end rediscover himself as such, if he has at any time really lost himself; solely the fruit of the optimism, which here rises like a sweetishly seductive column of vapour out of the depth of the Socratic conception of the world.

The features of the opera therefore do not by any means exhibit the elegiac sorrow of an eternal loss, but rather the cheerfulness of eternal rediscovery, the indolent delight in an idyllic reality which one can at least represent to one's self each moment as real: and in so doing one will perhaps surmise some day that this supposed reality is nothing but a fantastically silly dawdling, concerning which every one, who could judge it by the terrible earnestness of true nature and compare it with the actual primitive scenes of the beginnings of mankind, would have to call out with loathing: Away with the phantom! Nevertheless one would err if one thought it possible to frighten away merely by a vigorous shout such a dawdling thing as the opera, as if it were a spectre. He who would destroy the opera must join issue with Alexandrine cheerfulness, which expresses itself so naïvely therein concerning its favourite representation; of which in fact it is the specific form of art. But what is to be expected for art itself from the operation of a form of art, the beginnings of which do not at all lie in the æsthetic province; which has rather stolen over from a half-moral sphere into the artistic domain, and has been able only now and then to delude us concerning this hybrid origin? By what sap is this parasitic opera-concern nourished, if not by that of true art? Must we not suppose that the highest and indeed the truly serious task of art—to free the eye from its glance into the horrors of night and to deliver the "subject" by the healing balm of appearance from the spasms of volitional agitations—will degenerate under the influence of its idyllic seductions and Alexandrine adulation to an empty dissipating tendency, to pastime? What will become of the eternal truths of the Dionysian and Apollonian in such an amalgamation of styles as I have exhibited in the character of the stilo rappresentativo? where music is regarded as the servant, the text as the master, where music is compared with the body, the text with the soul? where at best the highest aim will be the realisation of a paraphrastic tone-painting, just as formerly in the New Attic Dithyramb? where music is completely alienated from its true dignity of being, the Dionysian mirror of the world, so that the only thing left to it is, as a slave of phenomena, to imitate the formal character thereof, and to excite an external pleasure in the play of lines and proportions. On close observation, this fatal influence of the opera on music is seen to coincide absolutely with the universal development of modern music; the optimism lurking in the genesis of the opera and in the essence of culture represented thereby, has, with alarming rapidity, succeeded in divesting music of its Dionyso- cosmic mission and in impressing on it a playfully formal and pleasurable character: a change with which perhaps only the metamorphosis of the Æschylean man into the cheerful Alexandrine man could be compared.

If, however, in the exemplification herewith indicated we have rightly associated the evanescence of the Dionysian spirit with a most striking, but hitherto unexplained transformation and degeneration of the Hellene—what hopes must revive in us when the most trustworthy auspices guarantee the reverse process, the gradual awakening of the Dionysian spirit in our modern world! It is impossible for the divine strength of Herakles to languish for ever in voluptuous bondage to Omphale. Out of the Dionysian root of the German spirit a power has arisen which has nothing in common with the primitive conditions of Socratic culture, and can neither be explained nor excused thereby, but is rather regarded by this culture as something terribly inexplicable and overwhelmingly hostile, mdash; namely, German music as we have to understand it, especially in its vast solar orbit from Bach to Beethoven, from Beethoven to Wagner. What even under the most favourable circumstances can the knowledge-craving Socratism of our days do with this demon rising from unfathomable depths? Neither by means of the zig-zag and arabesque work of operatic melody, nor with the aid of the arithmetical counting board of fugue and contrapuntal dialectics is the formula to be found, in the trebly powerful light25 of which one could subdue this demon and compel it to speak. What a spectacle, when our æsthetes, with a net of "beauty" peculiar to themselves, now pursue and clutch at the genius of music romping about before them with incomprehensible life, and in so doing display activities which are not to be judged by the standard of eternal beauty any more than by the standard of the sublime. Let us but observe these patrons of music as they are, at close range, when they call out so indefatigably "beauty! beauty!" to discover whether they have the marks of nature's darling children who are fostered and fondled in the lap of the beautiful, or whether they do not rather seek a disguise for their own rudeness, an æsthetical pretext for their own unemotional insipidity: I am thinking here, for instance, of Otto Jahn. But let the liar and the hypocrite beware of our German music: for in the midst of all our culture it is really the only genuine, pure and purifying fire-spirit from which and towards which, as in the teaching of the great Heraclitus of Ephesus, all things move in a double orbit-all that we now call culture, education, civilisation, must appear some day before the unerring judge, Dionysus.

Let us recollect furthermore how Kant and Schopenhauer made it possible for the spirit of German philosophy streaming from the same sources to annihilate the satisfied delight in existence of scientific Socratism by the delimitation of the boundaries thereof; how through this delimitation an infinitely profounder and more serious view of ethical problems and of art was inaugurated, which we may unhesitatingly designate as Dionysian wisdom comprised in concepts. To what then does the mystery of this oneness of German music and philosophy point, if not to a new form of existence, concerning the substance of which we can only inform ourselves presentiently from Hellenic analogies? For to us who stand on the boundary line between two different forms of existence, the Hellenic prototype retains the immeasurable value, that therein all these transitions and struggles are imprinted in a classically instructive form: except that we, as it were, experience analogically in reverse order the chief epochs of the Hellenic genius, and seem now, for instance, to pass backwards from the Alexandrine age to the period of tragedy. At the same time we have the feeling that the birth of a tragic age betokens only a return to itself of the German spirit, a blessed self-rediscovering after excessive and urgent external influences have for a long time compelled it, living as it did in helpless barbaric formlessness, to servitude under their form. It may at last, after returning to the primitive source of its being, venture to stalk along boldly and freely before all nations without hugging the leading-strings of a Romanic civilisation: if only it can learn implicitly of one people—the Greeks, of whom to learn at all is itself a high honour and a rare distinction. And when did we require these highest of all teachers more than at present, when we experience a re-birth of tragedy and are in danger alike of not knowing whence it comes, and of being unable to make clear to ourselves whither it tends.

It may be weighed some day before an impartial judge, in what time and in what men the German spirit has thus far striven most resolutely to learn of the Greeks: and if we confidently assume that this unique praise must be accorded to the noblest intellectual efforts of Goethe, Schiller, and Winkelmann, it will certainly have to be added that since their time, and subsequently to the more immediate influences of these efforts, the endeavour to attain to culture and to the Greeks by this path has in an incomprehensible manner grown feebler and feebler. In order not to despair altogether of the German spirit, must we not infer therefrom that possibly, in some essential matter, even these champions could not penetrate into the core of the Hellenic nature, and were unable to establish a permanent friendly alliance between German and Greek culture? So that perhaps an unconscious perception of this shortcoming might raise also in more serious minds the disheartening doubt as to whether after such predecessors they could advance still farther on this path of culture, or could reach the goal at all. Accordingly, we see the opinions concerning the value of Greek contribution to culture degenerate since that time in the most alarming manner; the expression of compassionate superiority may be heard in the most heterogeneous intellectual and non-intellectual camps, and elsewhere a totally ineffective declamation dallies with "Greek harmony," "Greek beauty," "Greek cheerfulness." And in the very circles whose dignity it might be to draw indefatigably from the Greek channel for the good of German culture, in the circles of the teachers in the higher educational institutions, they have learned best to compromise with the Greeks in good time and on easy terms, to the extent often of a sceptical abandonment of the Hellenic ideal and a total perversion of the true purpose of antiquarian studies. If there be any one at all in these circles who has not completely exhausted himself in the endeavour to be a trustworthy corrector of old texts or a natural-history microscopist of language, he perhaps seeks also to appropriate Grecian antiquity "historically" along with other antiquities, and in any case according to the method and with the supercilious air of our present cultured historiography. When, therefore, the intrinsic efficiency of the higher educational institutions has never perhaps been lower or feebler than at present, when the "journalist," the paper slave of the day, has triumphed over the academic teacher in all matters pertaining to culture, and there only remains to the latter the often previously experienced metamorphosis of now fluttering also, as a cheerful cultured butterfly, in the idiom of the journalist, with the "light elegance" peculiar thereto— with what painful confusion must the cultured persons of a period like the present gaze at the phenomenon (which can perhaps be comprehended analogically only by means of the profoundest principle of the hitherto unintelligible Hellenic genius) of the reawakening of the Dionysian spirit and the re-birth of tragedy? Never has there been another art-period in which so-called culture and true art have been so estranged and opposed, as is so obviously the case at present. We understand why so feeble a culture hates true art; it fears destruction thereby. But must not an entire domain of culture, namely the Socratic- Alexandrine, have exhausted its powers after contriving to culminate in such a daintily-tapering point as our present culture? When it was not permitted to heroes like Goethe and Schiller to break open the enchanted gate which leads into the Hellenic magic mountain, when with their most dauntless striving they did not get beyond the longing gaze which the Goethean Iphigenia cast from barbaric Tauris to her home across the ocean, what could the epigones of such heroes hope for, if the gate should not open to them suddenly of its own accord, in an entirely different position, quite overlooked in all endeavours of culture hitherto—amidst the mystic tones of reawakened tragic music.

Let no one attempt to weaken our faith in an impending

re-birth of Hellenic antiquity; for in it alone we find our hope of a renovation and purification of the German spirit through the fire-magic of music. What else do we know of amidst the present desolation and languor of culture, which could awaken any comforting expectation for the future? We look in vain for one single vigorously-branching root, for a speck of fertile and healthy soil: there is dust, sand, torpidness and languishing everywhere! Under such circumstances a cheerless solitary wanderer could choose for himself no better symbol than the Knight with Death and the Devil, as Dürer has sketched him for us, the mail-clad knight, grim and stern of visage, who is able, unperturbed by his gruesome companions, and yet hopelessly, to pursue his terrible path with horse and hound alone. Our Schopenhauer was such a Dürerian knight: he was destitute of all hope, but he sought the truth. There is not his equal.

But how suddenly this gloomily depicted wilderness of our exhausted culture changes when the Dionysian magic touches it! A hurricane seizes everything decrepit, decaying, collapsed, and stunted; wraps it whirlingly into a red cloud of dust; and carries it like a vulture into the air.

Confused thereby, our glances seek for what has vanished: for what they see is something risen to the golden light as from a depression, so full and green, so luxuriantly alive, so ardently infinite. Tragedy sits in the midst of this exuberance of life, sorrow and joy, in sublime ecstasy; she listens to a distant doleful song—it tells of the Mothers of Being, whose names are: Wahn, Wille, Wehe—Yes, my friends, believe with me in Dionysian life and in the re-birth of tragedy. The time of the Socratic man is past: crown yourselves with ivy, take in your hands the thyrsus, and do not marvel if tigers and panthers lie down fawning at your feet.

Dare now to be tragic men, for ye are to be redeemed! Ye

are to accompany the Dionysian festive procession from India to Greece! Equip yourselves for severe conflict, but believe in the wonders of your god!

21.

Gliding back from these hortative tones into the mood which befits the contemplative man, I repeat that it can only be learnt from the Greeks what such a sudden and miraculous awakening of tragedy must signify for the essential basis of a people's life. It is the people of the tragic mysteries who fight the battles with the Persians: and again, the people who waged such wars required tragedy as a necessary healing potion.

Who would have imagined that there was still such a uniformly powerful effusion of the simplest political sentiments, the most natural domestic instincts and the primitive manly delight in strife in this very people after it had been shaken to its foundations for several generations by the most violent convulsions of the Dionysian demon? If at every considerable spreading of the Dionysian commotion one always perceives that the Dionysian loosing from the shackles of the individual makes itself felt first of all in an increased encroachment on the political instincts, to the extent of indifference, yea even hostility, it is certain, on the other hand, that the state-forming Apollo is also the genius of the principium individuationis, and that the state and domestic sentiment cannot live without an assertion of individual personality. There is only one way from orgasm for a people,—the way to Indian Buddhism, which, in order to be at all endured with its longing for nothingness, requires the rare ecstatic states with their elevation above space, time, and the individual; just as these in turn demand a philosophy which teaches how to overcome the indescribable depression of the intermediate states by means of a fancy. With the same necessity, owing to the unconditional dominance of political impulses, a people drifts into a path of extremest secularisation, the most magnificent, but also the most terrible expression of which is the Roman imperium.

Placed between India and Rome, and constrained to a seductive choice, the Greeks succeeded in devising in classical purity still a third form of life, not indeed for long private use, but just on that account for immortality. For it holds true in all things that those whom the gods love die young, but, on the other hand, it holds equally true that they then live eternally with the gods. One must not demand of what is most noble that it should possess the durable toughness of leather; the staunch durability, which, for instance, was inherent in the national character of the Romans, does not probably belong to the indispensable predicates of perfection. But if we ask by what physic it was possible for the Greeks, in their best period, notwithstanding the extraordinary strength of their Dionysian and political impulses, neither to exhaust themselves by ecstatic brooding, nor by a consuming scramble for empire and worldly honour, but to attain the splendid mixture which we find in a noble, inflaming, and contemplatively disposing wine, we must remember the enormous power of tragedy, exciting, purifying, and disburdening the entire life of a people; the highest value of which we shall divine only when, as in the case of the Greeks, it appears to us as the essence of all the prophylactic healing forces, as the mediator arbitrating between the strongest and most inherently fateful characteristics of a people.

Tragedy absorbs the highest musical orgasm into itself, so that it absolutely brings music to perfection among the Greeks, as among ourselves; but it then places alongside thereof tragic myth and the tragic hero, who, like a mighty Titan, takes the entire Dionysian world on his shoulders and disburdens us thereof; while, on the other hand, it is able by means of this same tragic myth, in the person of the tragic hero, to deliver us from the intense longing for this existence, and reminds us with warning hand of another existence and a higher joy, for which the struggling hero prepares himself presentiently by his destruction, not by his victories. Tragedy sets a sublime symbol, namely the myth between the universal authority of its music and the receptive Dionysian hearer, and produces in him the illusion that music is only the most effective means for the animation of the plastic world of myth. Relying upon this noble illusion, she can now move her limbs for the dithyrambic dance, and abandon herself unhesitatingly to an orgiastic feeling of freedom, in which she could not venture to indulge as music itself, without this illusion. The myth protects us from the music, while, on the other hand, it alone gives the highest freedom thereto. By way of return for this service, music imparts to tragic myth such an impressive and convincing metaphysical significance as could never be attained by word and image, without this unique aid; and the tragic spectator in particular experiences thereby the sure presentiment of supreme joy to which the path through destruction and negation leads; so that he thinks he hears, as it were, the innermost abyss of things speaking audibly to him.

If in these last propositions I have succeeded in giving perhaps only a preliminary expression, intelligible to few at first, to this difficult representation, I must not here desist from stimulating my friends to a further attempt, or cease from beseeching them to prepare themselves, by a detached example of our common experience, for the perception of the universal proposition. In this example I must not appeal to those who make use of the pictures of the scenic processes, the words and the emotions of the performers, in order to approximate thereby to musical perception; for none of these speak music as their mother-tongue, and, in spite of the aids in question, do not get farther than the precincts of musical perception, without ever being allowed to touch its innermost shrines; some of them, like Gervinus, do not even reach the precincts by this path. I have only to address myself to those who, being immediately allied to music, have it as it were for their mother's lap, and are connected with things almost exclusively by unconscious musical relations. I ask the question of these genuine musicians: whether they can imagine a man capable of hearing the third act of Tristan und Isolde without any aid of word or scenery, purely as a vast symphonic period, without expiring by a spasmodic distention of all the wings of the soul? A man who has thus, so to speak, put his ear to the heart-chamber of the cosmic will, who feels the furious desire for existence issuing therefrom as a thundering stream or most gently dispersed brook, into all the veins of the world, would he not collapse all at once? Could he endure, in the wretched fragile tenement of the human individual, to hear the re-echo of countless cries of joy and sorrow from the "vast void of cosmic night," without flying irresistibly towards his primitive home at the sound of this pastoral dance-song of metaphysics? But if, nevertheless, such a work can be heard as a whole, without a renunciation of individual existence, if such a creation could be created without demolishing its creator— where are we to get the solution of this contradiction?

Here there interpose between our highest musical excitement and the music in question the tragic myth and the tragic hero—in reality only as symbols of the most universal facts, of which music alone can speak directly. If, however, we felt as purely Dionysian beings, myth as a symbol would stand by us absolutely ineffective and unnoticed, and would never for a moment prevent us from giving ear to the re-echo of the universalia ante rem. Here, however, the Apollonian power, with a view to the restoration of the well-nigh shattered individual, bursts forth with the healing balm of a blissful illusion: all of a sudden we imagine we see only Tristan, motionless, with hushed voice saying to himself: "the old tune, why does it wake me?" And what formerly interested us like a hollow sigh from the heart of being, seems now only to tell us how "waste and void is the sea." And when, breathless, we thought to expire by a convulsive distention of all our feelings, and only a slender tie bound us to our present existence, we now hear and see only the hero wounded to death and still not dying, with his despairing cry: "Longing! Longing! In dying still longing! for longing not dying!" And if formerly, after such a surplus and superabundance of consuming agonies, the jubilation of the born rent our hearts almost like the very acme of agony, the rejoicing Kurwenal now stands between us and the "jubilation as such," with face turned toward the ship which carries Isolde. However powerfully fellow- suffering encroaches upon us, it nevertheless delivers us in a manner from the primordial suffering of the world, just as the symbol-image of the myth delivers us from the immediate perception of the highest cosmic idea, just as the thought and word deliver us from the unchecked effusion of the unconscious will. The glorious Apollonian illusion makes it appear as if the very realm of tones presented itself to us as a plastic cosmos, as if even the fate of Tristan and Isolde had been merely formed and moulded therein as out of some most delicate and impressible material.

Thus does the Apollonian wrest us from Dionysian universality and fill us with rapture for individuals; to these it rivets our sympathetic emotion, through these it satisfies the sense of beauty which longs for great and sublime forms; it brings before us biographical portraits, and incites us to a thoughtful apprehension of the essence of life contained therein. With the immense potency of the image, the concept, the ethical teaching and the sympathetic emotion—the Apollonian influence uplifts man from his orgiastic self-annihilation, and beguiles him concerning the universality of the Dionysian process into the belief that he is seeing a detached picture of the world, for instance, Tristan and Isolde, and that, through music, he will be enabled to see it still more clearly and intrinsically. What can the healing magic of Apollo not accomplish when it can even excite in us the illusion that the Dionysian is actually in the service of the Apollonian, the effects of which it is capable of enhancing; yea, that music is essentially the representative art for an Apollonian substance?

With the pre-established harmony which obtains between perfect drama and its music, the drama attains the highest degree of conspicuousness, such as is usually unattainable in mere spoken drama. As all the animated figures of the scene in the independently evolved lines of melody simplify themselves before us to the distinctness of the catenary curve, the coexistence of these lines is also audible in the harmonic change which sympathises in a most delicate manner with the evolved process: through which change the relations of things become immediately perceptible to us in a sensible and not at all abstract manner, as we likewise perceive thereby that it is only in these relations that the essence of a character and of a line of melody manifests itself clearly. And while music thus compels us to see more extensively and more intrinsically than usual, and makes us spread out the curtain of the scene before ourselves like some delicate texture, the world of the stage is as infinitely expanded for our spiritualised, introspective eye as it is illumined outwardly from within. How can the word-poet furnish anything analogous, who strives to attain this internal expansion and illumination of the visible stage-world by a much more imperfect mechanism and an indirect path, proceeding as he does from word and concept? Albeit musical tragedy likewise avails itself of the word, it is at the same time able to place alongside thereof its basis and source, and can make the unfolding of the word, from within outwards, obvious to us.

Of the process just set forth, however, it could still be said as decidedly that it is only a glorious appearance, namely the afore-mentioned Apollonian illusion, through the influence of which we are to be delivered from the Dionysian obtrusion and excess. In point of fact, the relation of music to drama is precisely the reverse; music is the adequate idea of the world, drama is but the reflex of this idea, a detached umbrage thereof. The identity between the line of melody and the lining form, between the harmony and the character-relations of this form, is true in a sense antithetical to what one would suppose on the contemplation of musical tragedy. We may agitate and enliven the form in the most conspicuous manner, and enlighten it from within, but it still continues merely phenomenon, from which there is no bridge to lead us into the true reality, into the heart of the world. Music, however, speaks out of this heart; and though countless phenomena of the kind might be passing manifestations of this music, they could never exhaust its essence, but would always be merely its externalised copies. Of course, as regards the intricate relation of music and drama, nothing can be explained, while all may be confused by the popular and thoroughly false antithesis of soul and body; but the unphilosophical crudeness of this antithesis seems to have become—who knows for what reasons—a readily accepted Article of Faith with our æstheticians, while they have learned nothing concerning an antithesis of phenomenon and thing-in- itself, or perhaps, for reasons equally unknown, have not cared to learn anything thereof.

Should it have been established by our analysis that the Apollonian element in tragedy has by means of its illusion gained a complete victory over the Dionysian primordial element of music, and has made music itself subservient to its end, namely, the highest and clearest elucidation of the drama, it would certainly be necessary to add the very important restriction: that at the most essential point this Apollonian illusion is dissolved and annihilated. The drama, which, by the aid of music, spreads out before us with such inwardly illumined distinctness in all its movements and figures, that we imagine we see the texture unfolding on the loom as the shuttle flies to and fro,—attains as a whole an effect which transcends all Apollonian artistic effects. In the collective effect of tragedy, the Dionysian gets the upper hand once more; tragedy ends with a sound which could never emanate from the realm of Apollonian art.

And the Apollonian illusion is thereby found to be what it is,—the assiduous veiling during the performance of tragedy of the intrinsically Dionysian effect: which, however, is so powerful, that it finally forces the Apollonian drama itself into a sphere where it begins to talk with Dionysian wisdom, and even denies itself and its Apollonian conspicuousness. Thus then the intricate relation of the Apollonian and the Dionysian in tragedy must really be symbolised by a fraternal union of the two deities: Dionysus speaks the language of Apollo; Apollo, however, finally speaks the language of Dionysus; and so the highest goal of tragedy and of art in general is attained.

22.

Let the attentive friend picture to himself purely and simply, according to his experiences, the effect of a true musical tragedy. I think I have so portrayed the phenomenon of this effect in both its phases that he will now be able to interpret his own experiences. For he will recollect that with regard to the myth which passed before him he felt himself exalted to a kind of omniscience, as if his visual faculty were no longer merely a surface faculty, but capable of penetrating into the interior, and as if he now saw before him, with the aid of music, the ebullitions of the will, the conflict of motives, and the swelling stream of the passions, almost sensibly visible, like a plenitude of actively moving lines and figures, and could thereby dip into the most tender secrets of unconscious emotions. While he thus becomes conscious of the highest exaltation of his instincts for conspicuousness and transfiguration, he nevertheless feels with equal definitiveness that this long series of Apollonian artistic effects still does not generate the blissful continuance in will-less contemplation which the plasticist and the epic poet, that is to say, the strictly Apollonian artists, produce in him by their artistic productions: to wit, the justification of the world of the individuatio attained in this contemplation,—which is the object and essence of Apollonian art. He beholds the transfigured world of the stage and nevertheless denies it. He sees before him the tragic hero in epic clearness and beauty, and nevertheless delights in his annihilation. He comprehends the incidents of the scene in all their details, and yet loves to flee into the incomprehensible. He feels the actions of the hero to be justified, and is nevertheless still more elated when these actions annihilate their originator. He shudders at the sufferings which will befall the hero, and yet anticipates therein a higher and much more overpowering joy. He sees more extensively and profoundly than ever, and yet wishes to be blind. Whence must we derive this curious internal dissension, this collapse of the Apollonian apex, if not from the Dionysian spell, which, though apparently stimulating the Apollonian emotions to their highest pitch, can nevertheless force this superabundance of Apollonian power into its service? Tragic myth is to be understood only as a symbolisation of Dionysian wisdom by means of the expedients of Apollonian art: the mythus conducts the world of phenomena to its boundaries, where it denies itself, and seeks to flee back again into the bosom of the true and only reality; where it then, like Isolde, seems to strike up its metaphysical swan-song:—

In des Wonnemeeres wogendem Schwall, in der Duft-

Wellen tönendem Schall, in des Weltathems wehendem All—
ertrinken—versinken unbewusst—höchste Lust!26

In the sea of pleasure's Billowing roll,

In the ether-waves Knelling and toll,

In the world-breath's Wavering whole—

To drown in, go down in— Lost in swoon—greatest boon!

We thus realise to ourselves in the experiences of the truly æsthetic hearer the tragic artist himself when he proceeds like a luxuriously fertile divinity of individuation to create his figures (in which sense his work can hardly be understood as an "imitation of nature")—and when, on the other hand, his vast Dionysian impulse then absorbs the entire world of phenomena, in order to anticipate beyond it, and through its annihilation, the highest artistic primal joy, in the bosom of the Primordial Unity. Of course, our æsthetes have nothing to say about this return in fraternal union of the two art-deities to the original home, nor of either the Apollonian or Dionysian excitement of the hearer, while they are indefatigable in characterising the struggle of the hero with fate, the triumph of the moral order of the world, or the disburdenment of the emotions through tragedy, as the properly Tragic: an indefatigableness which makes me think that they are perhaps not æsthetically excitable men at all, but only to be regarded as moral beings when hearing tragedy. Never since Aristotle has an explanation of the tragic effect been proposed, by which an æsthetic activity of the hearer could be inferred from artistic circumstances. At one time fear and pity are supposed to be forced to an alleviating discharge through the serious procedure, at another time we are expected to feel elevated and inspired at the triumph of good and noble principles, at the sacrifice of the hero in the interest of a moral conception of things; and however certainly I believe that for countless men precisely this, and only this, is the effect of tragedy, it as obviously follows therefrom that all these, together with their interpreting æsthetes, have had no experience of tragedy as the highest art. The pathological discharge, the catharsis of Aristotle, which philologists are at a loss whether to include under medicinal or moral phenomena, recalls a remarkable anticipation of Goethe. "Without a lively pathological interest," he says, "I too have never yet succeeded in elaborating a tragic situation of any kind, and hence I have rather avoided than sought it. Can it perhaps have been still another of the merits of the ancients that the deepest pathos was with them merely æsthetic play, whereas with us the truth of nature must co-operate in order to produce such a work?" We can now answer in the affirmative this latter profound question after our glorious experiences, in which we have found to our astonishment in the case of musical tragedy itself, that the deepest pathos can in reality be merely æsthetic play: and therefore we are justified in believing that now for the first time the protophenomenon of the tragic can be portrayed with some degree of success. He who now will still persist in talking only of those vicarious effects proceeding from ultra-æsthetic spheres, and does not feel himself raised above the pathologically-moral process, may be left to despair of his æsthetic nature: for which we recommend to him, by way of innocent equivalent, the interpretation of Shakespeare after the fashion of Gervinus, and the diligent search for poetic justice.

Thus with the re-birth of tragedy the æsthetic hearer is also born anew, in whose place in the theatre a curious quid pro quo was wont to sit with half-moral and half-learned pretensions,—the "critic." In his sphere hitherto everything has been artificial and merely glossed over with a semblance of life. The performing artist was in fact at a loss what to do with such a critically comporting hearer, and hence he, as well as the dramatist or operatic composer who inspired him, searched anxiously for the last remains of life in a being so pretentiously barren and incapable of enjoyment. Such "critics," however, have hitherto constituted the public; the student, the school-boy, yea, even the most harmless womanly creature, were already unwittingly prepared by education and by journals for a similar perception of works of art. The nobler natures among the artists counted upon exciting the moral- religious forces in such a public, and the appeal to a moral order of the world operated vicariously, when in reality some powerful artistic spell should have enraptured the true hearer. Or again, some imposing or at all events exciting tendency of the contemporary political and social world was presented by the dramatist with such vividness that the hearer could forget his critical exhaustion and abandon himself to similar emotions, as, in patriotic or warlike moments, before the tribune of parliament, or at the condemnation of crime and vice:—an estrangement of the true aims of art which could not but lead directly now and then to a cult of tendency. But here there took place what has always taken place in the case of factitious arts, an extraordinary rapid depravation of these tendencies, so that for instance the tendency to employ the theatre as a means for the moral education of the people, which in Schiller's time was taken seriously, is already reckoned among the incredible antiquities of a surmounted culture. While the critic got the upper hand in the theatre and concert-hall, the journalist in the school, and the press in society, art degenerated into a topic of conversation of the most trivial kind, and æsthetic criticism was used as the cement of a vain, distracted, selfish and moreover piteously unoriginal sociality, the significance of which is suggested by the Schopenhauerian parable of the porcupines, so that there has never been so much gossip about art and so little esteem for it. But is it still possible to have intercourse with a man capable of conversing on Beethoven or Shakespeare? Let each answer this question according to his sentiments: he will at any rate show by his answer his conception of "culture," provided he tries at least to answer the question, and has not already grown mute with astonishment.

On the other hand, many a one more nobly and delicately endowed by nature, though he may have gradually become a critical barbarian in the manner described, could tell of the unexpected as well as totally unintelligible effect which a successful performance of Lohengrin, for example, exerted on him: except that perhaps every warning and interpreting hand was lacking to guide him; so that the incomprehensibly heterogeneous and altogether incomparable sensation which then affected him also remained isolated and became extinct, like a mysterious star after a brief brilliancy. He then divined what the æsthetic hearer is.

23.

He who wishes to test himself rigorously as to how he is related to the true æsthetic hearer, or whether he belongs rather to the community of the Socrato-critical man, has only to enquire sincerely concerning the sentiment with which he accepts the wonder represented on the stage: whether he feels his historical sense, which insists on strict psychological causality, insulted by it, whether with benevolent concession he as it were admits the wonder as a phenomenon intelligible to childhood, but relinquished by him, or whether he experiences anything else thereby.

For he will thus be enabled to determine how far he is on the whole capable of understanding myth, that is to say, the concentrated picture of the world, which, as abbreviature of phenomena, cannot dispense with wonder. It is probable, however, that nearly every one, upon close examination, feels so disintegrated by the critico-historical spirit of our culture, that he can only perhaps make the former existence of myth credible to himself by learned means through intermediary abstractions.

Without myth, however, every culture loses its healthy, creative natural power: it is only a horizon encompassed with myths which rounds off to unity a social movement. It is only by myth that all the powers of the imagination and of the Apollonian dream are freed from their random rovings. The mythical figures have to be the invisibly omnipresent genii, under the care of which the young soul grows to maturity, by the signs of which the man gives a meaning to his life and struggles: and the state itself knows no more powerful unwritten law than the mythical foundation which vouches for its connection with religion and its growth from mythical ideas.

Let us now place alongside thereof the abstract man proceeding independently of myth, the abstract education, the abstract usage, the abstract right, the abstract state: let us picture to ourselves the lawless roving of the artistic imagination, not bridled by any native myth: let us imagine a culture which has no fixed and sacred primitive seat, but is doomed to exhaust all its possibilities, and has to nourish itself wretchedly from the other cultures—such is the Present, as the result of Socratism, which is bent on the destruction of myth. And now the myth- less man remains eternally hungering among all the bygones, and digs and grubs for roots, though he have to dig for them even among the remotest antiquities. The stupendous historical exigency of the unsatisfied modern culture, the gathering around one of countless other cultures, the consuming desire for knowledge—what does all this point to, if not to the loss of myth, the loss of the mythical home, the mythical source? Let us ask ourselves whether the feverish and so uncanny stirring of this culture is aught but the eager seizing and snatching at food of the hungerer—and who would care to contribute anything more to a culture which cannot be appeased by all it devours, and in contact with which the most vigorous and wholesome nourishment is wont to change into "history and criticism"?

We should also have to regard our German character with despair and sorrow, if it had already become inextricably entangled in, or even identical with this culture, in a similar manner as we can observe it to our horror to be the case in civilised France; and that which for a long time was the great advantage of France and the cause of her vast preponderance, to wit, this very identity of people and culture, might compel us at the sight thereof to congratulate ourselves that this culture of ours, which is so questionable, has hitherto had nothing in common with the noble kernel of the character of our people. All our hopes, on the contrary, stretch out longingly towards the perception that beneath this restlessly palpitating civilised life and educational convulsion there is concealed a glorious, intrinsically healthy, primeval power, which, to be sure, stirs vigorously only at intervals in stupendous moments, and then dreams on again in view of a future awakening. It is from this abyss that the German Reformation came forth: in the choral-hymn of which the future melody of German music first resounded. So deep, courageous, and soul-breathing, so exuberantly good and tender did this chorale of Luther sound,—as the first Dionysian-luring call which breaks forth from dense thickets at the approach of spring. To it responded with emulative echo the solemnly wanton procession of Dionysian revellers, to whom we are indebted for German music—and to whom we shall be indebted for the re-birth of German myth.

I know that I must now lead the sympathising and attentive friend to an elevated position of lonesome contemplation, where he will have but few companions, and I call out encouragingly to him that we must hold fast to our shining guides, the Greeks. For the rectification of our æsthetic knowledge we previously borrowed from them the two divine figures, each of which sways a separate realm of art, and concerning whose mutual contact and exaltation we have acquired a notion through

Greek tragedy. Through a remarkable disruption of both these primitive artistic impulses, the ruin of Greek tragedy seemed to be necessarily brought about: with which process a degeneration and a transmutation of the Greek national character was strictly in keeping, summoning us to earnest reflection as to how closely and necessarily art and the people, myth and custom, tragedy and the state, have coalesced in their bases.

The ruin of tragedy was at the same time the ruin of myth. Until then the Greeks had been involuntarily compelled immediately to associate all experiences with their myths, indeed they had to comprehend them only through this association: whereby even the most immediate present necessarily appeared to them sub specie æterni and in a certain sense as timeless. Into this current of the timeless, however, the state as well as art plunged in order to find repose from the burden and eagerness of the moment. And a people—for the rest, also a man—is worth just as much only as its ability to impress on its experiences the seal of eternity: for it is thus, as it were, desecularised, and reveals its unconscious inner conviction of the relativity of time and of the true, that is, the metaphysical significance of life. The contrary happens when a people begins to comprehend itself historically and to demolish the mythical bulwarks around it: with which there is usually connected a marked secularisation, a breach with the unconscious metaphysics of its earlier existence, in all ethical consequences. Greek art and especially Greek tragedy delayed above all the annihilation of myth: it was necessary to annihilate these also to be able to live detached from the native soil, unbridled in the wilderness of thought, custom, and action. Even in such circumstances this metaphysical impulse still endeavours to create for itself a form of apotheosis (weakened, no doubt) in the Socratism of science urging to life: but on its lower stage this same impulse led only to a feverish search, which gradually merged into a pandemonium of myths and superstitions accumulated from all quarters: in the midst of which, nevertheless, the Hellene sat with a yearning heart till he contrived, as Græculus, to mask his fever with Greek cheerfulness and Greek levity, or to narcotise himself completely with some gloomy Oriental superstition.

We have approached this condition in the most striking manner since the reawakening of the Alexandro—Roman antiquity in the fifteenth century, after a long, not easily describable, interlude. On the heights there is the same exuberant love of knowledge, the same insatiate happiness of the discoverer, the same stupendous secularisation, and, together with these, a homeless roving about, an eager intrusion at foreign tables, a frivolous deification of the present or a dull senseless estrangement, all sub speci sæculi, of the present time: which same symptoms lead one to infer the same defect at the heart of this culture, the annihilation of myth. It seems hardly possible to transplant a foreign myth with permanent success, without dreadfully injuring the tree through this transplantation: which is perhaps occasionally strong enough and sound enough to eliminate the foreign element after a terrible struggle; but must ordinarily consume itself in a languishing and stunted condition or in sickly luxuriance. Our opinion of the pure and vigorous kernel of the German being is such that we venture to expect of it, and only of it, this elimination of forcibly ingrafted foreign elements, and we deem it possible that the German spirit will reflect anew on itself. Perhaps many a one will be of opinion that this spirit must begin its struggle with the elimination of the Romanic element: for which it might recognise an external preparation and encouragement in the victorious bravery and bloody glory of the late war, but must seek the inner constraint in the emulative zeal to be for ever worthy of the sublime protagonists on this path, of Luther as well as our great artists and poets. But let him never think he can fight such battles without his household gods, without his mythical home, without a "restoration" of all German things I And if the German should look timidly around for a guide to lead him back to his long-lost home, the ways and paths of which he knows no longer—let him but listen to the delightfully luring call of the Dionysian bird, which hovers above him, and would fain point out to him the way thither.

24.

Among the peculiar artistic effects of musical tragedy we had to emphasise an Apollonian illusion, through which we are to be saved from immediate oneness with the Dionysian music, while our musical excitement is able to discharge itself on an Apollonian domain and in an interposed visible middle world. It thereby seemed to us that precisely through this discharge the middle world of theatrical procedure, the drama generally, became visible and intelligible from within in a degree unattainable in the other forms of Apollonian art: so that here, where this art was as it were winged and borne aloft by the spirit of music, we had to recognise the highest exaltation of its powers, and consequently in the fraternal union of Apollo and Dionysus the climax of the Apollonian as well as of the Dionysian artistic aims.

Of course, the Apollonian light-picture did not, precisely with this inner illumination through music, attain the peculiar effect of the weaker grades of Apollonian art. What the epos and the animated stone can do— constrain the contemplating eye to calm delight in the world of the individuatio—could not be realised here, notwithstanding the greater animation and distinctness. We contemplated the drama and penetrated with piercing glance into its inner agitated world of motives—and yet it seemed as if only a symbolic picture passed before us, the profoundest significance of which we almost believed we had divined, and which we desired to put aside like a curtain in order to behold the original behind it. The greatest distinctness of the picture did not suffice us: for it seemed to reveal as well as veil something; and while it seemed, with its symbolic revelation, to invite the rending of the veil for the disclosure of the mysterious background, this illumined all-conspicuousness itself enthralled the eye and prevented it from penetrating more deeply He who has not experienced this,—to have to view, and at the same time to have a longing beyond the viewing,— will hardly be able to conceive how clearly and definitely these two processes coexist in the contemplation of tragic myth and are felt to be conjoined; while the truly æsthetic spectators will confirm my assertion that among the peculiar effects of tragedy this conjunction is the most noteworthy. Now let this phenomenon of the æsthetic spectator be transferred to an analogous process in the tragic artist, and the genesis of tragic myth will have been understood. It shares with the Apollonian sphere of art the full delight in appearance and contemplation, and at the same time it denies this delight and finds a still higher satisfaction in the annihilation of the visible world of appearance. The substance of tragic myth is first of all an epic event involving the glorification of the fighting hero: but whence originates the essentially enigmatical trait, that the suffering in the fate of the hero, the most painful victories, the most agonising contrasts of motives, in short, the exemplification of the wisdom of Silenus, or, æsthetically expressed, the Ugly and Discordant, is always represented anew in such countless forms with such predilection, and precisely in the most youthful and exuberant age of a people, unless there is really a higher delight experienced in all this?

For the fact that things actually take such a tragic course would least of all explain the origin of a form of art; provided that art is not merely an imitation of the reality of nature, but in truth a metaphysical supplement to the reality of nature, placed alongside thereof for its conquest. Tragic myth, in so far as it really belongs to art, also fully participates in this transfiguring metaphysical purpose of art in general: What does it transfigure, however, when it presents the phenomenal world in the guise of the suffering hero? Least of all the "reality" of this phenomenal world, for it says to us: "Look at this! Look carefully! It is your life! It is the hour-hand of your clock of existence!"

And myth has displayed this life, in order thereby to transfigure it to us? If not, how shall we account for the æsthetic pleasure with which we make even these representations pass before us? I am inquiring concerning the æsthetic pleasure, and am well aware that many of these representations may moreover occasionally create even a moral delectation, say under the form of pity or of a moral triumph. But he who would derive the effect of the tragic exclusively from these moral sources, as was usually the case far too long in æsthetics, let him not think that he has done anything for Art thereby; for Art must above all insist on purity in her domain. For the explanation of tragic myth the very first requirement is that the pleasure which characterises it must be sought in the purely æsthetic sphere, without encroaching on the domain of pity, fear, or the morally-sublime. How can the ugly and the discordant, the substance of tragic myth, excite an æsthetic pleasure?

Here it is necessary to raise ourselves with a daring bound into a metaphysics of Art. I repeat, therefore, my former proposition, that it is only as an æsthetic phenomenon that existence and the world, appear justified: and in this sense it is precisely the function of tragic myth to convince us that even the Ugly and Discordant is an artistic game which the will, in the eternal fulness of its joy, plays with itself. But this not easily comprehensible proto-phenomenon of Dionysian Art becomes, in a direct way, singularly intelligible, and is immediately apprehended in the wonderful significance of musical dissonance: just as in general it is music alone, placed in contrast to the world, which can give us an idea as to what is meant by the justification of the world as an æsthetic phenomenon. The joy that the tragic myth excites has the same origin as the joyful sensation of dissonance in music. The Dionysian, with its primitive joy experienced in pain itself, is the common source of music and tragic myth.

Is it not possible that by calling to our aid the musical relation of dissonance, the difficult problem of tragic effect may have meanwhile been materially facilitated? For we now understand what it means to wish to view tragedy and at the same time to have a longing beyond the viewing: a frame of mind, which, as regards the artistically employed dissonance, we should simply have to characterise by saying that we desire to hear and at the same time have a longing beyond the hearing. That striving for the infinite, the pinion-flapping of longing, accompanying the highest delight in the clearly-perceived reality, remind one that in both states we have to recognise a Dionysian phenomenon, which again and again reveals to us anew the playful up-building and demolishing of the world of individuals as the efflux of a primitive delight, in like manner as when Heraclitus the Obscure compares the world-building power to a playing child which places stones here and there and builds sandhills only to overthrow them again.

Hence, in order to form a true estimate of the Dionysian capacity of a people, it would seem that we must think not only of their music, but just as much of their tragic myth, the second witness of this capacity.

Considering this most intimate relationship between music and myth, we may now in like manner suppose that a degeneration and depravation of the one involves a deterioration of the other: if it be true at all that the weakening of the myth is generally expressive of a debilitation of the Dionysian capacity. Concerning both, however, a glance at the development of the German genius should not leave us in any doubt; in the opera just as in the abstract character of our myth-less existence, in an art sunk to pastime just as in a life guided by concepts, the inartistic as well as life-consuming nature of Socratic optimism had revealed itself to us. Yet there have been indications to console us that nevertheless in some inaccessible abyss the German spirit still rests and dreams, undestroyed, in glorious health, profundity, and Dionysian strength, like a knight sunk in slumber: from which abyss the Dionysian song rises to us to let us know that this German knight even still dreams his primitive Dionysian myth in blissfully earnest visions. Let no one believe that the German spirit has for ever lost its mythical home when it still understands so obviously the voices of the birds which tell of that home. Some day it will find itself awake in all the morning freshness of a deep sleep: then it will slay the dragons, destroy the malignant dwarfs, and waken Brünnhilde—and Wotan's spear itself will be unable to obstruct its course!

My friends, ye who believe in Dionysian music, ye know also what tragedy means to us. There we have tragic myth, born anew from music,—and in this latest birth ye can hope for everything and forget what is most afflicting. What is most afflicting to all of us, however, is— the prolonged degradation in which the German genius has lived estranged from house and home in the service of malignant dwarfs. Ye understand my allusion—as ye will also, in conclusion, understand my hopes.

25.

Music and tragic myth are equally the expression of the

Dionysian capacity of a people, and are inseparable from each other. Both originate in an ultra Apollonian sphere of art; both transfigure a region in the delightful accords of which all dissonance, just like the terrible picture of the world, dies charmingly away; both play with the sting of displeasure, trusting to their most potent magic; both justify thereby the existence even of the "worst world." Here the Dionysian, as compared with the Apollonian, exhibits itself as the eternal and original artistic force, which in general calls into existence the entire world of phenomena: in the midst of which a new transfiguring appearance becomes necessary, in order to keep alive the animated world of individuation. If we could conceive an incarnation of dissonance—and what is man but that?—then, to be able to live this dissonance would require a glorious illusion which would spread a veil of beauty over its peculiar nature. This is the true function of Apollo as deity of art: in whose name we comprise all the countless manifestations of the fair realm of illusion, which each moment render life in general worth living and make one impatient for the experience of the next moment.

At the same time, just as much of this basis of all existence—the Dionysian substratum of the world—is allowed to enter into the consciousness of human beings, as can be surmounted again by the Apollonian transfiguring power, so that these two art-impulses are constrained to develop their powers in strictly mutual proportion, according to the law of eternal justice. When the Dionysian powers rise with such vehemence as we experience at present, there can be no doubt that, veiled in a cloud, Apollo has already descended to us; whose grandest beautifying influences a coming generation will perhaps behold.

That this effect is necessary, however, each one would most surely perceive by intuition, if once he found himself carried back—even in a dream—into an Old-Hellenic existence. In walking under high Ionic colonnades, looking upwards to a horizon defined by clear and noble lines, with reflections of his transfigured form by his side in shining marble, and around him solemnly marching or quietly moving men, with harmoniously sounding voices and rhythmical pantomime, would he not in the presence of this perpetual influx of beauty have to raise his hand to Apollo and exclaim: "Blessed race of Hellenes! How great Dionysus must be among you, when the Delian god deems such charms necessary to cure you of your dithyrambic madness!"—To one in this frame of mind, however, an aged Athenian, looking up to him with the sublime eye of Æschylus, might answer: "Say also this, thou curious stranger: what sufferings this people must have undergone, in order to be able to become thus beautiful! But now follow me to a tragic play, and sacrifice with me in the temple of both the deities!"

APPENDIX

[Late in the year 1888, not long before he was overcome by his sudden attack of insanity, Nietzsche wrote down a few notes concerning his early work, the Birth of Tragedy. These were printed in his sister's biography (Das Leben Friedrich Nietzsches, vol. ii. pt. i. pp. 102 ff.), and are here translated as likely to be of interest to readers of this remarkable work.

They also appear in the Ecce Homo.—TRANSLATOR'S NOTE.]

"To be just to the Birth of Tragedy(1872), one will have to forget some few things. It has wrought effects, it even fascinated through that wherein it was amiss—through its application to Wagnerism, just as if this Wagnerism were symptomatic of a rise and going up. And just on that account was the book an event in Wagner's life: from thence and only from thence were great hopes linked to the name of Wagner. Even to-day people remind me, sometimes right in the midst of a talk on Parsifal, that I and none other have it on my conscience that such a high opinion of the cultural value of this movement came to the top.

More than once have I found the book referred to as 'the Re-birth of Tragedy out of the Spirit of Music': one only had an ear for a new formula of Wagner's art, aim, task,—and failed to hear withal what was at bottom valuable therein. 'Hellenism and Pessimism' had been a more unequivocal title: namely, as a first lesson on the way in which the Greeks got the better of pessimism,—on the means whereby they overcame it. Tragedy simply proves that the Greeks were no pessimists: Schopenhauer was mistaken here as he was mistaken in all other things. Considered with some neutrality, the Birth of

Tragedy appears very unseasonable: one would not even dream that it was begun amid the thunders of the battle of Wörth. I thought these problems through and through before the walls of Metz in cold September nights, in the midst of the work of nursing the sick; one might even believe the book to be fifty years older. It is politically indifferent— un-German one will say to-day,—it smells shockingly Hegelian, in but a few formulæ does it scent of Schopenhauer's funereal perfume. An 'idea'— the antithesis of 'Dionysian versus Apollonian'—translated into metaphysics; history itself as the evolution of this 'idea'; the antithesis dissolved into oneness in Tragedy; through this optics things that had never yet looked into one another's face, confronted of a sudden, and illumined and comprehended through one another: for instance, Opera and Revolution. The two decisive innovations of the book are, on the one hand, the comprehension of the Dionysian phenomenon among the Greeks (it gives the first psychology thereof, it sees therein the One root of all Grecian art); on the other, the comprehension of Socratism: Socrates diagnosed for the first time as the tool of Grecian dissolution, as a typical decadent. 'Rationality' against instinct! 'Rationality' at any price as a dangerous, as a life-undermining force! Throughout the whole book a deep hostile silence on Christianity: it is neither Apollonian nor Dionysian; it negatives all æsthetic values (the only values recognised by the Birth of Tragedy), it is in the widest sense nihilistic, whereas in the Dionysian symbol the utmost limit of affirmation is reached. Once or twice the Christian priests are alluded to as a 'malignant kind of dwarfs,' as 'subterraneans.'"

2.

"This beginning is singular beyond measure. I had for my own inmost experience discovered the only symbol and counterpart of history,—I had just thereby been the first to grasp the wonderful phenomenon of the Dionysian. And again, through my diagnosing Socrates as a decadent, I had given a wholly unequivocal proof of how little risk the trustworthiness of my psychological grasp would run of being weakened by some moralistic idiosyncrasy—to view morality itself as a symptom of decadence is an innovation, a novelty of the first rank in the history of knowledge. How far I had leaped in either case beyond the smug shallow-pate-gossip of optimism contra pessimism! I was the first to see the intrinsic antithesis: here, the degenerating instinct which, with subterranean vindictiveness, turns against life (Christianity, the philosophy of Schopenhauer, in a certain sense already the philosophy of Plato, all idealistic systems as typical forms), and there, a formula of highest affirmation, born of fullness and overfullness, a yea-saying without reserve to suffering's self, to guilt's self, to all that is questionable and strange in existence itself. This final, cheerfullest, exuberantly mad- and-merriest Yea to life is not only the highest insight, it is also the deepest, it is that which is most rigorously confirmed and upheld by truth and science. Naught that is, is to be deducted, naught is dispensable; the phases of existence rejected by the Christians and other nihilists are even of an infinitely higher order in the hierarchy of values than that which the instinct of decadence sanctions, yea durst sanction. To comprehend this courage is needed, and, as a condition thereof, a surplus of strength: for precisely in degree as courage dares to thrust forward, precisely according to the measure of strength, does one approach truth. Perception, the yea-saying to reality, is as much a necessity to the strong as to the weak, under the inspiration of weakness, cowardly shrinking, and flight from reality—the 'ideal.' ...

They are not free to perceive: the decadents have need of the lie,—it is one of their conditions of self-preservation. Whoso not only comprehends the word Dionysian, but also grasps his self in this word, requires no refutation of Plato or of

Christianity or of Schopenhauer—he smells the putrefaction."

3.

"To what extent I had just thereby found the concept 'tragic,' the definitive perception of the psychology of tragedy, I have but lately stated in the Twilight of the Idols, page 139 (1st edit.): 'The affirmation of life, even in its most unfamiliar and severe problems, the will to life, enjoying its own inexhaustibility in the sacrifice of its highest types,—that is what I called Dionysian, that is what I divined as the bridge to a psychology of the tragic poet. Not in order to get rid of terror and pity, not to purify from a dangerous passion by its vehement discharge (it was thus that Aristotle misunderstood it); but, beyond terror and pity, to realise in

fact the eternal delight of becoming, that delight which even involves in itself the joy of annihilating![27] In this sense I have the right to understand myself to be the first tragic philosopher—that is, the utmost antithesis and antipode to a pessimistic philosopher. Prior to myself there is no such translation of the Dionysian into the philosophic pathos: there lacks the tragic wisdom,—I have sought in vain for an indication thereof even among the great Greeks of philosophy, the thinkers of the two centuries before Socrates. A doubt still possessed me as touching Heraclitus, in whose proximity I in general begin to feel warmer and better than anywhere else. The affirmation of transiency and annihilation, to wit the decisive factor in a [27] Mr. Common's translation, pp. 227-28.

Dionysian philosophy, the yea-saying to antithesis and war, to becoming, with radical rejection even of the concept 'being,'—that I must directly acknowledge as, of all thinking hitherto, the nearest to my own. The doctrine of 'eternal recurrence,' that is, of the unconditioned and infinitely repeated cycle of all things—this doctrine of

Zarathustra's might after all have been already taught by

Heraclitus. At any rate the portico28 which inherited well-nigh all its fundamental conceptions from Heraclitus, shows traces thereof."

Facsimile of Nietzsches handwriting.

"In this book speaks a prodigious hope. In fine, I see no reason whatever for taking back my hope of a Dionysian future for music. Let us cast a glance a century ahead, let us suppose my assault upon two millenniums of anti-nature and man-vilification succeeds! That new party of life which will take in hand the greatest of all tasks, the upbreeding of mankind to something higher,—add thereto the relentless annihilation of all things degenerating and parasitic, will again make possible on earth that too-much of life, from which there also must needs grow again the Dionysian state. I promise a tragic age:

the highest art in the yea-saying to life, tragedy, will be born anew, when mankind have behind them the consciousness of the hardest but most necessary wars, without suffering therefrom. A psychologist might still add that what I heard in my younger years in Wagnerian music had in general naught to do with Wagner; that when I described Wagnerian music I described what I had heard, that I had instinctively to translate and transfigure all into the new spirit which I bore within myself "

THE BIRTH OF TRAGEDY